SYSTEMS DESIGN AND HCI -
a practical handbook

Brian Shorrock

SIGMA PRESS
Wilmslow, Cheshire, U.K.

Copyright © B Shorrock, 1988.

All Rights Reserved. No part of this publication may be reproduced, stored in a retrieval system, or transmitted in any form or by any means, electronic, mechanical, photocopying, recording or otherwise, without prior written permission.

First published in 1988 by
Sigma Press 98a Water Lane, Wilmslow, SK9 5BB, England.

Printed in Malta by Interprint Limited

British Library Cataloguing in Publication Data

Shorrock, Brian
    Systems Design and HCI: a practical handbook
    1. Computer systems. Design. Human factors
    I. Title
    004.2'1'019

ISBN: 1 85058 101 0

Distributed by
John Wiley & Sons Ltd., Baffins Lane, Chichester, West Sussex, England.

Cover design by
Professional Graphics, Warrington, UK

Acknowledgments:

PCW 8256 is a trademark of Amstrad PLC.
LocoScript is a trademark of Locomotive Software Ltd.
The PICK® operating system is a proprietary software product of Pick Systems.
This book may include descriptions of other products, the names of which may be trademarks or registered trademarks, and due acknowledgment is hereby made.

Preface

This book presents a definitive and essentially practical guide to the design of data processing systems. It is aimed at four basic classes of people:

* *Executives* - who need to know what sort of systems they should demand from designers.

* *Systems Designers* - who need to know how best to satisfy the demands of executives.

* *Human Computer Interaction Researchers* - who need to see how their work fits into the overall problem of Systems Design.

* *Students of Computing* - who wish to become better designers than their forebears.

The Guide is concerned primarily with the design of commercial data processing systems, but most of the concepts described are equally applicable to all kinds of computer systems, including the evaluation of established Packages, Data Base Management Systems and 4th Generation Languages.

Data Processing (DP) is essentially a very simple process, which should have been made even simpler by the power, versatility and relative cheapness of modern computers. In general, this is not what has happened.

Many users are still far from satisfied with their computer systems. Most systems still take far too long to develop and install, and many potential users are deterred by the apparent complexity of the systems on offer. In nearly every case, the problems can be attributed to one single neglected aspect - namely, poor Systems Design. This being the case, there is little doubt that improving standards of Systems Design will not only benefit users and potential users, it will also promote the more widespread use of computers.

With so much at stake, one may well ask why are designs still so bad? The answer is very simple, because it is only in very recent years that very large numbers of people have come into direct contact with computers and more recently people have begun to realise that systems which were suitable for a few specialists to run were not suitable for mass consumption. So it is only now that the importance of Human Computer Interaction (HCI) is beginning to be appreciated.

I have called the book Systems Design and HCI because it looks at Systems Design primarily from the users point of view. Indeed the main aim of the methodology described is to produce systems which are more than just 'user-friendly'. In fact, it aims to produce systems to which users can readily relate.

This is a major departure from conventional programmer orientated design methodologies. However, what makes the approach particularly attractive is that the very things that make it easy for users to relate to systems also make systems easier to design, easier to program and easier to maintain.

The techniques involved can be applied to any make of computer and are neither difficult nor costly. The effects of the approach can be summed-up in terms of cheaper, faster and more flexible systems - designed for users. Taken in combination, these effects are such that the HCI of Systems Design seems certain to have a significant effect on both users and suppliers. Indeed, HCI seems set to prove to be the key to growth throughout the computer industry.

The book is based on a standardised approach developed for designing systems called Patterned Systems Design.

In his mammoth survey of 4th Generation Languages, James Martin (MARTIN, 1985) compares the current state of computing with that of the early automobile industry in the USA. Apparently, when car production was just beginning to expand a well known sociologist was asked to predict how many cars would eventually be required. After due deliberation, the sociologist suggested a figure of 2 million (based on the assumption that no more than 2 million people would be prepared to serve as chauffeurs.)

This was, of course, before Henry Ford introduced the Model T Ford which could be mass-produced - and was easier to control.

Martin then goes on to point out, that computers can now be mass-produced and that the limited number of professional programmers available is the main restriction to growth. He suggests, user-orientate programming languages are the key to future expansion.

There can be little doubt that he is partly right and in perhaps five years time his pronouncements will certainly become more relevant. What Martin doesn't follow up, however, is that the key to the success of the Model T Ford was that virtually anybody could readily learn to drive it.

Today there is a glut of computers and programs, and the real problem is that there aren't enough people who know how to drive the computers.

To return to the analogy. Although some people may want to customise their car, most people today buy a standard mass-produced car. They do not want to modify it, merely to drive it.

So, the next step in the development of computer systems must be to ensure that systems are produced in such a way that anybody can use them.

This is what this handbook is about. It covers six main aspects:

An Introduction to Systems Design and Data Processing. (Chapters 1 and 2).

Patterned Systems Design - The standard user interface. (Chapters 3 to 10).

Steps in Developing a System. (Chapters 11 to 14).

Special applications. (Chapter 15).

High-level Language Designs. (Chapters 16 to 18).

Dos and Don'ts of Systems Design. (Chapter 19).

Contents

1: Introduction 1
Modern Computer Systems...1
User-friendliness 2
What is Systems Design?..3
Patterned Systems Design..4
Why Executives? 4
State of the Art...5

2: Data Processing is Simple 7
Introduction 7
What is Data Processing? 10
What can be done to a Single Record?..10
Reports..10
Key Fields..12
Record Sequencing and Access..12
Search for Rectangular Files..14
Counters and Tables 18
Checking Data...19
Appraisal...20

3: The Basic Principles of PSD..21
Introduction 21
Key features of a Modern Computer...21
Why Patterned Systems Design? 22
The 'Record' is the key...23
PSD Modules...24
PSD High-level Structuring..26
Appraisal...28

4: The Basic PSD Structure..29
Introduction 29
The Keyboard..29
PSD Menus..31
PSD Headers...32
Menu *v* Command Systems...34
Skilled Users...35
Appraisal...36

5: PSD Record Processing 38
Introduction 38
Across-screen Input. 38
Down-screen Input 40
Random-Input 42
Question & Answer Input. 43
Typing into Fields 44
Error Detection 45
The 'Create' Record Function.. 46
Foot-of-Screen Routines. 47
The 'Amend' Record Function.. 48
The 'Erase' Record Function 49
The 'Display' Record Function. 50
The 'Print' Record Function. 50
Appraisal.. 51

6: More About PSD Records 53
Introduction 53
Multi-screen Records 53
Scrolling or Racking. 56
Large Fields 57
Multiple Record Entries and Displays 58
Repetitive Keys... 59
Counters and Default Values 60
Record Processing. 61
Format Conventions. 61
Appraisal.. 62

7: Report Displays and Prints.. 65
Introduction 65
Secondary Processing... 65
Report Format - Displays... 66
Report Format - Prints.. 67
Local v Central Printing... 69
Designing for A4 Paper.. 71
Other Type Sizes. 74
Design for Ease of Use. 75
Copies of Reports. 78
Stopping a Print. 78

8: Password Control, Record Keys and Codes 79
Introduction 79
Log-on.. 79
Levels of Authority.. 81
Function levels of Authority.. 81
Record keys 84

Codes 89

9: Miscellaneous Features 92
Introduction 92
Colour 92
Mice, Joysticks and Roller-Balls 92
Touch Sensitive Screens 94
Automatic Data Entry 94
Special Keys 96
Word-processing 96
Voice Input and Output 98
Keyboards 98
Floppy Discs 100

10: Designing Records and Normalisation 101
Introduction 101
Terminology 101
Normalisation 102
First Normal Form 103
Second Normal Form 103
Third Normal Form 104
Comparison with PSD 105
Appraisal 106

11: Design Phases 109
Introduction 109
Project Initiation 109
Project Identification 111
Feasibility Study 112
The System Specification 115
System Testing 119
User Guides and Procedures 119
Implementation 120
Maintenance 120
Appraisal 121

12: The Methodology of Design - The Rough Design Phase 122
Introduction 122
Background to Case Study 122
Appraisal of Existing System 124
Search for Modules 125
The next Module - Life Policies 127
Household Insurance Policies 129
Solution to Problem of Major in the WRAC 130

13: The Methodology of Design - Refining The Rough Design .. 133
Introduction 133
Life policy Reports 135
Summarising the Design 142

14: Finalising The Design 144
Introduction 144
What if...? 145
Documenting Modules 146
Input Formats 148
Field Validation 148
Record Processing 149
Specifying Reports 149
Re-Appraising Designs 150
Completing the Design 150
Additional Details 150

15: Special Applications 153
Introduction 153
Customised Devices 153
Early Cash-point Designs 154
Appraisal 157
WP on the Amstrad PCW8256 157
The Keyboard 158
Locoscript 1.2 160
Conclusion 168

16: DBMS's and 4GL's 169
Introduction 169
What are 4GL's 169
User/Designers 171
Terminology 172
Hierarchical Systems 173
Structuring 176
Screen Design Facilities 179
Menus, Views and Security 180
Conclusion 181

17: Outline Specification for A 4GL+ - Record Processing 182
Introduction 182
Abbreviation 182
Entry to the 4GL+ 183
Record Definition 185
File Definition 187
Procedure Definition 189
Menu Building 190

Authorisation Levels 192

18: Outline Specification for a 4GL+ - Report Processing 194
Introduction 194
Types of Reports 195
File-listing Reports - Format Definition... 197
Report Procedure Definition... 200
Page Layout Definition... 201
Report Format Definition - Simple Reports... 203
Report Procedure Definition - Simple Reports...................................... 205
Complex Reports.. 207
Conclusion.. 207

19: Dos and Don'ts of Systems Design 208

Postscript... 213

References.. 214

Index... 215

Chapter 1

Introduction

Modern Computer Systems

During the last 25 years the progress that has been made in both the design and cost of computers has been quite remarkable. Similarly, a great deal of progress has been made in speeding-up and simplifying programming. At the same time there have been subtle, but important changes in the basic methods of data processing (DP).

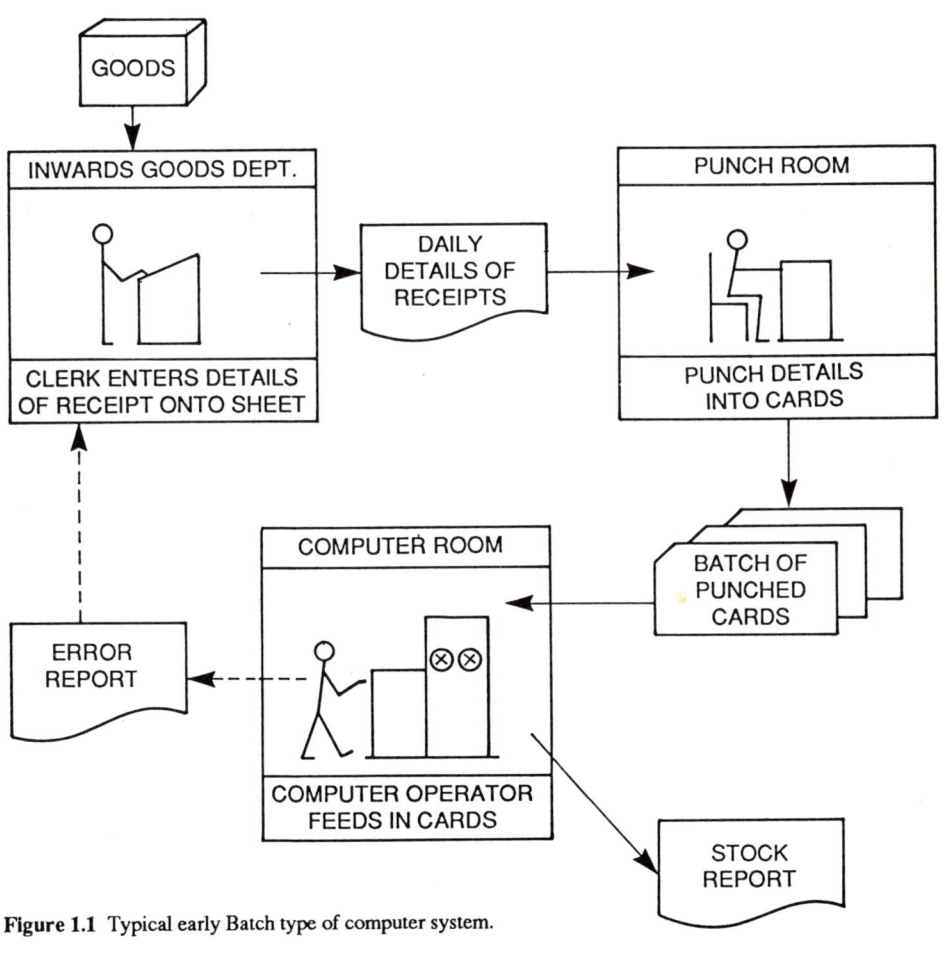

Figure 1.1 Typical early Batch type of computer system.

1

Early commercial computer systems were Batch Systems (Figure 1.1), run by specialists in the form of computer operators. User involvement was strictly limited to providing data (ie. details of transactions) for input to the computer and to periodically receiving reports printed out by the computer.

At best batch systems were slow, mainly because of the time taken to submit and prepare batches of data and delays in getting reports back to users. Turnaround times of the order of a week were not uncommon, particularly if errors were detected during processing.

Modern computer systems now generally operate in what is known either as on-line, real-time or transaction processing (TP) mode. In TP mode details of transactions can be entered directly into the computer by one or a number of operators and can be processed immediately (Figure 1.2).

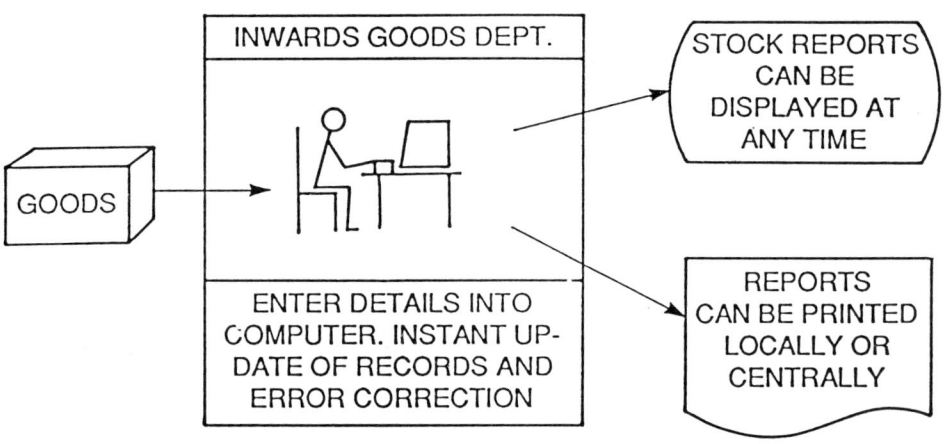

Figure 1.2 Typical modern Transaction Processing type of system.

TP clearly has many advantages, particularly since data can be entered at source and any errors highlighted and corrected as soon as the data is entered. What previously took days can now be achieved in a matter of seconds. However, TP does give rise to some new and important problems.

User-Friendliness

Today, instead of systems being designed to be run by a few specialist operators, any system of any consequence, must be designed so that it can be understood and used by large numbers of people; people who often know little or nothing about computers.

This has added an important new dimension to the design of modern computer systems, namely the subject of HCI or, as it is frequently called user-friendliness. As will become clear later, HCI is concerned with more than just user-friendliness, but this term will suffice for the moment.

User-friendliness depends on a wide variety of things, ranging from the aptness of the system to the way in which user-manuals are presented and so on. Its importance can best be judged from the fact that the annual cost of a user is usually over 200 times more than the cost of their computers. Whilst the cost of computers is falling rapidly, year by year, the salaries of users are still rising.

A prime aim of this guide, therefore, is to show how to produce systems designs which are user-friendly.

What is Systems Design?

One of the main problems in producing user-friendly systems is computer jargon. If users and potential users cannot understand the terminology used, this immediately creates a barrier between them and systems designers. In presenting this guide every effort has been made to avoid jargon or where necessary to explain it.

In designing or presenting any system, designers must make sure that they avoid computer jargon or where necessary explain it.

At first sight, this stricture may appear to be somewhat difficult, probably because the term 'Systems Design' has often been misunderstood. A number of books have been produced on what is claimed to be systems design. Some have also been produced on what may be considered to be the same subject under the title of 'structured design'. Generally, these books are concerned with programming, rather than design, problems. Ironically, many of the complex problems posed in these books arise because systems have not been properly designed in the first place.

A more detailed examination of the steps involved in developing and implementing systems is shown later in this guide. In the meantime, suffice it to say, that in the context of this guide systems design does not include programming.

Systems Design is the process whereby a definitive specification of a system is produced.

As will become clear later, the system specification should be couched in lay terms. In this way it will serve, firstly, to allow users to verify that their requirements are being met and, secondly, to provide programmers with the details that they need.

There is currently a school of thought which suggests that 'Prototyping' is the real way to tackle this problem, but there appears to be little point in programming a system if it is not going to satisfy users' needs, particularly if this is going to encourage slipshod analysis of users' requirements.

So the sensible approach seems to be the one recommended, whereby users' requirements are clearly defined before programming starts.

Patterned Systems Design

Users who have been confronted with systems specifications running to several hundred pages may well feel that the aforementioned is something of an over-simplification of the problems. It is in so far as the designing of systems is almost invariably an iterative process, where a variety of alternatives have to be explored before the design is finalised. The key to success lies in what has been called Patterned Systems Design or PSD for short.

Much of what follows is devoted to explaining in detail the principles of PSD. Briefly PSD consists essentially of a series of algorithms, which are designed to ensure that systems are produced in the form of standardised modules.

The modularity of PSD means that designers, users and later programmers can concentrate their attention on small parts of a system at a time. The fact that modules conform to rigid standards means that much of what would normally have to be specified is implicit.

The basic concepts of PSD were initially developed on a major project, where it was felt that the system should not look as though it had been programmed by four different programmers. In other words, it was developed to ensure consistency and hence user-friendliness, but experience in its use has shown that significant benefits are achieved at every stage in the development and implementation of DP systems even to the extent that staff, who in the past had been unable to design systems, suddenly found that they could produce system specifications using PSD.

Why Executives?

The fact that this guide on systems design is addressed among others to Executives may be somewhat puzzling at first. This is not a subtle attempt to elevate the status of the book. Nor, indeed is it intended to encourage Executives to become Systems Designers. It is, however, a vital pointer to the scope for improving systems design and a guide to what needs to be done to realise the potential. Firstly, consider the scope. The ability of modern computers to display all kinds of vital information virtually at the touch of a button would seem to make a computer terminal a must for every executive. Yet, very few executives have terminals and still fewer know how to use one.

A variety of reasons have been put forward to explain this. Notably, that executives consider using a terminal to be degrading, but to have all kinds of vital facts and figures about a business at one's fingertips hardly seems degrading.

A far more plausible explanation is that the busy executive has never been able to find time to master computer systems. This in turn can be attributed primarily to the fact that insufficient attention has been given to ensuring that systems are designed so that they can readily be understood.

Clearly if systems are designed so that they can quickly be absorbed this will not only save valuable training time and the frustration of mastering new systems, it will also open up important new markets for computers.

Turning now to the second aspect - what needs to be done to achieve this?. A prime requirement of any successful computer system is that it must satisfy users' needs. Many contemporary systems do not and some sources have even suggested that the only solution is for users to design their own systems (JONES, 1986). Many users have successfully used a variety of packages to design minor but useful systems. However, experience has shown that to rely on inexperienced designers to produce major systems is a hazardous and often extremely costly business. It seems certain, therefore, that the need for professional systems designers will continue for many years to come. The problem of striking a satisfactory compromise between what users feel that they want and what the systems designer can produce will remain.

Any systems designer worthy of the name will have been trained in the art of eliciting details of what is required from potential users. This is by no means a rigidly defined process and misunderstandings can occur, particularly when jargon is used by either party. What seems clear is that the more executives (or any other senior staff) know about the design of computer systems, the better they will be able to express their needs and the better they will be able to judge whether or not what is proposed will truly satisfy their requirements.

The guide has, therefore, been addressed to executives in the hope that it will help them to gain a better understanding of what should be expected from modern, well-designed, computer systems.

State of the Art

The current state of the art of systems design can perhaps best be illustrated by an anecdote, related by a consultant friend.

The consultant was visiting a high-technology plant which had large numbers of modern terminals linked to other plants and the head-office. He asked the manager he was visiting about Systems Design Standards and was told that there were none. However, the manager volunteered to show the consultant some of the current systems and chose the electronic mailing system. This system, he explained, allowed letters to be transmitted throughout the company. To log-on he had to enter his name. The system responded with the message 'Surname missing'.

He tried again and got the same response, even though he had in fact typed in his surname on both occasions. He then realised that he had left out his middle initial.

Once into the system, he was advised that there were three letters waiting for him. He then selected the option which lists who the letters were from and when they had been sent. There were only two letters.

As the manager was pointing out what was on the screen, the screen suddenly cleared. He explained that the screen was touch-sensitive and he must have accidentally touched it. Eventually, the two-letter display was retrieved. The manager then explained that he knew what was in the letters, because he had spoken to the sender on the phone. It then transpired that the letters had been in the system for three months and he still hadn't found out how to display the actual letters.

The consultant, who considered himself an expert at mastering difficult computer systems, then tried to work out how to display the letters. He failed. End of anecdote.

The above may not be typical of all systems, but it shows very clearly the gap which exists between the progress that has been made on computer hardware and the progress on systems design and on HCI in particular.

In many ways the situation as far as computers are concerned is closely analagous to television. The modern TV Set (Hardware) is excellent and relatively cheap, but the programmes (Software) cost a great deal and frequently leave a lot to be desired. This must not be taken to imply that all computer-hardware developments have been progressive. As will be seen later, a variety of 'gimmicks' have been introduced and these have often made things more difficult for users.

It is hoped that what has been described is sufficient to emphasise the importance of the HCI of Systems Design.

Chapter 2

Data Processing is Simple

Introduction

The ways in which modern computers can be applied are virtually unlimited. They can, for example, be used to produce and edit letters, to control machine tools, to produce and evaluate complex designs, and to navigate space craft. Alternatively, they can be used for commercial Electronic Data Processing (EDP). In other words, to simply process information of an every day nature in conventional ways. It has been estimated that about 80% of all computing falls into this category.

Commercial EDP is the form of computing to which most people are exposed. It is also the form of computing where users are most likely to know little or nothing about computers - and where user-friendliness is vital.

As has been suggested earlier, data processing is not normally complex, but, EDP has been made to appear to be complex, mainly due to poor systems design and jargon. The main aim of this chapter is to demonstrate that EDP can be simple and to show how jargon can and must be avoided. It also looks at the fundamental principles of EDP and the design of EDP systems. Experienced designers may be tempted to skip the chapter. Don't. The more experienced the designer, the greater the danger that jargon will be used.

Effective systems design depends very largely on the ability of users and systems designers to communicate with each other. Effective communication can only take place if users and designers speak the same language.

To the systems designer terms like Database, Sets, Entities, Attributes, Interfaces, Data Flows, DOS and so on, may seem clear, but the terms will not be clear to the average user and will only serve to cause confusion. They must, therefore, be avoided.

What is Data Processing?

DP is not new. In one form or another we all do it every day (Figure 2.1). Shopping lists are written out, telephone directories are scanned, new names are added to address books and cash is totalled and so on.

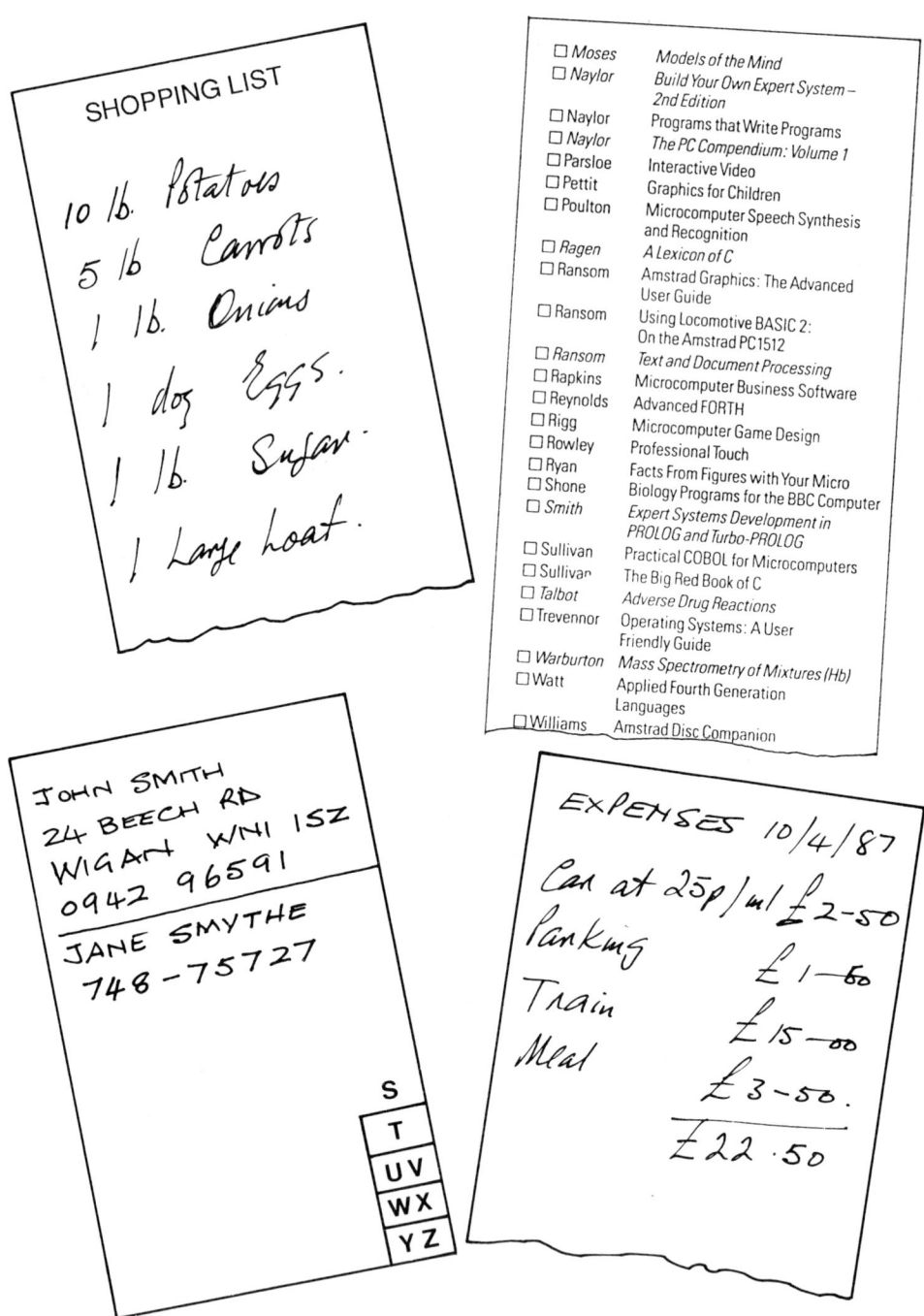

Figure 2.1 Data Processing is not new. Virtually everybody performs some form of data processing every day.

In each of the above examples data (ie. information) was processed manually and the processes described may not appear to have much in common with each other, let alone with computer systems. The key to recognising their commonality is to think in terms of 'records'. Once this is done, then it should become clear that all DP systems have a great deal in common and that computer systems differ very little from their manual equivalent.

Consider an 'address book', for example. To picture this in terms of records it is best to think of providing a card for each person (Figure 2.2). Each card will have 'Fields' into which details can be entered and the pack of records will be held in a file. It will become clear later that it is important that only one type of record must be held in any one file, and that all the records must have provision for the same fields of information. In other words, the file must be thought of as a box-file, rather than as a folder in which a variety of documents may be filed. This very simple and logical way of filing information is also the simplest and most flexible way of storing data on computers.

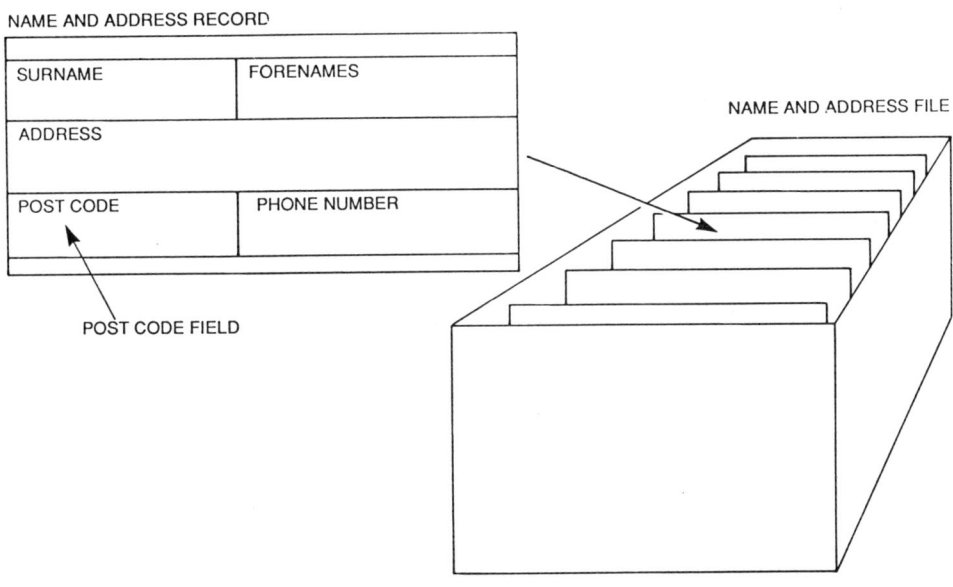

Figure 2.2 A box-file, holding Records on which Fields of information are recorded.

Using the technique of thinking of computer records, as fixed-format cards, held in a box-file is the first step in visualising any manual system as a computer system, and vice versa.

Note that the terms file, record and field are all terms that should readily be grasped by both users and designers.

What Can be Done to A Single Record?

To further the analogy between manual and computer systems the next step is to consider what can be done to a single record in isolation. Returning to the address book example, it should be clear that the answer is - not a lot.

There are in fact only five basic 'Functions' that can be performed on a single record (Figure 2.3).

```
1. CREATE Record
2. AMEND Record
3. ERASE Record
4. DISPLAY Record
5. PRINT Record
```

Figure 2.3 These are common features for all computer and manual records.

In terms of a computer system, CREATE Record is the process of adding a new record to a file, whilst AMEND Record allows what has already been created to be changed. ERASE Record results in the record being removed altogether.

DISPLAY record extracts a record so that it can be viewed, but not changed. Finally, PRINT record reproduces what is on the record on paper. When a particular Function has been selected a computer is said to be in a particular mode. For example, Create mode.

The five basic Functions are the key to effective systems design. They show what must be provided for on all records. A record and its associated facilities is called a Module.

Note that imprecise terms such as Update and Edit have been avoided. The terms Create, Amend and so on, should be clear to most people and can be applied equally well to either computer or manual systems. Users should readily be able to visualise what a computer system will do, by thinking about the manual equivalent.

The five basic Functions form the core of the PSD methodology. They also give designers the first clue as to what they should be looking for when they are designing systems. More about these two aspects later.

Reports

So far only single records have been considered, but it is when reports are required, either across records or files, that computers generally begin to excel. The reports required will differ significantly from system to system and they cannot be standardised.

Reporting requirements will also normally figure prominently in the way in which a system is programmed. If programming considerations are set aside, however, the logic associated with producing reports from computers is exactly the same as for the manual equivalent.

To ensure that designs can readily be understood programming considerations and in particular programming terminology must not be allowed to confuse the design process.

Computer generated Reports can take two basic forms:

* REPORT DISPLAYS, the equivalent of looking through a manual file.

* REPORT PRINTS, the equivalent of writing out details from a file.

For example, in the case of the address book two typical reporting requirements may be to list details in Surname or in Post Code sequence (Figure 2.4).

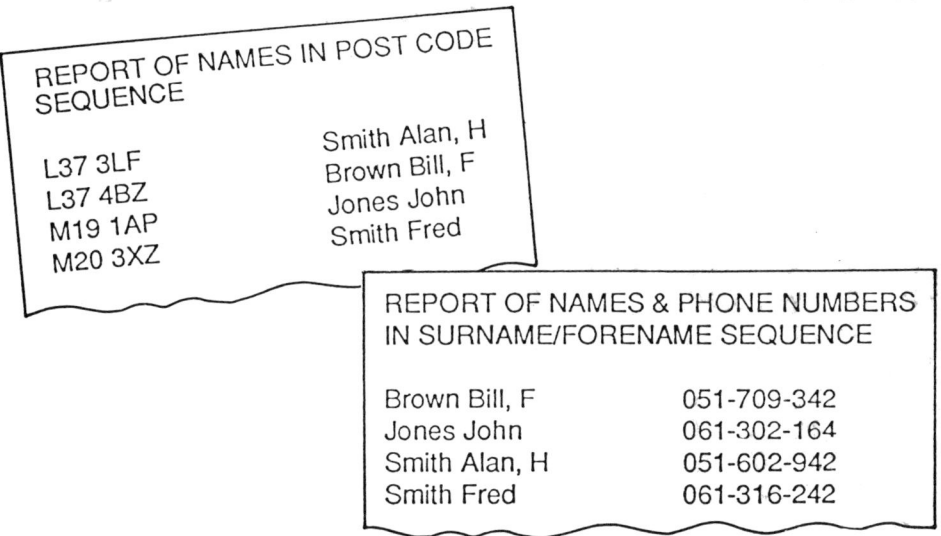

Figure 2.4 Reports from a computer will usually involve printing or displaying details from a number of records or files, in a variety of formats.

On either a manual or computer system it is not, of course, necessary to list all the details shown on the records nor to list the details in the same sequence as they appear on the file, but the details required must be available.

On all systems, Reporting is a secondary process and the records from which a Report is to be produced must be on file.

An essential step in the systems design process is to consider what reports are required, and to ensure that provision has been made for the necessary records to be established.

Key Fields

The term 'Key Field' usually figures prominently in the description of a computer system. Although the term is not normally used in connection with manual systems, the principles involved are exactly the same on both types of systems.

To be able to select a particular record, it is essential that there is a unique way of identifying the record.

The fields which uniquely identify a record are called the Key Fields. So, in the case of the address book, the Surname and Forenames are the Key Fields. The Post Code is also used as a key, but in this case it is a Secondary Key.

Systems Designers must ensure that each record has a unique key, and that any secondary keys are identified.

Note that in the case of the address book, the Surname on its own is not unique. Because there can be many Smiths and so on, the Surname on its own does not identify a particular record.

Programs can be devised to search for 'key data' in amongst other data in a field. But, this is a highly inefficient process. Key data should, therefore, be held in separate fields. Thus, for example, the Post Code should not be put in a field holding the rest of the address.

Record Sequencing and Access

Introducing a Post Code as a Secondary Key highlights one of the main problems facing systems developers, namely the problem of how to sequence records in a file.

In the case of the example shown earlier, the address cards would normally be filed in Surname/Forename sequence. Clearly, this is ideal for listing records in this sequence, but the task of listing details in Post Code sequence, however, obviously presents problems, particularly on a manual system.

One solution would be to re-sort the cards by Post Code before attempting to list them, or, if listings in this sequence, are frequently required, two sets of cards could be held, with one in each sequence. But the task of maintaining two copies of the same information is clearly not attractive.

There are other manual alternatives. If each card is numbered, for example, the task can be simplified by holding an Index of Post Codes and reference numbers (Figure 2.5).

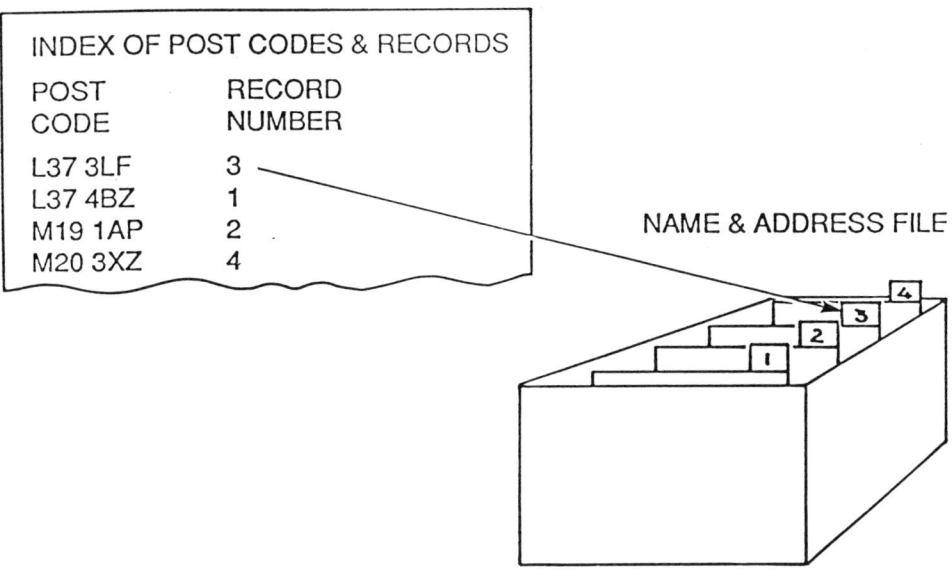

Figure 2.5 Holding an index can facilitate access to a file in a variety of different ways.

From what has been said, it will be apparent that there are a large number of ways in which this problem can be resolved on manual systems. There is also a correspondingly large number of ways in which the problem can be resolved using computers. There is unfortunately no one 'best' solution to this problem. Each application will involve finding the best compromise, depending on the speed and frequency with which reports are required, processing and storage costs, and development costs.

This may seem to cast certain doubts about the assertion that DP is simple. At this point it is perhaps appropriate to admit that there is one fundamental problem in computing.

The problem is that once a record has been stored on a disc, which may hold thousands or even millions of records, then it can be a very difficult job to find the record again without searching through the whole of the disc. Not surprisingly, the subject of how to ensure that records can be retrieved quickly and efficiently is one that has captivated large parts of the computer industry for many years.

The most unfortunate bit about this is that with many of the approaches adopted the industry insists on getting users and systems designers embroiled in these problems. Approaches of this nature must be avoided.

To determine how best to store and handle data in a computer is a task which calls for an intimate knowledge of the working of a computer. Indeed, in many cases, knowledge of the current loading of different parts of the computer is required.

Clearly, this is a task for a programmer, not a systems designer. In other words, systems designers must stick to specifying what must be done and not how the computer will actually do it. If this is the case, then in the context of this guide the problem can be dismissed and it can be reaffirmed that data processing is simple.

Search for Rectangular Files

As was suggested earlier, the first step in thinking about computer files is to think in terms of box-files. Once this has been done then it is not difficult to see that the details on a card could be put onto a strip, so that all the data for each record is on a single line. The Address Book box-file can conveniently be illustrated as shown in Figure 2.6.

RECORD No.	SURNAME	FORENAME	ADDRESS	POST CODE	PHONE No.
1	BROWN	BILL	22 POND RD.	L40 2FL	051-228-960
2	JONES	JOHN	10 MILL ST.	M69 2QT	061-234-529
3	SMITH	ALAN	4 KEY RD.	L92 1YQ	051-194-098
4	SMITH	BILL	98 QUAY ST.	M82 9RT	061-567-432

Figure 2.6 A Rectangular file, an essential feature of effective systems design.

Fortunately, this is not only the most convenient way of illustrating what is on a file, it is also the most convenient and flexible way of actually storing computer files. A file of this type is called a Rectangular file and is the form of file recommended for holding all data on systems.

A Rectangular file is one where provision is made for all the records in the file to have identical fields, in terms of both the size and number of fields (Figure 2.6).

Rectangular files are sometimes called Flat or Two-dimensional files, but it is felt that the term Rectangular is more graphic and this will be used throughout the text.

Rectangular files can be wasteful in terms of the space that they take up, because every record must be big enough to hold the maximum number of fields and each field must allow for the biggest piece of data expected.

On early computer systems Complex files were frequently used and a great deal of time and effort was expended on packing data to avoid waste. Generally, the complexity which this introduced was extremely costly and error prone.

Today the overriding considerations of simplicity and flexibility are such that all live data must be held in Rectangular files. Or, it must appear that this is the case.

The qualification in the last paragraph has been introduced because there are systems which can in fact automatically pack and unpack Rectangular files. Again this is essentially a programming problem. Designers should, however, assure themselves that this facility is going to be totally transparent under all circumstances.

The term 'transparent' is commonly used in computing to mean that users are unaware of what is actually happening. In this case it must appear at all times as if fixed length fields are being used.

As has been suggested, this is essentially a programming problem, but since designers are ultimately responsible for systems, they must ensure that any deviations from the logical design of a system are not going to introduce unnecessary restrictions and costs in the future.

Often Rectangular files are the logical way to develop a system, as in the case of the address book. Looking at this from a manual point of view, nobody would consider using different sizes of cards for people with short or long names. It makes sense to do the same on a computer. However, in other cases a certain amount of thought is required. Consider, for example, a simplified Delivery Note (Figure 2.7). On a manual system a copy of each Delivery Note would normally be filed in a folder. One may expect to find a similar file on an EDP version of the system. This will not be the case.

The Delivery Note is a complex document consisting of a Header and a series of Item Details (Figure 2.8). There is what is called a one-to-many relationship between the Header and the Details. In other words, a customer may have more than one item delivered.

Complex records must be simplified by assigning data to separate Rectangular files.

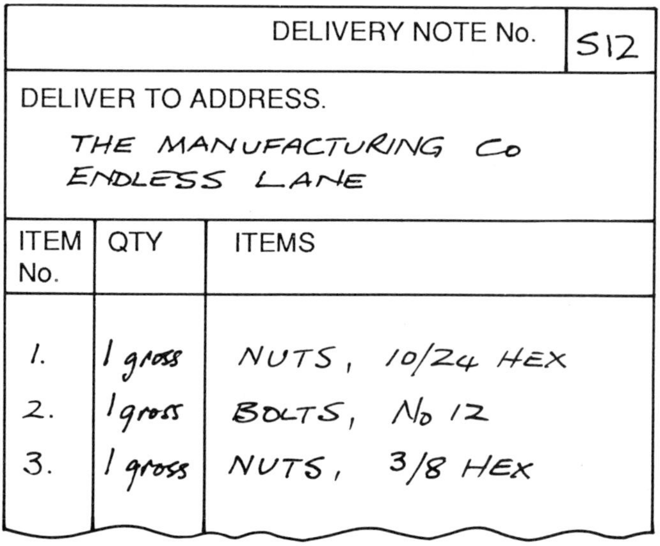

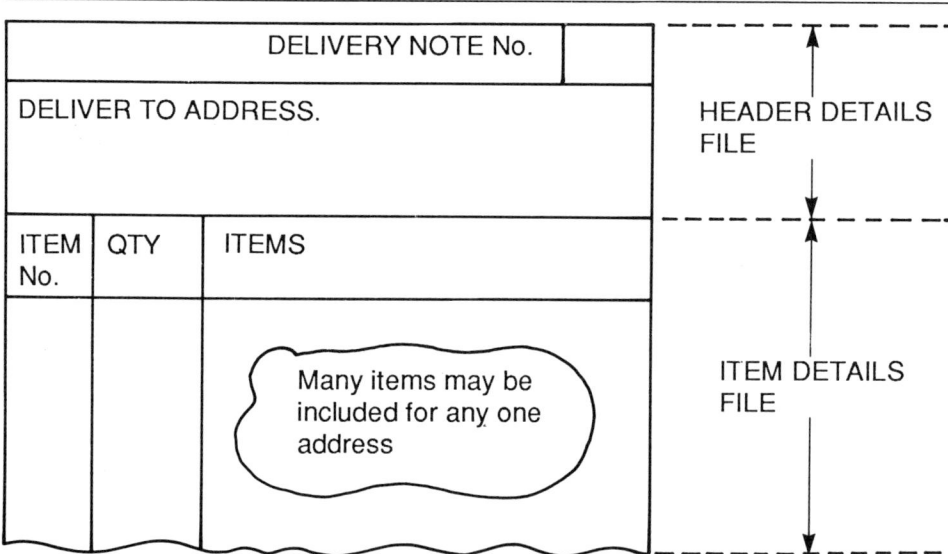

Figure 2.7 Typical simplified Delivery Note.

Figure 2.8 The Delivery Note is a complex document. Header and Item Details must be held in separate files.

In practice, further simplifications would be introduced into the example shown, but for the moment it should be clear that if the Header is put into one file and the details into another, these can readily be held on Rectangular files - providing each item on the Details file has the 'Delivery Note No.' on it to link it to the Header (Figure 2.9).

DELIVERY NOTE HEADER FILE

DELIVERY NOTE No.	DELIVER TO ADDRESS
S12 S13 etc.	The Manufacturing Co., Endless Lane, Spondon. AND Co., Sweet St., Southampton

DELIVERY NOTE ITEMS FILE

DELIVERY NOTE No.	ITEM	QTY	U/M	ITEM DESCRIPTION
S12	1	1	Gross	Nuts, 10/24 Hex.
S12	2	1	Gross	Bolts, No. 12.
S12	3	1	Gross	Nuts, 3/8 Hex.
S13	1	2	Cwt	Cement.
etc.				

Figure 2.9 Header and Item details assigned to separate Rectangular files.

The Header and Item Details will, of course, be the subject of separate Modules. Since each Item Detail will be held in a separate record and the Header will be on a different file, Delivery Notes cannot be displayed or printed using the basic Functions. They must be produced via Report Displays or Prints.

Breaking down files in this way makes the task of designing and programming systems very much easier. It also makes the task of producing reports about Customers or Item Details very much simpler.

On a commercial system, Delivery Notes would normally be part of an Invoice/Delivery Note set and would be part of a much wider system. Similarly, Customers and Items would normally be coded. The wider implications of this will be examined later, but the basic principles remain exactly the same.

Before leaving this section it is worth noting that splitting the files leads the designer on. For example, once the Header details are put in a separate file it quickly becomes apparent, that when a second delivery is made a great deal of data will be duplicated on the system as it stands.

In fact, the only piece of data which wouldn't be duplicated on the Header each time a repeat delivery is made would be the delivery note number. So the system as it stands leaves a lot of food for thought.

Splitting data into Rectangular files will normally reveal duplications, which indicate the scope for further rationalisation.

For the sake of completeness, it should perhaps be stated that more subtle links may be introduced at the programming stage, between the Header and the Item Details. These must augment, rather than replace, the logical link. Failure to ensure that this is done can often turn the production of even the simplest reports into an unnecessarily difficult task.

Counters and Tables

In addition to records, computer systems will normally have two other features, both of which are again common to manual systems, namely Counters and Tables.

Counters can be used in a variety of ways. For example, on an Invoicing system, Counters would normally be used to keep a running total of the number of items on the invoice and of their value. Similarly, the number of the last invoice printed would also be held, so that invoices can be numbered automatically. Counters should not normally present any problems, although care is required to ensure that they are incremented at the right time and that provision has been made for start-up. The start-up provisions must include, where necessary, facilities to handle documents which are already in existence.

Counters will usually be incremented automatically by the system, but if they have to be changed manually from time to time, this is best achieved by treating the counter as a field on a Control record.

Tables can also be used in a variety of ways. For example, to hold conversion factors for weights and measures, extended descriptions for coded abbreviations and/or lists of acceptable abbreviations and so on. Again they should not present any difficulties, but care is required to ensure that they do not unduly restrict a system.

If frequent changes to Tables are required, the table must be treated as a series of records on a file. Working in this way allows users to alter the 'Table' in the normal way, without a programme change being required. This can be either an advantage or a disadvantage, depending upon whether it is desirable/acceptable for users to change the values in the Tables.

In the case of weights and measures conversion tables (Figure 2.10) it would not normally be desirable for users to change the conversion factors, although a new range of measures may need to be added to change from Imperial to Metric. In the case of currency exchange rates it is clearly essential that users should be able to change these to reflect day to day changes.

CODE	DESCRIPTION	INCHES PER.
IN	INCHES	1
FT	FEET	12
YD	YARDS	36

Figure 2.10 Typical conversion Table.

Checking Data

An important feature of computer systems is that they can automatically check details as they are entered. This is not possible on manual systems, but the concept should not present users with any difficulties - providing care is taken in deciding what checks to apply.

The most common check is that the number of characters entered does not exceed the size of the corresponding Field. This is usually essential, since most systems will be programmed to allow for a particular number of characters. If more are entered, then the effect is rather like that of a typist typing past the edge of a page.

Computers can also check whether data should be purely Numeric (N) or should consist of letters and symbols in the form of Alphabetic (A) data. The symbol 'X' is commonly used to indicate that data may be either Numeric or Alpha.

This checking facility is particularly useful, as the most common source of confusion on computer systems arises when users type the letter 'O', instead of zero, or when the letter 'I' is typed instead of the number one.

Where necessary the precise format of a field can be checked, for example, NN/NN/NN for a date, or a check can be made that values lie within sensible ranges, for example, that the month must lie in the range 01 to 12.

As far as users are concerned, these checks should help them to avoid problems rather than present problems. However, designers must take particular care to avoid including checks which are too restrictive. There is nothing more frustrating to users than a system which doesn't allow them to do what they should be able to do.

One of the most common forms of irritation arises from the use of upper and lower-case letters. On many systems only upper-case letters will be accepted. On more enlightened systems the computer will, where appropriate, accept either and convert what is typed into the form required.

Computers can also help with other tests, such as checking whether or not a particular record already exists on a file, or if a particular value appears in a Table. Tests of this nature can be vital to ensure that a system reacts in a sensible way when an unexpected situation arises.

At each stage in the design process, the designer must ask the question, "What if ... ?", and assume the worst.

For example, if a user wishes to Amend a particular Customer record, the system must be designed to cater for the situation where no such record exists. Conversely, if a user attempts to Create a record for a 'new' Customer when a record already exists, the system must point this out.

One of the most common mistakes in designing systems is to assume that what exists today will exist tomorrow. The commercial world is never static and the demands which are made on systems will continually change. Organisations change from day to day; New products will be created and old ones disappear; New Tax and VAT laws will be introduced, and indeed newer and better computers will appear. Systems must therefore be designed to adjust to change. Clearly, not all changes can be anticipated. The effects of changes can, however, be minimised.

Systems must be designed with simplicity and flexibility foremost, and checks must be limited to the minimum necessary to ensure the integrity of the system.

Appraisal

In this chapter almost all the basic principles of the HCI of systems design have been touched upon, hopefully, in a way and in terms that can readily be understood by both users and designers. The primary aim has been to show that in essence EDP is simple and that there is no real reason why people should not readily be able to understand computer systems, providing the systems are designed so that people can readily relate to them, and that jargon is avoided.

This chapter has covered a lot of ground very briefly and this will be examined in more detail in subsequent chapters.

The concept of Rectangular files may take a bit of getting used to as far as users of purely manual systems are concerned. Similarly, the file structures that these introduce may seem to be somewhat unusual at first. Apart from this, computer systems should differ very little from their manual counterpart. So both users and designers should benefit from thinking of computer systems in terms of their manual equivalent.

Chapter 3.

The Basic Principles of PSD

Introduction

This chapter is devoted in the main to describing the basic principles of Patterned Systems Design (PSD). The methodology is aimed primarily at the design of everyday commercial EDP, as opposed to specialised applications such as Computer Aided Design and Word Processing, and so on.

As will become clearer later, most of the concepts are equally applicable to all forms of modern computing. This includes dedicated systems, such as Bank Cash-Dispensers, and systems with advanced forms of input such as Bar-Code Readers. Initially, only conventional EDP is considered and for this a clear understanding is required of what is meant by a modern computer.

Key Features of a Modern Computer

Modern computers come in a wide variety of shapes and forms. As far as PSD is concerned, there are only a very limited number of major features that need to be considered. The modern computer must have (Figure 3.1):

*   One or more Visual Display Units (VDUs), or Monitors, with a screen on which data can be displayed.

*   Processing and Storage Units. In the case of a small micro-computer these units may be an integral part of the VDU or of the Keyboard. On larger systems the units may be many miles away, linked to the VDU by telephone lines. As far as PSD is concerned, all of these systems are the same, providing that they permit working in TP mode.

*   One or more Keyboards, which will allow details to be entered onto the screen of the VDU and into the processing and storage units.

*   Printers. These may be situated centrally, and be shared by many users. Or each user may have a printer or share one with a neighbour.

As was suggested earlier, the main feature which distinguishes modern systems from their Batch Processing predecessors is their ability to perform Transaction Processing (TP) or, in other words, to allow users to determine what program should be run and to enter and process data at will.

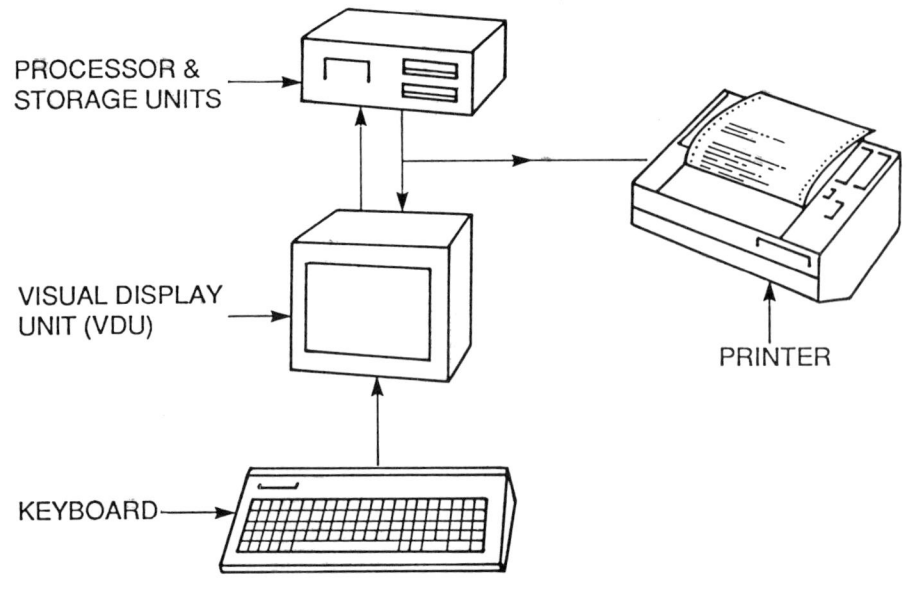

Figure 3.1 The main elements of a modern computer.

Apart from TP working, the other key feature that distinguishes the modern computer from its predecessors is the VDU. This allows a full screen of data to be displayed (normally 24 lines of 80 characters). This display is usually simply called 'a Screen' and the display is, in most cases, virtually instantaneous.

A bright flashing line or character-sized block on the screen, known as the Cursor, determines where what is typed into the Keyboard will appear on the screen. By manipulating the Cursor, users can return to what has previously been typed and correct or erase it.

These features represent a very significant advance from earlier teletype systems, where output was limited by the slowness of the teleprinter and typing errors could not be corrected. They have also opened the way for major improvements in systems design and it is these features that PSD is aimed at exploiting.

Why Patterned Systems Designs?

The concept of PSD first began to take shape in 1977 on a project which was part of a major factory automation scheme.

Initially, four programmers were to be involved in the project and after unhappy experiences with similar projects it was agreed at the start that the system must not look as though it had been developed by a number of different people. So the first part of the project was devoted to establishing a series of standards and standard programs to cover input, output and screen-handling. The results of this work far exceeded expectation and in spite of the time taken to develop the standards, the project was completed ahead of schedule.

It was some time before the reasons for this achievement were fully appreciated. Indeed, it took the works of a number of eminent authors (BEER, 1979, de BONO, 1969 and FURST, 1979), to make clear what should have been obvious, namely the impact of pattern recognition.

Pattern recognition is probably the most truly remarkable and the most powerful of all human attributes. There is a popular misconception that people are good at thinking. This is not the case. Try to think of the answer to (273x796) if there is any doubt about this.

What people are in fact extremely good and quick at is pattern recognition. Very complex objects such as trees, houses, chairs or cars can instantly be recognised for what they are, even where items, within a classification, differ significantly in shape and size. What is perhaps even more remarkable is that objects which have never been seen before can be 'recognised'. For example, a new car, a new painting by a well-known artist or a new song by a familiar group.

Clearly, therefore, if computer systems are designed, so that they conform to patterns, then people will quickly become familiar with the patterns. Better still, if systems are designed so that they conform to patterns with which users are already familiar and only call for skills which users already have, then users will readily relate to the systems and feel at ease with them.

The term PSD has, therefore, been used to describe the collection of algorithms, which have been devised to ensure that systems conform to patterns to which users can readily relate.

These algorithms are expanded upon in this chapter and the ones which follow it.

The 'Record' is the Key

At first sight, the task of attempting to produce systems which conform to familiar patterns may appear to be formidable. This is particularly so if conventional batch-type systems are considered, where Files and File Handling considerations predominate.

Initially, a Stock Control system may appear to have little in common with a Payroll or Invoicing system. The key to finding commonality has already been suggested in Chapter 2, and this is to think in terms of Records rather than Files.

PSD is based on standardisation at Record-level. As has already been demonstrated, there are only a limited number of Functions that can be performed on a single record and these are a common requirement for all Records.

Records will obviously differ from one system to another in terms of the number of fields, their size and their contents, but this will not present any problems for either users or designers, providing all Records are handled in a standardised way.

PSD Modules

The basic building block of a PSD system is called a Module. This brings together all the basic Functions associated with a Record.

Each Record will be the subject of a Module. And, each Module will be entered through a 'Menu of Functions' which must be the same for all Modules (Figure 3.2).

```
            MENU OF FUNCTIONS
        Enter selection number ... ?[ ]

        1. CREATE Record

        2. AMEND Record

        3. ERASE Record

        4. DISPLAY Record

        5. PRINT Record

        6. REPORT DISPLAYS

        7. REPORT PRINTS
```

Figure 3.2 Standard PSD Menu of Functions.

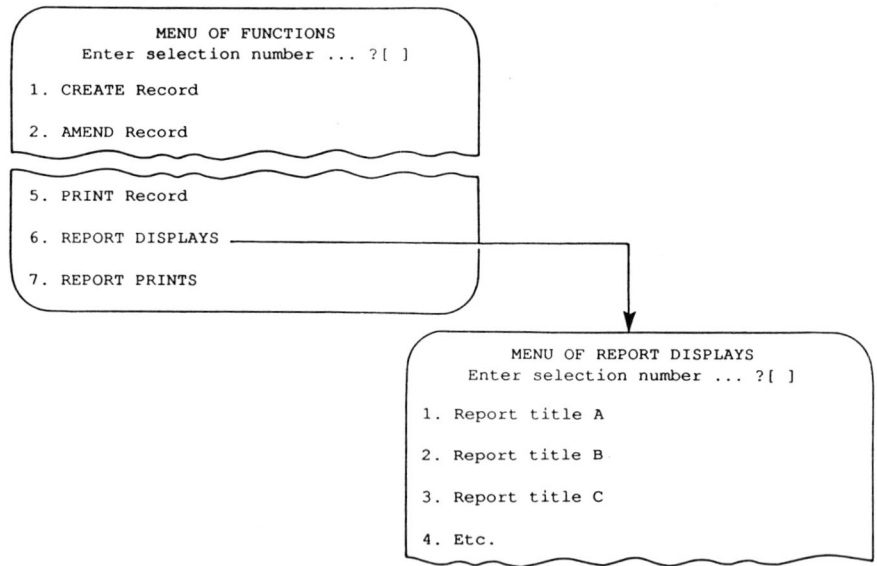

Figure 3.3 Reports are selected from secondary menus.

Note that the selections 6 & 7 make provision for Reports. These selections take users to secondary 'Menus of Reports', in which the reports associated with each module will be listed for selection (Figure 3.3).

Working in this way ensures that the Menu of Functions can be standard for all Modules on all Systems. This has two basic advantages:

* Because the menu is standard, users will quickly memorise it and will hardly need to look at it. More about this later.

* Relegating reports to secondary menus reflects the natural structuring of a system. It also allows large numbers of reports to be accommodated.

Compare the simplicity of PSD with the confusion that arises on a typical badly-structured system (Figure 3.4). The menu shown in fact covers two modules and the basic functions are mixed in with the report selections.

Similarly, the menu does not reflect the structure of the system, so users cannot relate to it. The menu is further complicated by the failure to rationalise Display and Print facilities.

```
                BILL OF MATERIALS MENU

             ENTER SELECTION NUMBER ? ...

       1.   SINGLE LEVEL EXPLOSION DISPLAY
       2.   SINGLE LEVEL EXPLOSION PRINT
       3.   INDENTED EXPLOSION DISPLAY
       4.   INDENTED EXPLOSIION PRINT
       5.   INDENTED WHERE-USED DISPLAY
       6.   INDENTED WHERE-USED PRINT
       7.   SINGLE LEVEL WHERE-USED DISPLAY
       8.   SINGLE LEVEL WHERE-USED PRINT
       9.   MASTER PARTS CREATE
      10.   MASTER PARTS UPDATE
      11.   PRODUCT STRUCTURE CREATE
      12.   PRODUCT STRUCTURE UPDATE
```

Figure 3.4 Typical badly organised menu.

PSD High Level Structuring

Once the modules required for a system have been identified, the task of completing the system is essentially a matter of grouping modules into logical Sub-systems and grouping the Sub-systems into logical Systems (Figure 3.5).

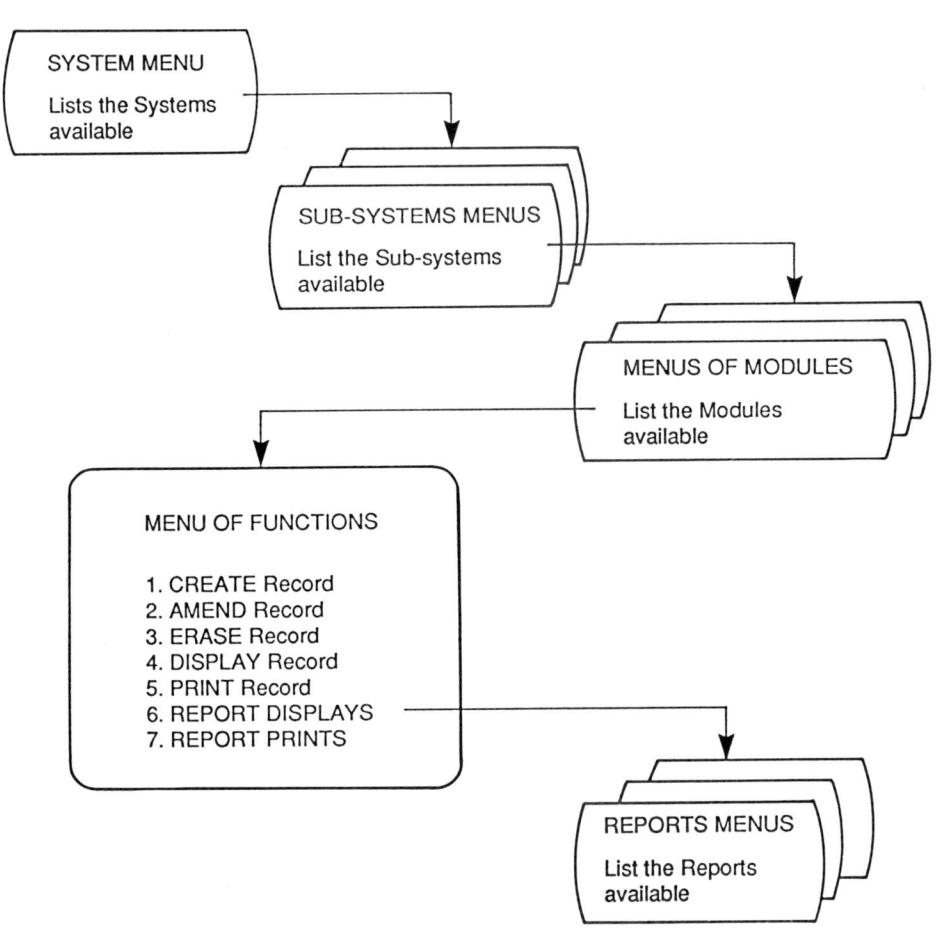

Figure 3.5 The full PSD structure.

Menus must be provided at each level, so that when users select the System that they require the appropriate menu of Sub-systems will be displayed. Selection of a particular Sub-system will then result in the modules available being displayed and so on to the Menu of Functions, etc. Figure 3.6 shows a typical selection path through a PSD system.

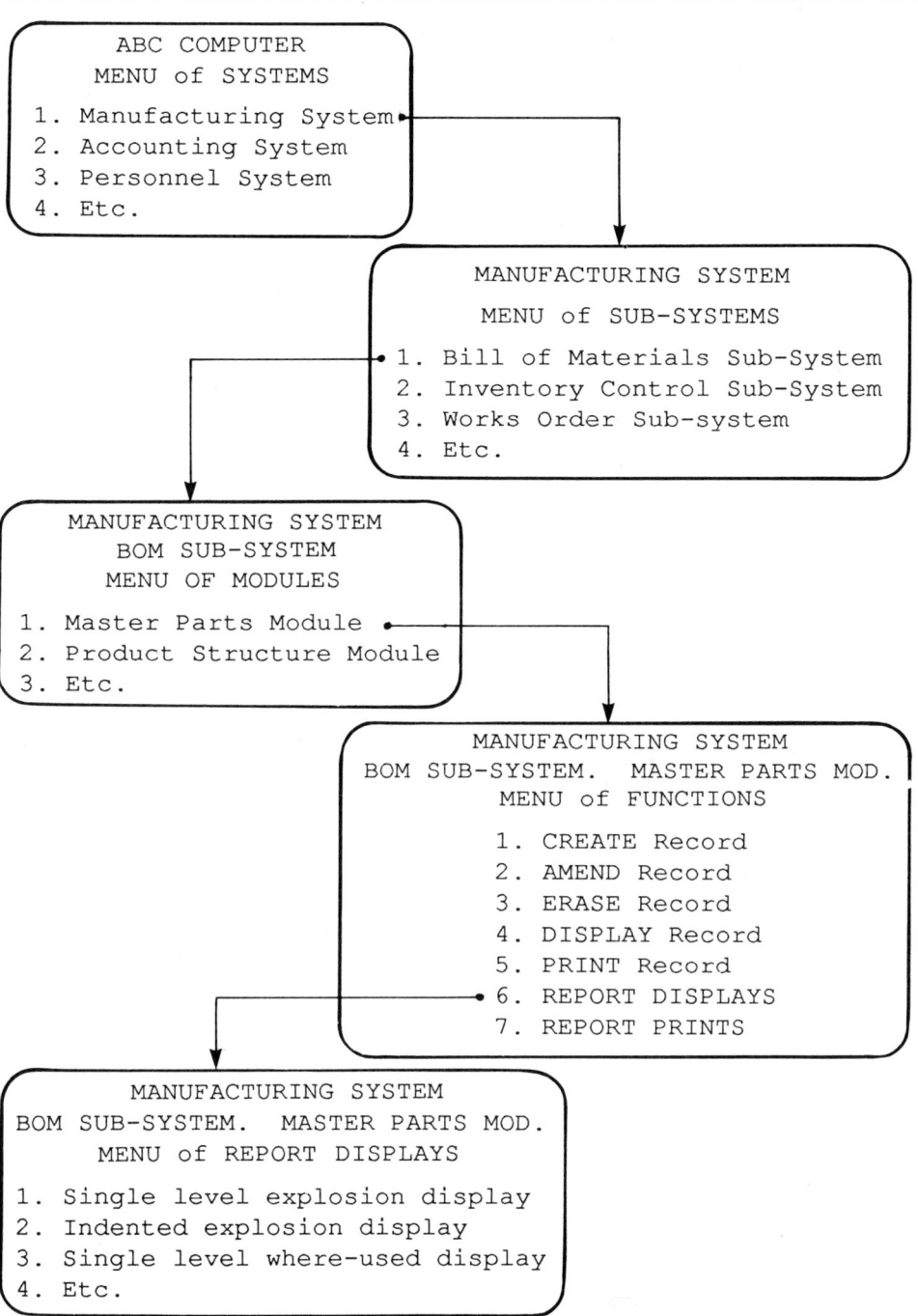

Figure 3.6 Typical section through a PSD system.

As will become clear later, up to 16 selections can conveniently be listed on each menu and this is about the limit of what people can conveniently scan. Longer menus, particularly those with cryptic details, must be avoided. Where less than nine options have to be displayed these can be double spaced to advantage.

With 16 selections per menu, the structure can accommodate over 4000 modules and an unlimited number of reports. This should be more than adequate for most applications and further levels of structuring must be avoided.

In the unlikely event that a total system cannot be accommodated within the recommended structure, a totally separate set of systems, another Package, should be established. The choice of which of the alternative Menus of Systems is then accessed would then be determined by the I/D which the user uses to Log-on. In this way, the shallow nature of the structure can be preserved. This, coupled with the logical basis of PSD, ensures that facilities are not hidden away under layer upon layer of structuring. So users find it easy to navigate through the systems and the structure lends itself to the task of ensuring the security of the system and making sure that users know where they are in a system.

Appraisal

As will become clearer later, the standard PSD Structuring plays a simple but vital role in the task of effective systems design. It is not just a desirable feature - it is essential.

The key lies in recognising the fact that there are only five Basic Functions (ie. Create, Amend, etc.) and that these are a common requirement for all Records.

At the same time, the structure reflects the way in which systems are normally structured in the outside world, and so users can readily relate to it.

As users work down through a package, the menus guide them logically from the broad area of their requirements to their precise needs. For example, in Figure 3.6, what the menus are saying to users as they work down through the menus is:

What System do you want? - Manufacturing.

What Sub-system of Manufacturing? - Bill of Materials.

What Module of the BOM? - Master Parts Module.

Do you want to Create, Amend, Erase, Display or Print a record?

Or do you want to Report on the Master Parts Records?

If so, which report do you want?

What could be simpler?

Chapter 4

The Basic PSD Structure

Introduction

This chapter examines in more detail the problems of how to structure systems, so that users can readily navigate through them. It also describes the recommended PSD approach.

The Keyboard

The PSD approach is based on the use of a conventional computer Keyboard (Figure 4.1), although it can be adapted to most types of keyboard. A conventional Keyboard consists essentially of a QWERTY (Typewriter) keyboard and a varying number of other keys.

The fact that there are varying numbers of 'other keys' is highly significant from the HCI point of view, and affects both users and designers;

* There are a large number of people who are reasonably proficient in the use of a typewriter. These people will, therefore readily relate to systems that do not require the use of 'special' keys.

* Using special keys may restrict a system to one particular type of keyboard.

There are two major exceptions to the above. Firstly, EDP systems must have a facility which is not found on a normal typewriter, namely a facility to 'Enter' data from the VDU into the Processing unit. (Technically, the data is in an input buffer, but it is convenient to think of it as in the VDU.) So all EDP Keyboards must have an <ENTER> key.

Some Keyboards, unfortunately, do not have a special enter-key, or even a key labelled 'Enter'. The <CARRIAGE RETURN> or <TAB> keys may have to be used. This is distinctly unfriendly and obviously leads to problems when Word-processing is introduced.

The second exception is the Numeric Keypad. Normally, pressing a number on the keypad has exactly the same effect as typing the number, so users can use whichever alternative they prefer.

Since virtually everybody can use a Numeric Keypad or calculator, use of the keypad is attractive and PSD navigation is based on this.

Users should, however, beware of systems where the Numeric Keypad is not always live.

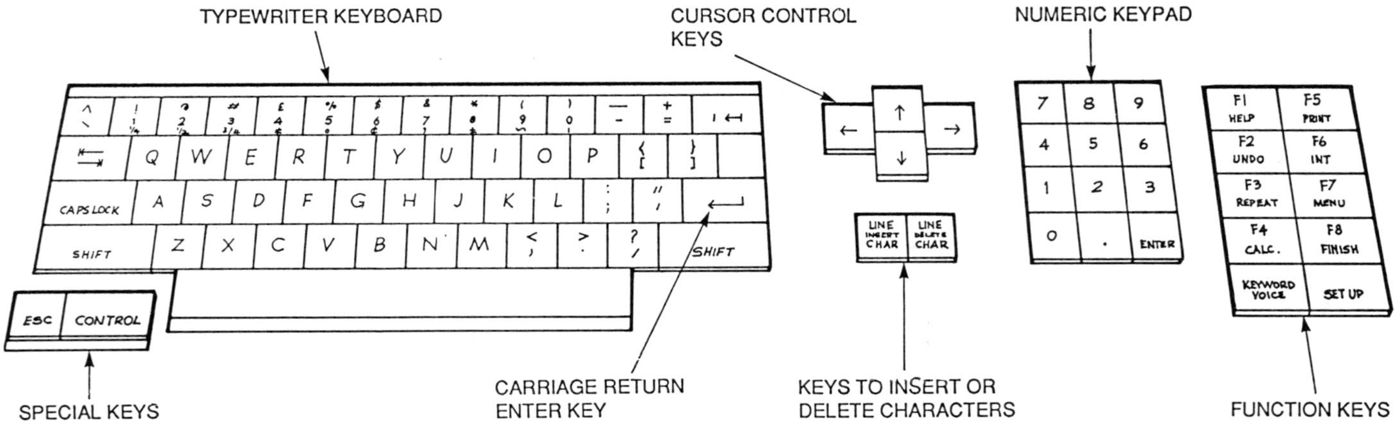

Figure 4.1 The main elements of a conventional computer keyboard.

PSD Menus

In the light of the above the most important features of PSD Menus (Figure 4.2) are that:

* All menus must be presented in precisely the same format and must be handled by standard routines.

* All selections must be numbered down the left-hand side of the screen.

* Users must be prompted to 'Enter selection number ... ', and this prompt must always appear in the same place on the screen.

Using this approach, anyone who can use a Keypad can readily progress down through a PSD system from menu to menu, one level at a time. To return back up the structure users must enter an asterisk in respose to the selection prompt.

Initially, leaving the selection number blank and pressing <ENTER> was used to indicate that users wished to go back up the structure. But experience showed that if users lingered a little too long on the <ENTER> key, a fast system could jump two levels at a time. This can cause confusion and the slightly longer but more positive approach is recommended.

```
01:32   16/04/87   MANUFACTURING SYSTEM.    01+01+03+6
Bill of Materials Sub-system.   Product Structure Module.
                     REPORT DISPLAYS.
               Enter selection number ...?[ ]

1. Single level explosion display

2.  "         "    where-used display

3. Indented explosion display

4.     "         where-used display

5. Etc.
```

Figure 4.2 Typical PSD Menu. The same format is used for all PSD menus.

It is highly disturbing to users if a system reacts in an unexpected way, due to a user error. Systems must be designed to respond positively.

On some systems a <CANCEL> key is provided to exit from a menu, back up a structure. This is straight forward but can suffer from the same problem as a blank <ENTER>. It will of course restrict systems to keyboards which have a <CANCEL> key and a skilled typist will find an asterisk easier.

PSD Headers

On any major system, it is essential that users should not only be able to navigate through a system with ease - they must know precisely where they are at all times.

This is achieved by means of the PSD Screen Header (Figure 4.3).

The PSD Screen Header is common to all screens, all prints and all standard reports. It occupies the top four lines of each screen and does not include the ruler, which is shown in the illustration.

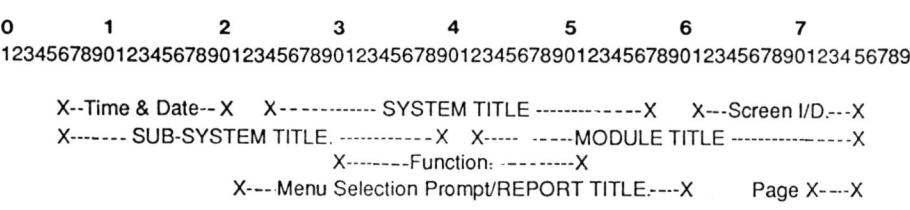

```
        0         1         2         3         4         5         6         7         8
        12345678901234567890123456789012345678901234567890123456789012345678901234 567890

        X--Time & Date-- X    X------------ SYSTEM TITLE -------------X    X---Screen I/D.---X
        X------- SUB-SYSTEM TITLE. ------------X   X----- -----MODULE TITLE ------------- ----X
                             X--------Function: ----------X
                        X--- Menu Selection Prompt/REPORT TITLE.----X       Page X----X
```

Figure 4.3 PSD Screen Header Standard

The Header is automatically built up on a progressive basis as users move through a system. It shows:

*   Time and Date. (Line 1, 34 characters, positions 6 to 20.) This displays the system clock in the form HH:MM DD/MM/YY.

*   System Title. (Line 1, 34 characters, positions 24 to 57.) Initially, this will display the name of the computer. It will then change to show the title of whatever System is selected, when the first menu selection is made.

* Screen I/D. (Line 1, 15 characters, positions 61 to 75.) This allows an identifier to be displayed to cross-reference the display to user guides and programmes. The structure lends itself to an I/D of the form shown in Figure 4.4, based on menu selection numbers.

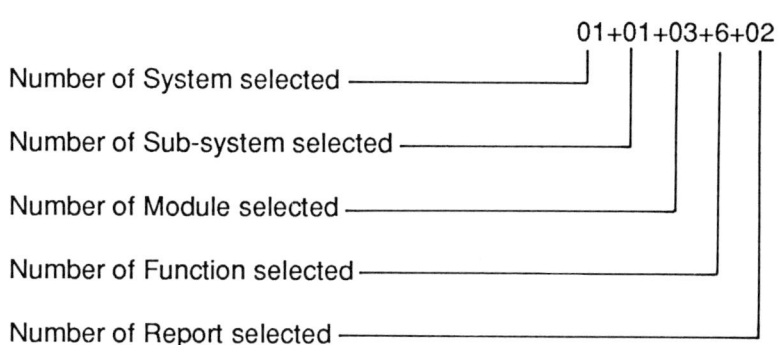

Figure 4.4 Format of Screen I/D numbers. Note that '+' is used as a delimiter to avoid confusion with times and/or dates.

* Sub-system Title. (Line 2, 34 characters, positions 6 to 39.) Initially, this will show an asterisk. When a selection is made from a Menu of Sub-systems, the title of the selection will be displayed.

* Module Title. (Line 2, 34 characters, positions 42 to 75.) Initially this will show an asterisk. When a Module has been selected, it will show the title of the module.

* Function. (Line 3, 22 characters, positions 30 to 51.) This is used to show which Function has been selected from the Menu of Functions.

* Report Title. (Line 4, 40 characters, positions 21 to 60.) This is used to display the title of whatever report is selected. It is also used to display the prompt for menu selection.

* Page. (Line 4, 5 characters, positions 71 to 75.) This allows the page number of a report to be displayed.

On minor systems with fewer levels, some of the details shown in the Screen Header may be superfluous, but the same standard format must be used throughout. This will ensure that users quickly become familiar with the structure and that new facilities can readily be added without any major revisions.

For example, whilst many systems may not have a clock initially, making provision for the display will ensure that wholesale modifications to screen designs are avoided when one is introduced.

Many systems designers do not appear to have recognised the importance of Screen Headers, or perhaps feel that to devote four lines of screen to this is wasteful. But lines of screen cost virtually nothing, whereas confused users cost a great deal.

The PSD Header logically reflects the actual structure of the systems and the standardised nature of the header makes it easy for users to know where to look. Similarly, once a standard method of handling the Header has been determined, the designer's task is reduced to one of simply deciding upon the title to be used at each stage.

The selected titles must conform to the prescribed limits. To ensure that this is the case a pro-forma of the form shown in Figure 4.5 is useful.

In common with all PSD displays, the Screen Header is limited to 70 characters per line. This is to allow what is displayed on the screen to be printed on A4 paper in exactly the same format. It assumes that the maximum type-size that will be used is 10 characters per inch (Pica).

The same restriction is normally applied to all PSD displays. In this way, many of the problems associated with copying and filing larger sheets of paper can be avoided. And, only one format has to be devised to serve for both Displays and Prints.

```
SYSTEM TITLE (34 characters)
_ _ _ _ _ _ _ _ _ _ _ _ _ _ _ _ _ _ _ _ _ _ _ _ _ _ _ _ _ _ _ _ _ _
SUB-SYSTEM TITLE (34 characters)
_ _ _ _ _ _ _ _ _ _ _ _ _ _ _ _ _ _ _ _ _ _ _ _ _ _ _ _ _ _ _ _ _ _
MODULE TITLE (34 characters)
_ _ _ _ _ _ _ _ _ _ _ _ _ _ _ _ _ _ _ _ _ _ _ _ _ _ _ _ _ _ _ _ _ _
REPORT TITLE (40 characters)
_ _ _ _ _ _ _ _ _ _ _ _ _ _ _ _ _ _ _ _

_ _ _ _ _ _ _ _ _ _ _ _ _ _ _ _ _ _ _ _
```

Figure 4.5 A design aid for Screen Headers

Menu v Command Systems

What has been described so far is what is called a Menu-driven System. The main alternative to this is to use a command-based approach.

In command-based systems, after logging-on, users are invited to 'Enter a Command'. In most cases, this is done in a distinctly unfriendly way, by simply displaying a cryptic prompt, such as '>' or 'A>'.

Commands usually take the form of mnemonics, such as 'STKREP', and each function and report on a system has its own mnemonic. By entering a command, users can go directly to whatever they wish to run. This clearly has attractions - providing that users can remember the appropriate command.

Not surprisingly, there has been a considerable amount of debate about the relative merits of the two alternatives. The general consensus of opinion appears to be that skilled users prefer command systems, whilst unskilled users prefer Menus (WATTS, 1984).

What appears to have been overlooked, however, is that Command systems do not give users any feel for the structure of the systems, and as systems get bigger and bigger, the task of remembering an ever increasing number of commands becomes more and more formidable, particularly when complex commands are introduced.

On many systems users are still expected to use commands which are controlled by parameters. For example, users may be expected to enter a command of the form 'COPY B:*.*A:' to copy what is on one disc to another. In this day and age, expecting users to operate in this way seems inexcusable, particularly when a comma or colon out of place can result in the command being rejected.

A primary aim of most computer systems must be to attract as many users as possible, and by definition all new users will be untrained. It seems clear that in the first instance all systems must be based on the Menu approach. Whether it is then worth overlaying this with a Command system seems highly doubtful.

Skilled Users

Notwithstanding the above, there is one way in which PSD can be speeded-up for skilled users. As was suggested earlier, the Menu of Functions is common to all modules. It will therefore quickly be memorised by experienced users.

Provision can be made for skilled users to skip this menu by entering a double-selection at the level of the Menu of Modules. This can be achieved by typing in the selection number of the module required, followed either by:

* The initial letter(s) of the Function required (Figure 4.6), or

* A '+' delimiter followed by the menu selection number of the Function required.

For example, entering a multiple selection of '3A' or '3+2' at the Menu of Modules stage would take user directly to Module 3, in AMEND mode.

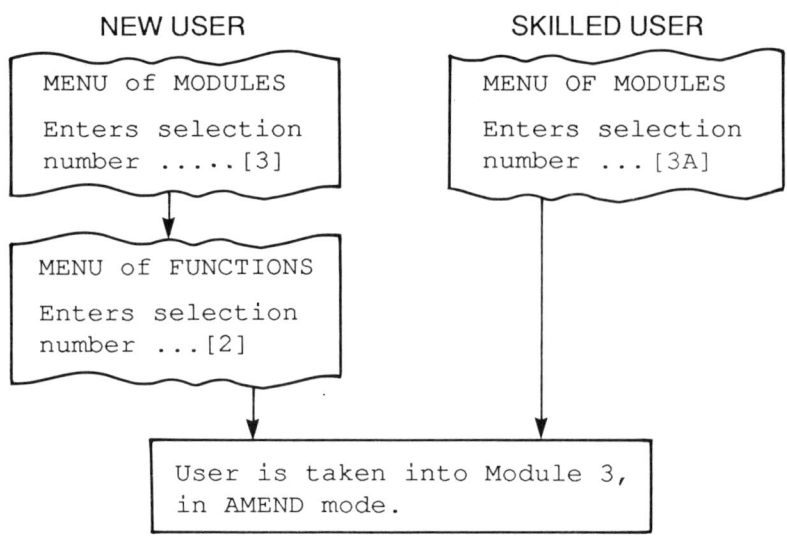

Figure 4.6 Skilled users can enter multiple menu selections.

Appraisal

PSD structuring enables systems to be produced in a way which can readily be understood by all concerned. It is essentially very simple and hence flexible. It also helps to ensure that EDP systems mirror their manual equivalents. This is a vital factor in enabling users to relate to systems and in avoiding what one author has aptly described as '... immense difficulties' (MARTIN, 1975).

No special features such as Mice, Touch-screens or even colour are required. And the intelligence of users is not insulted by cluttered screens showing icons of filing cabinets and waste paper baskets (Figure 4.7).

The restrictions imposed by the use of Special Function Keys are avoided, as is also the curse of so many systems, namely the need to become skilled in the art of cursor manipulation. With PSD, busy executives can quickly get the displays and reports that they require using little more than the keypad.

The PSD Screen Header shows users precisely where the are in the system at any time and with an overview of the structure they can quickly see how to get to where they want to be.

This may seem to be fairly elementary, but it is vital. To fully appreciate the importance of it, consider for a moment the analogy of the London Underground (System). Imagine trying to find one's way round it, without a map.

Consider also how much more difficult navigation would be if a map was provided, but different Lines (Sub-systems) were not identified. Imagine also the difficulties which travellers would have if Stations (Modules) were not clearly labelled or if station names were shown, but in a different way and place at each station.

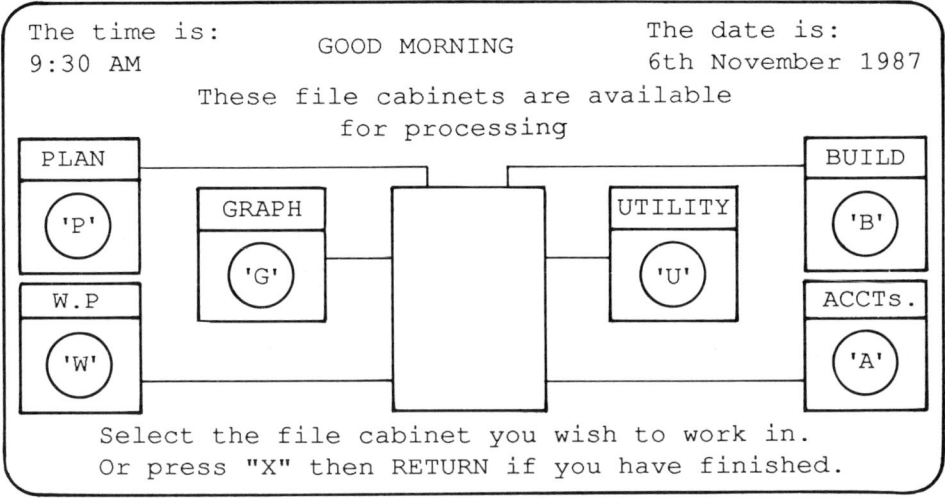

Figure 4.7 Menu selection can be made difficult.

Clearly, with time and effort one could master these difficulties. One could learn the hard way, as on so many computer systems, but the alternatives are simple and the benefits are highly significant.

This is particularly so, because the benefits apply not only to users, but also to designers and programmers. Indeed, they extend to all concerned with any aspect of the development, implementation, running and maintenence of a PSD System.

These benefits together with more detailed aspects of PSD are examined in the next chapter.

Chapter 5

PSD Record Processing

Introduction

In the previous chapter, it was demonstrated how easy it was for users to get to where they want to be in a PSD system. This chapter looks in more detail at the PSD methodology for actually processing records.

The task of actually creating, amending and erasing records is normally the one where users are most closely involved with the workings of computers. It is usually the one that takes the most user-time, and more often than not, it is performed by relatively junior staff.

The user-friendliness of this aspect of the design of systems is therefore a vital factor in determining the success or failure of a system. It is also the sphere where the biggest mistakes are most often made and where PSD can contribute the most.

This chapter looks in more detail at data-input and display formats, and then goes on to consider correction and filing processes. It should be noted that the standardised methods described are concerned purely with the processing of individual records, as opposed to reporting on numbers of records. Thus each transaction will normally require a unique key to be entered to identify the record to be processed.

The text assumes that the appropriate module and function have been selected and for simplicity Screen Headers are not shown.

Across-Screen Input

One of the most common design faults on systems is the use of across-screen input. On early VDU-based systems, users still had to remember what fields had to be entered and had to insert commas between fields (Figure 5.1). This was an exceptionally difficult task, a hang over from the days of punched cards and missing commas frequently caused errors.

```
LS1798624, NUT 3/16 HEX, EA, , , , 100, 50, 15/02/86
```

Figure 5.1 Early form of VDU input. Users had to refer to guides to find out what to put in and to delineate fields with commas.

Today the format of what has to be entered is normally shown on the input screen. On many systems, however, across-screen input has still been retained (Figure 5.2). This is a fundamental mistake.

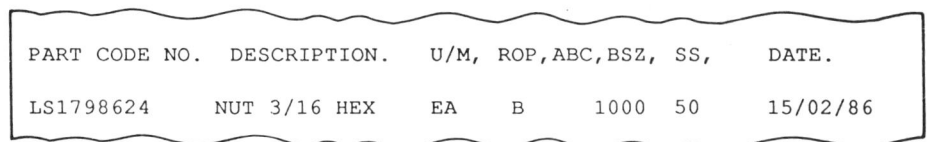

```
PART CODE NO.   DESCRIPTION.     U/M,   ROP,ABC,BSZ,  SS,      DATE.

LS1798624       NUT 3/16 HEX     EA     B    1000     50       15/02/86
```

Figure 5.2 Across-screen input showing cryptic field names.

In part, across-screen layout is probably a carry over from early systems. Generally it can be attributed to the fact that designers have failed to recognise the difference between Records and Reports.

In other words, the mistake that has been made is to try to design systems in such a way that what is put into a system is in the form in which it is expected out of the system.

The blame for this cannot be put purely on designers. It is natural for users to think that what is put into a system should look like what they want out of the system. If, for example, a system is to produce a Delivery Note (Figure 5.3), users may well expect what is put into the system to look like what is currently produced.

Designers may even encounter user resistance if they propose alternative formats. They must therefore be fully prepared to justify the avoidance of across-screen input.

Across-screen input creates major problems in virtually all aspects of the development and implementation of a system.

Many of the problems associated with across-screen input will become clearer later, once the preferred PSD approach has been considered, namely down-screen input. At this stage suffice it to say that the main problems with across-screen input are:

* Cryptic field headings, which confuse users and necessitate extensive user guides.

* Wrap-round difficulties, if there are more than 80 characters to a line of data.

* Error correction difficulties, due mainly to the vagaries of cursor controlled correction.

* Non-standard layout.

* Users and Designers become confused about what is a Record and what is a Report, and hence about the true structure of the system.

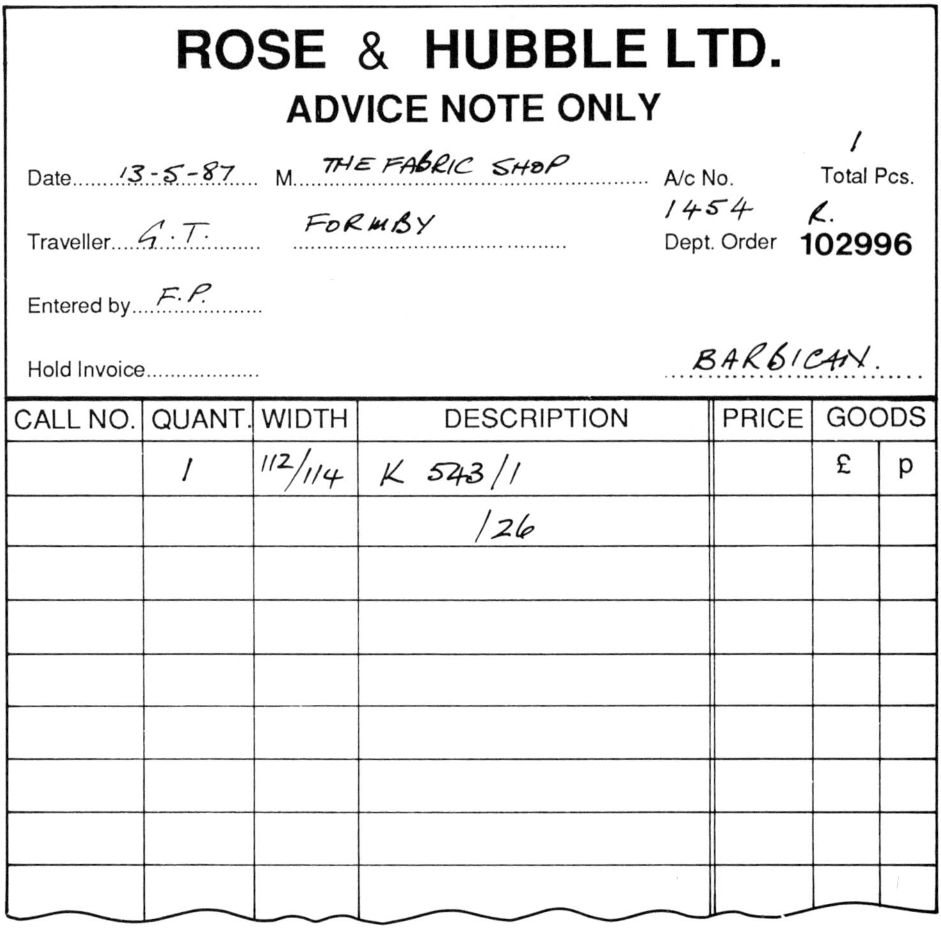

		ROSE & HUBBLE LTD.			
		ADVICE NOTE ONLY			
Date *13-5-87*	M *THE FABRIC SHOP*		A/c No *1454*	Total Pcs. *1*	
Traveller *G.T.*	*FORMBY*		Dept. Order	**102996** *K.*	
Entered by *F.P.*					
Hold Invoice			*BARBICAN.*		
CALL NO.	QUANT.	WIDTH	DESCRIPTION	PRICE	GOODS
	1	*112/114*	*K 543/1*		£ p
			/26		

Figure 5.3 Typical Delivery Note. Users may expect to put details into the computer in this format. They must not.

Down-Screen Input

Using PSD, all records employ the same basic format, based on down-screen input (Figure 5.4).

The main advantages of down-screen input are as follows:

* Adequate field descriptions can be shown and field sizes can be indicated.

* Where appropriate, details of the input format can be included, as for fields 4 and 8.

* Each field can be numbered, to facilitate corrections and for cross-referencing to user guides.

* The problems confronting both designers and users are considerably simplified.

```
1. Part Code    ...[          ]
2. Description  ...[                    ]
3. Unit of measure ...[     ]
4. Reorder policy (M) or (B) ...[ ]
5. ABC class ... [ ]
6. Batch size ... [      ]
7. Safety stock ... [      ]
8. Date active 'DD/MM/YY' ...[           ]
```

Figure 5.4 Down-screen input, recommended throughout.

Using this approach, the task of 'designing' screens is essentially reduced to one of listing the fields in sequence down the left-hand side of the screen. A task which can readily be performed by a standard program.

Thus, once the designer has specified what fields have to be accommodated, the design of the screen is implicit. A great deal of time and documentation can therefore be saved.

The same format must be used for all the basic Functions associated with a record. Thus, whether users are in Create or Display mode etc., the same data will always appear in the same place on the screen.

The same format must also be used for the Print function, so that printed details will be in precisely the same format. To this end each line of input must be limited to a width of 70 characters to facilitate printing on A4 paper.

Brackets are the simplest way of indicating field sizes. They are also probably the best way. There are other ways, such as the use of broken underlining. This has the advantage that users can count how many characters can be put into a field, although the instances when a user would want to do this must be few and far between.

Normally, a skilled user will not look at the screen during input and the main reason for showing the field size is so that users can see what has happened if they try to put too many characters into a field. Generally, the choice between the use of brackets or underlining is not significant. Certainly, the use of partially illuminated boxes or anything else which reduces the legibility of what is on the screen must be avoided.

There is also scope for further thought as far as the position of the input field is concerned. A somewhat tidier layout is shown in Figure 5.5. Unfortunately, whilst this makes the data stand out more clearly, it makes it more difficult for users to relate the data to its description. Again there is little to choose between the alternatives.

```
1. Part Code ...                      [_            ]
2. Description...                     [             ]
3. Unit of measure ...                [ ]
4. Reorder policy (M) or (B)          [ ]
5. ABC class...                       [    ]
6. Batch size...                      [    ]
7. Safety stock ...                   [    ]
8. Date active 'DD/MM/YY' ....        [       ]
```

Figure 5.5 Down-screen input. A tidier alternative.

Random Input

For the sake of completeness, there are two other forms of screen layout which should be mentioned, the first of which is Random Input. Random input is similar in many ways to down-screen input except that fields are not restricted to the left hand side of the screen (Figure 5.6).

```
Part Code            Description
[        ]           [                              ]

Unit of measure      Reorder policy       ABC class
[   ]                [    ]                      [ ]

Batch size           Safety stock         Date active
[     ]              [       ]            [           ]
```

Figure 5.6 Random input. Not recommended.

Fields can be numbered, but generally they are not. Similarly, colour is often used to excess on systems employing random input. The method has the advantage that more than 16 fields can be displayed on one screen, but, 'saving' screens is almost always counter-productive.

The method can also be used to devise input screens in the same format as source documents, assuming that a fixed form of source data is used. The benefits of this could, however, be achieved much more readily by numbering the fields on the source document and using down-screen input.

Better still, forms should where possible be redesigned so that they lend themselves to down-screen input. It is easy to forget that most forms are designed to serve a particular purpose. So if the main purpose of a form is to be used as computer input, it must be designed as such.

Random input has significant disadvantages. In particular, each screen has to be individually designed, programmed and documented. Also, users cannot readily determine where to look on the screen for a particular field number. The simpler, more systematic form of down-screen input is therefore preferred.

Question and Answer Input

The final form of input which is still commomly used takes the form of a question and answer session. The questions are posed one at a time with the next question being displayed when a question is answered (Figure 5.7).

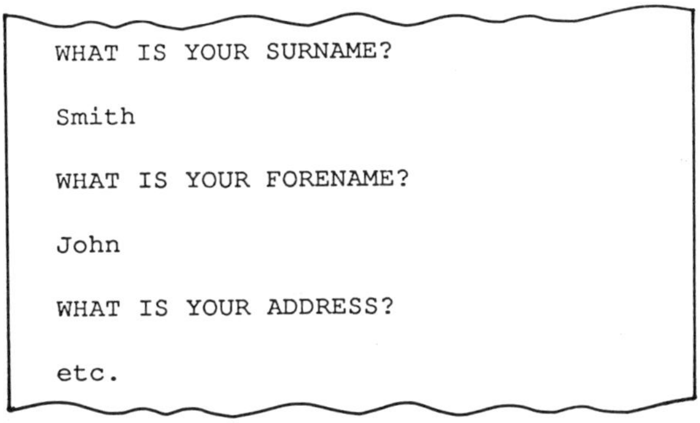

```
WHAT IS YOUR SURNAME?

Smith

WHAT IS YOUR FORENAME?

John

WHAT IS YOUR ADDRESS?

etc.
```

Figure 5.7 Question and Answer Input - Not recommended for general use.

This method of input is extremely easy to program and does have attractions for totally unskilled users or young children. Generally, however, its use is a hangover from the days when teletypes were the main form of input.

The method is not convenient for commercial DP and as such it is probably advisable to avoid its use altogether. The method lacks the crispness of the 'form-filling' alternatives, and although input is easy, everything else creates problems.

Input is usually scrolled and error correction is a major problem. Similarly, the input format is inappropriate for display and printing, and so special routines have to be programmed to cover each application.

The method is not recommended.

Typing into Fields

The fields into which data is to be inserted will be indicated by a flashing cursor and what is typed will normally appear on the screen in the designated field.

Pressing <ENTER> causes what has been typed into a field to be read in to a temporary file, the brackets are removed from the display and the cursor moves to the next field.

Until such time as <ENTER> is pressed, users must be able to correct what has been typed into a field. Correction after <ENTER> is dealt with later.

This correction process is the only one in PSD where a limited amount of cursor manipulation is unavoidable, and where special function keys are required.

Nearly every operating system seems to tackle the correction process in a different way, thus making what should be a simple process more difficult. The simplest approach appears to be to use two keys <INSERT> and <DELETE> as follows:

* Over typing is achieved by moving the cursor back to where a character is to be replaced and simply retyping.

* To remove an unwanted character, cursor to the character and press <DELETE>. The field will then be re-displayed without the deleted character.

* To insert a character, cursor to the point where a character is to be inserted and press <INSERT>. This will result in a space being created into which a character can then be typed.

This approach seems simple and logical, but users may find that they are stuck with more complex methods for the time being.

Note that the use of the cursor manipulation keys and special function keys for correction is justified, because the task which is being performed cannot be performed using conventional keys.

Note also that users are only expected to cursor within a field, rather than from one field to another.

After each of the above operations the cursor will move to the next character, so that successive overtyping or deletion can readily be achieved. This again can lead to confusion.

On some systems, when <ENTER> is pressed, what is to the right of the cursor is ignored. A much more positive approach is to ignore the position of the cursor and read in whatever is displayed in the field on the screen.

On many systems further confusion is also caused by using the <TAB> key to enter data in some circumstances and <ENTER> in other cases.

The keys to be used, and the functions performed by keys must be consistent throughout systems.

Error Detection

As each field is entered it must be checked against whatever criteria have been specified for the field. The criteria may include an indication as to whether the field can be left blank or must be filled in, the field size, the format and perhaps a range of acceptable values.

When an error is detected this must be indicated immediately by a 'Bell' (an audible warning) and an error message must be displayed. The system must then re-prompt for the field to be entered again. On early systems the Bell was used to indicate that a field had been entered correctly. However, this was quickly found to be distracting for users and disturbing for nearby staff. The quieter alternative of only sounding the Bell for errors is therefore preferrable.

A particular line on the screen must be reserved for error messages, usually line 21, and these should be displayed flashing. This saves users having to search the screen for the error messages and avoids the possibility of vital data on the screen being over-written by error messages.

Care must be taken to ensure that error messages are clear and explicit. For example, 'Data must be numeric' is much more helpful than 'Error 26'.

Flagging errors as each field is entered can slow down the input process, particularly if the system has to search a disc to check whether a particular key already exists on a file. However, the essential simplicity of the approach makes it vital from the point of view of both users and designers.

Designers must, therefore, make sure that adequate processing power is available and that provision is made to ensure fast response times during input.

The alternative is to wait until all the fields on a Record have been entered before flagging errors. But this introduces unnecessary complications and frustration for users and should be avoided.

Because users can get locked into a field, if they cannot come up with a valid input, provision must be made for mid-record exits.

Again there are a bewilderingly wide variety of ways in which this can be achieved. The recommended way is to use the same approach as the exit from a menu. In other words, to type an asterisk in the first character position in a field.

The effects of entering an asterisk in this way will depend on the field:

* An asterisk in the first field of an input record will result in a return to the calling menu.

* An asterisk in any other field will result in a return to the start of the record entry.

The first alternative will normally be used when a user has selected the wrong item from a menu, the second alternative when a series of mistakes makes it easier to go back to the start of a record and enter the data again.

The 'Create' Record Function

In Create mode, the format for the record will be displayed and the system will prompt for data to be typed into the first field.

When <ENTER> is pressed the data will be checked and if it is satisfactory the prompt will move to the next field and so on.

A common mistake at this stage is to try to save key-strokes, by introducing the principle of automatic-entry when a field is filled.

Since the average time for a key-stroke is of the order of 0.005 of a minute, saving key-strokes is obviously not a very profitable business. At the same time, the uncertainty which is introduced, about when <ENTER> should or should not be pressed, will add significantly to the costs of a system.

Skilled operators do not normally look at the screen during input until a record has been fully entered. So they should not have to do so to check if a field has been fully filled. If operators do not realise that the system has done an auto-enter and they press <ENTER> then a field could be left blank.

Similarly, all kinds of problems can arise if corrections have to be made to a field. Operators will not have a chance to correct the last character in a field before the system moves on. It is also common for a field to be temporarily filled during correcting, if insertions are carried out before deletions.

Data must only be read into the computer when <ENTER> is pressed.

In Create mode an additional check will always be carried out to ensure that no record can be created with the same key as a record already on file.

When the last field of a record has been entered, the system will then engage one of a series of standard 'Foot-of-Screen' routines.

Foot-of-Screen Routines

Foot-of-Screen (FOS) routines are used throughout PSD systems to advise users what to do next and to facilitate error correction.

Screen lines 22 and 23 must be reserved for FOS routines. These help to ensure that at all times users know what to do next.

The form of the display will vary slightly from mode to mode, although, there are only a limited number of routines and they are all very similar.

In Create mode, the FOS routine is called FOSC (Figure 5.8). The message will appear as soon as the last field of data has been entered and it will prompt for a response at the end of line 23.

```
ENTER: (F) to File, (*) to Abort, or a Field Number to
enable corrections                              .... ? [ ]
```

Figure 5.8 Foot-of-Screen Message for Create mode (FOSC). Allows users to check an input record before the details are filed.

The main purpose of FOSC is to allow users to check what has been entered into a record before the record is committed to the main files of the computer.

At this stage what has been entered will in fact be in a temporary file (Figure5.9) and users have a number of choices:

* Entering 'F' will result in the record being filed.

* Entering '*' will result in the record entry being ignored.

* Entering a valid field number will result in the cursor moving to the field indicated, ready for corrections to be made.

The fact that the user is shown clearly and concisely what to do is important. However, what is more important is that the features offered and the way in which they are offered closely resemble the way in which an operator would produce a manual record.

Because users are shown what features are available and because these features are closely akin to manual processing, users can readily relate to the record creation process.

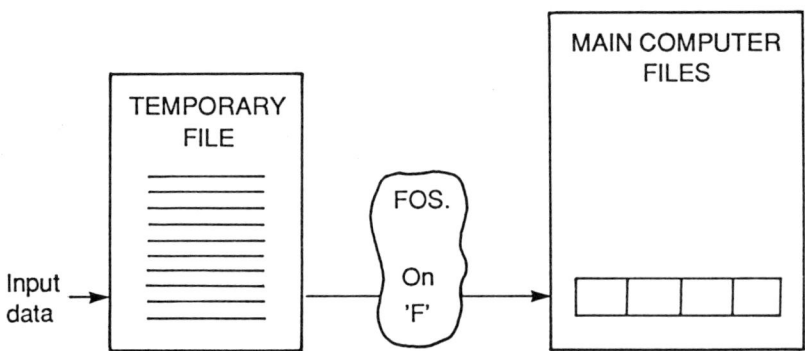

Figure 5.9 Data Entry. All data is held in a temporary file until its validity is confirmed.

As on manual systems, users must be encouraged to check a record before it is filed. They must also have the option to scrap the record and start again, and be able to correct individual fields.

On many systems correcting a field involves using cursor manipulation to direct the cursor to the field to be corrected. This is a time consuming and often erratic process at which users are not normally skilled. It can and must be avoided.

When a field number is entered in response to a FOS prompt, the cursor must be moved directly to the field ready for it to be corrected.

Once the cursor has been positioned the facilities for correction described earlier can be used. After a correction has been entered the system will return to the FOS routine, so that as many fields as necessary can be corrected.

Again key-strokes could have been saved by, for example, only requiring 'F' to be Pressed rather than Entered. Clearly, field numbers cannot be read in without using <ENTER> or a similar key to show when the number is complete.

To maintain a consistent approach, all FOS responses must be followed by <ENTER>.

Working in this way makes data entry simple and straight forward, and ensures that users can quickly learn what to do.

The Amend Record Function

The function of Amending records is very similar to Create, but in this case the data currently on file will be displayed once the record Key has been entered.

On many systems confusion is caused by data being displayed in different formats for Create and Amend. With PSD, the same format must be used throughout.

The only significant differences between Create and Amend are:

* The system will check that the record to be amended actually exists on file.

* A FOS routine will be invoked as soon as the data on a record has been displayed.

The FOS routine for Amend is exactly the same as for Create (ie. FOSC). Again the data will be held in a temporary file (Figure 5.10). In this case, Aborting will leave the records on the main file unchanged.

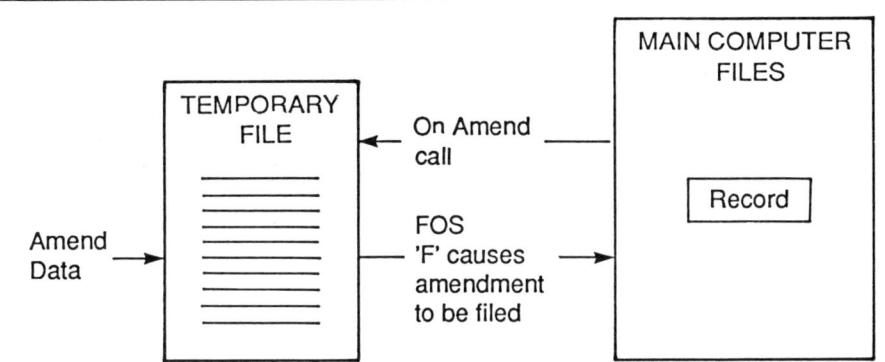

Figure 5.10 Amend Record. Changes are held in a temporary file until their validity is confirmed.

On some systems trying to amend a non-existent record doesn't result in the Key being rejected as not valid. On these systems a message is displayed such as 'No such record. Do you wish to create a record for this key ?'. This again causes un-necessary complications and should be avoided.

The Erase Record Function

When the Erase function is selected the contents of the record will be displayed in the standard format for verification purposes. The FOS for the Erase function (FOSE) will then be invoked (Figure 5.11).

Working in this way may seem to be a bit laborious, but it ensures that users have a chance to see what they are going to erase, before valuable data is accidentally destroyed.

The use of the letter 'E' is designed to concentrate the attention of users on what they are doing.

```
ENTER: (E) to confirm Erasure, or (*) to Abort      ... ?[ ]
```

Figure 5.11 Foot-of-Screeen for the Erase Function (FOSE).

The Display Record Function

From the aforementioned the way in which the Display function should operate should be self-apparent. In this case the FOS routine is FOSD (Figure 5.12).

```
ENTER: (D) to Display another record            ...? [ ]
```

Figure 5.12 Foot-of-Screen for the Display Record Function (FOSD).

In this case, since simply displaying data doesn't put anything at risk in the system, a simpler approach using a single key depression rather than an <ENTER> could have been used. Similarly, provision could have been included for an exit from the FOSD back to the calling menu.

Again, however, the over-riding consideration has been to maintain a simple consistent pattern of operation.

If users have to remember to press <ENTER> at some times and not at others, they will inevitably make mistakes and become disenchanted and disorientated.

The Print Record Function

The Print record function must display records before printing, so that time and paper are not wasted on printing unwanted records.

The FOS routine associated with this is FOSP. This allows the user two options (Figure 5.13) to confirm or abort.

```
ENTER (C) to Confirm print required, or (*) to abort printing
                                                        ... ? [ ]
```

Figure 5.13 FOS For Print Record (FOSP).

Appraisal

The way in which records are handled is the key to the HCI of systems, which in turn is the key to successful systems design.

```
10:20 16/08/87      THE MANUFACTURING SYSTEM      01+01+01+2
BILL OF MATERIALS SUB-SYSTEM         MASTER PARTS MODULE
                                  AMEND RECORD

1. Part Code...                   L1876-678

2. Description...                 NUT,3/8" HEX.

3. Unit of measure...             EA

4. Reorder policy (M) or (B)..    B

5. ABC class...                   C

6. Batch size...                ? [5000 ]

7. Safety stock...                1000

8. Date active 'DD/MM/YY'...      16/10/85


ENTER: (F) to File Record, (*) to Abort, or a Field Number to enable
corrections                                                  ...[6]
```

Figure 5.14 Typical PSD Screen, shows users where they are in a system and what they can do in a standardised manner. Note the use of ( ) to show where what is illustrated must be entered (Field 4), and ' ' to indicate that only the format is shown (Field 8).

What has been demonstrated in this chapter is that all records can be handled in a very positive, very simple, standardised way. The effects of this are far reaching and the benefits are too great to be ignored:

*   Designs are easier to formulate and document. Once users have been introduced to the basic method of handling one Record this doesn't have to be repeated for other Records. It is implicit that all records will have exactly the same functions and will be set out and handled in exactly the same way.

*   Programming is made easier, because of the highly standardised nature of the systems and by extensive use of standard programmes.

*   Users can readily relate to systems, because the systems conform rigidly to simple standardised patterns (Figure 5.14).

In spite of these advantages, some designers will almost certainly be feeling that PSD is too constraining. But if EDP is ever to achieve more than a fraction of its true potential, PSD is essential.

Chapter 6

More About PSD Records

Introduction

The basic PSD Functions that have been covered so far are summarised in Figure 6.1. This chapter covers a number of miscellaneous aspects of PSD Records and their handling in more detail.

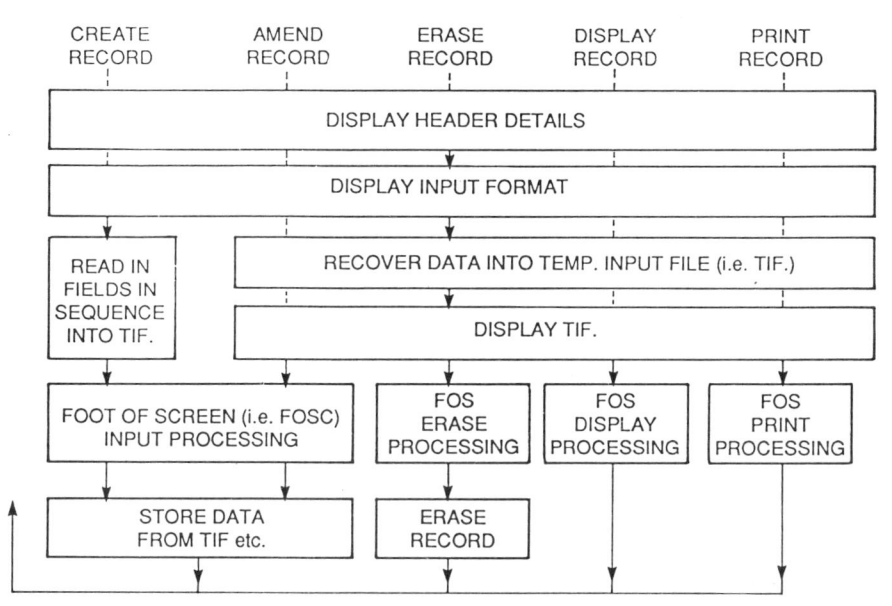

Figure 6.1 Summary of basic PSD Functions and facilities.

Multi-Screen Records

From what has been described so far, it should be apparent that the effective number of lines of screen that are available for processing Records is limited to 16 (Figure 6.2). That is lines 5 to 20 inclusive.

Similarly, as has been suggested, all record details must be restricted to a line length of 70 characters, so that they can be printed in the same format on A4 paper. Character positions 6 to 75 are recommended to allow adequate margins all round.

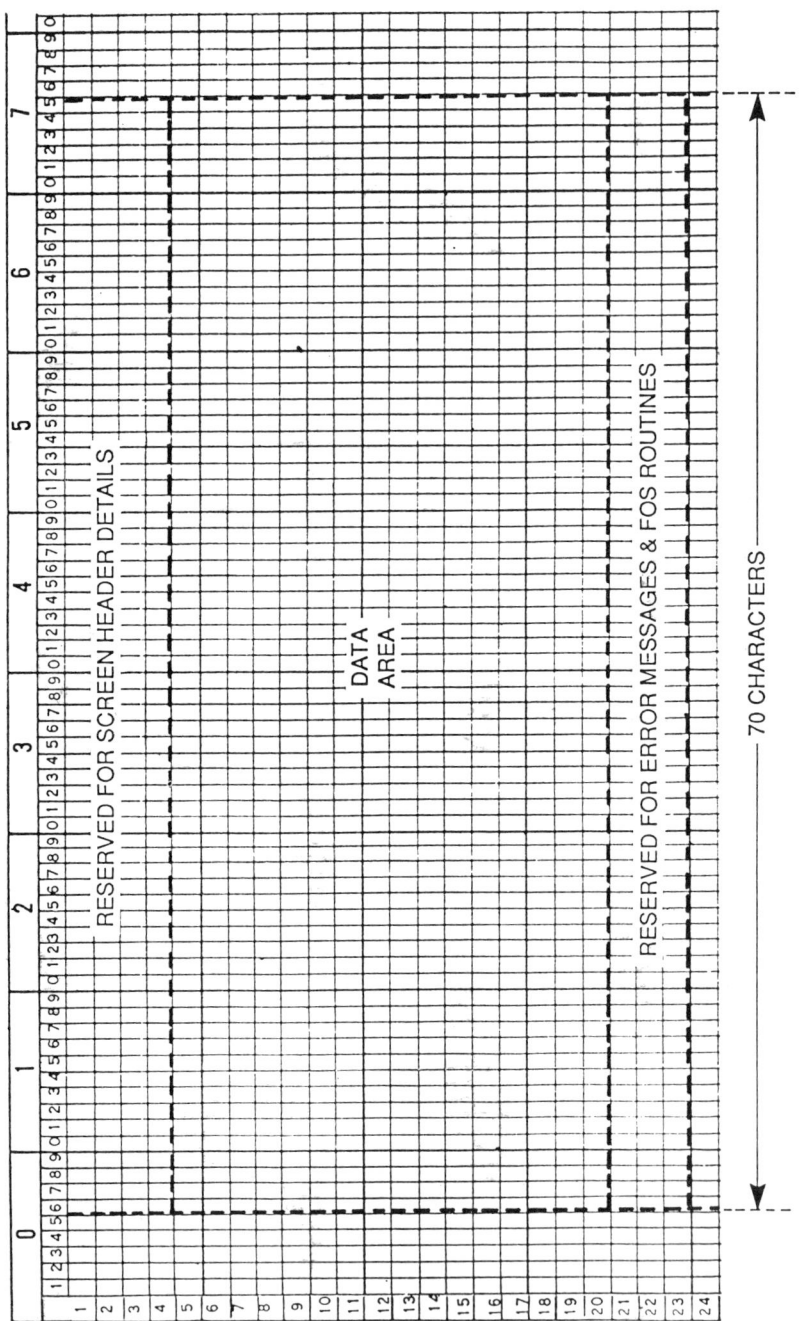

Figure 6.2 Standard VDU Screen Layout showing PSD reserved areas. Basic size 24 lines of 80 characters.

With only 16 lines available per screen, if there are more than 16 fields to a Record, the fields cannot be fitted down the left-hand side of a single screen.

The temptation to make provision for more than 16 fields on a screen must be avoided.

The way to avoid the problem is simply to continue onto another page. That is onto another standard screen. If still further screens are required these can readily be added, until the required number of fields has been accommodated.

Up to three standard screens can be fitted onto a sheet of A4 paper. It is therefore convenient to page number the screens, 1a, 1b, 1c; 2a, 2b, and 2c and so on. The numerical part of the page number will then indicate the printed page number (Figure 6.3).

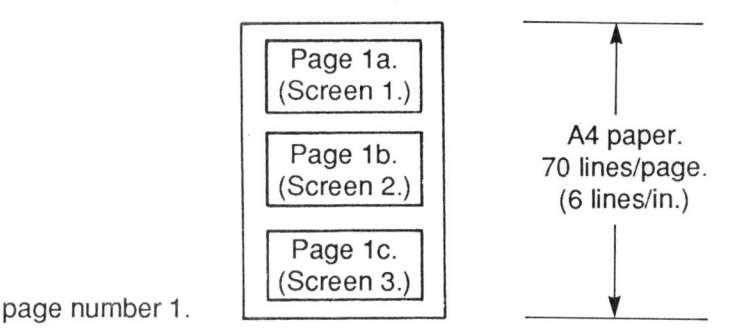

Figure 6.3 Printing VDU screens onto A4 paper.

Line 24 is usually reserved for operating system messages and is not normally printed. Even so, with 23 lines per screen, printing three screens onto an A4 sheet is very tight. However, if Screen Header details are only printed once per page, and/or the FOS details are suppressed, three screens will fit comfortably onto a single sheet.

Where a Record requires more than one screen (page) provision must be made to move from one page to another. In Create mode this will happen automatically when the last field on a screen is entered.

Similarly, in Amend mode the system must display the appropriate page, when a field is identified. In all other cases paging is achieved by extending the FOS routines to include the options '... (N) for Next page, (P) for Previous page.' (Figure 6.4).

```
ENTER: (F) to file, (*) to Abort, a Field Number to enable
corrections, (N) for Next page or (P) for Previous page...?[ ]
```

Figure 6.4 Provision for multi-screen accesses via the FOS.

Scrolling or Racking

So far the way in which multi-screen records have been handled is by Paging, which is very closely analagous to thumbing through a book and can quickly be grasped by users.

The main advantage of paging is that details always appear on the screen in the same place

Scrolling, or Racking as it is sometimes called, is frequently used as an alternative to Paging. Scrolling produces the same effect on the screen as winding a roll of data through a viewer (Figure 6.5).

Many systems Scroll automatically on input once the bottom line of the screen is reached. The main problem with this is that after scrolling details can appear anywhere on the screen, so users do not know where to look for a particular field.

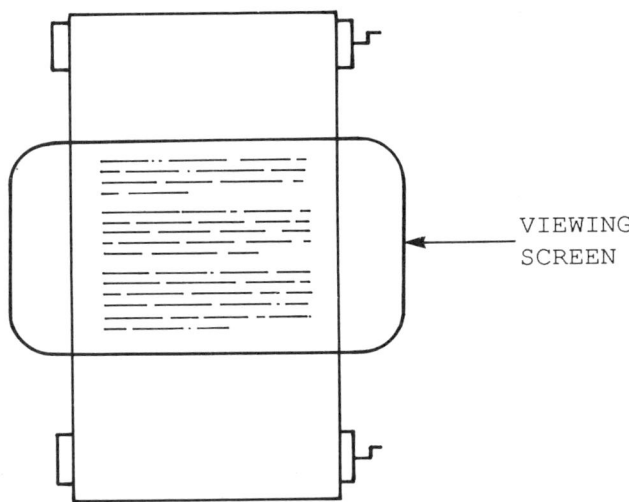

Figure 6.5 Scrolling or Racking, is like winding details through a viewer. It is not recommended.

Frequently the whole screen is racked, including the header (assuming that one has been provided), so the header will disappear and users will no longer be able to see where they are in the system.

Virtually every system uses a different key to invoke Scrolling, including such unlikely keys as <SPACE> and <SHIFT>. On many systems no provision is made for scrolling back up a display.

Whatever keys are used there is usually a time lag between the key being pressed or released and scrolling starting or stopping. It is therefore difficult to scroll to a precise place.

All in all, Scrolling can give rise to a great deal of confusion and the simpler, more positive approach of Paging is recommended.

Large Fields

So far the examples that have been used have been based on the description of a field and its data fitting onto a single line of 70 characters. Most EDP fields will fall into this category.

However, if extended text has to be accommodated a field may run to several lines. An Action File (Figure 6.6) is a typical example. There are a number of ways in which this could be handled.

```
   5. Action required...
   [X---------------------------------------]
   [----------------------------------------]
   [---------------------------------------X]
```

Figure 6.6 Multi-Line Fields. Input on separate lines under the field description.

The recommended way is to put the data on separate lines under the description, as shown. This allows users to input data in the form in which it will normally be printed and avoids the problem of split words at the end of lines (Figure 6.7). The basic rule is that if the description and data for a field will occupy more than 70 characters, the data must be entered on a separate line. (Note that the effective number of characters will be reduced if brackets are used as field de-limiters.)

Figure 6.7 is on the next page

```
    5. Action required ...[AAAAAAAAAAAAAAAAAAAAA]
    [BBBBBBBBBBBBBBBBBBBBBBBBBBBBBBBBBBBBBBBBB]
    [CCCCCCCCCCCCCCCCCCCCCCCCCCCCCCCCCCCCCCCC]
```
a) Details put in.

```
    AAAAAAAAAAAAAAAAAAAABBBBBBBBBBBBBBBBBBBBB
    BBBBBBBBBBBBBBBBBBBBCCCCCCCCCCCCCCCCCCCCC
    CCCCCCCCCCCCCCCCCCC
```
b) Details as printed.

Figure 6.7 Multi-Line-Fields. Data alongside the description creates problems with split lines and words

Multiple Record Entries and Displays

In the previous chapter details of the standard processing associated with each of the main record Functions were examined. The description stopped short at the point where a single record had been filed or deleted. This section looks at what should happen next. Basically there are two options:

* To return to the Menu of Functions, so that another function or the Reports Menus can be selected.

* To return to the start of the function, so that another record can be processed in the current mode.

In most commercial applications users will largely be concerned with repetitive processing on records of a particular type. There is clearly a need for the second alternative, so that users can continue to perform the same basic task without returning to a menu.

In many other cases, users may wish to move from one function to another or to another module after each record has been filed. For example, a clerk who is charged with entering a revised inflation factor would not wish to be invited to enter another one, if one factor applies to all products.

Using the repetitive entry approach users can, of course, return to the calling menu by putting an asterisk in the first data field. Users may find this somewhat tedious on some applications, so, although the repetitive entry approach is the simplest, because a single method is used throughout, it would appear that both alternative must be admitted.

Designers should normally use the repetitive entry approach, but the possibility of a single entry function must be considered. The method to be used must form part of the specification for each module.

Repetitive Keys

Another aspect of systems which users often find tedious is the task of creating rectangular files, when a part of the key is common to a number of records. On a Customers Order, for example, the key to each item on the order will be the Order Number and Item Number (Figure 6.8).

The order number will of course be common to all items on an order, and users should not have to type it into every record. At the same time this must be achieved within the basic PSD framework.

It is possible to arrange for systems to retain the first field and then to skip it on data entry, until some predetermined code is entered.

A simpler and more flexible approach is to retain what is in designated fields, but to require users to press <ENTER> to confirm the value shown.

	← RECORD KEY. →		
Order No.	Item No.	Part No.	QUANTITY
10962	1	B7890	1
10962	2	L56432	100
10962	3	D288	20
10963	1	XZ980	600
10963	2	Y43267	30

Figure 6.8 Repetitive data entry with common key-data

Using this approach, users can either re-use the same key or change the key, although the latter may not be admissible in some circumstances. On an order processing system, for example, it may be considered essential that details of carriage charges should be entered before moving on to another order. To cover this condition an additional FOS message is required. This is FOS@ (Figure 6.9).

```
ENTER: (@) in Field 1 to show that all items have been entered
```

Figure 6.9 FOS@, allows repetitive entry to be terminated.

FOS@ will be displayed in the normal FOS area after each record has been filed. If details of another record are then entered the FOS@ message will then be replaced by the normal FOS routines.

If '@' is entered, this will indicate to the system that the repeating entry must be terminated. The system must only test the first character of the field for '@', so that it is not necessary for users to erase what is in the rest of the field.

Repetitive key input can give rise to confusion in the eyes of both users and designers, particularly with regard to the use of the Abort feature in FOS processing. If, for example, a user has entered details of a number of items for a Customer's Order, Abort must only result in the record currently displayed being ignored. Other records already filed must not be affected.

In other words the basic Functions of PSD are at all times concerned solely with the processing of single records.

To remove details of all the items on an order is an 'across record' process. This is examined in the next chapter.

Counters and Default Values

Counters and default values should be used wherever possible to simplify the task of putting data into fields.

For example, in the case of the Customers Order, the Item Number should normally be incremented and displayed. Similarly, if the date of an order is normally the current date, this should also be displayed.

In all cases the same principle as before must be employed. That is, users must normally have a chance to change the default value, and must press <ENTER> to confirm the value. In some cases it may be unwise to allow users to alter values produced by counters. Allowing for Invoice Numbers to be altered could, for example, pose a threat to the security of a system.

Particular care must be taken to ensure that any unnecessary restrictions are avoided. Sooner or later, and generally sooner, these will lead to user frustration.

Thus, for example, if no provision is made for users to change Item Numbers, an important customer will almost certainly demand that its own numbers must be used - and they will not be in sequence and may not be numeric.

Record Processing

At the time when records are filed and details that have been entered are added to the main files, further processing may have to be specified.

The processing required will depend on what each system is supposed to do and cannot be standardised. For example, on a Stock Control System, filing details of a receipt would result in the stock total being increased and the quantity on order being reduced.

Care is obviously needed to ensure that what is specified is correct. This is particularly true as far as Amend is concerned. In this mode nothing on the main files must be changed until 'F' is entered. Then stock totals and so on must be adjusted by the difference between the original quantity received and the amended quantity.

Once the processing that needs to be done has been identified and the system has been tested, the special processing need not concern users. In computer terminology, it is said to be 'transparent' - in other words, users will not know that it is there.

Format Conventions

Before summarising the processing of PSD Records one minor but important aspect must be amplified, namely the subject of Format Conventions. On many systems it is usually minor details which create the greatest problems, particularly for new users. This is certainly true as far as Format Conventions are concerned, that is, about how users should be shown what format to use, either on an input screen or in User Guides.

The main problem arises because there are two basic forms of help which can be given:

a) The actual values which are permitted can be shown. For example:

 '4. Reorder policy, M or B ...   [ ]'

or

b) The form of the input may be shown. For example:

 '8. Date active, DD/MM/YY ...   [   ]'

In the above examples what is required should be apparent, although a naive user may be forgiven for actually typing in 'DD/MM/YY', instead of a date. In many cases, what is actually required will not be obvious. To avoid this problem it is recommended that the following conventions should be adopted:

* Where what is to be typed in is shown, this should be in brackets. For example:

    '4. Reorder policy, (M) or (B) ...   [ ]'

* Where what is illustrated merely shows the format of the input, this should be in 'quotes'. For example:

    '8. Date active, 'DD/MM/YY' ...   [   ]'

These conventions should be applied to all aspects of user interaction including dialogue. For example:

   'Is a print-out required, (Y) or (N) ...   [ ]'

Similar problems can arise due to confusion about whether letters should be typed or a key should be depressed. These problems can readily be avoided by the use of angular brackets to indicate that the text refers to a key. For example:

   'Press <CR>' , 'Press <CTRL>' , or 'Press <F1>'.

Use of the word 'Press' rather than 'Type' should in itself be sufficient to indicate that a single key should be depressed. But experience suggests that a great deal of confusion can arise and reinforcing the nature of the instruction is a simple and useful safeguard.

Appraisal

Much of what has been written so far has been concerned with comparing the advantages of PSD with other alternatives. If the alternatives are ignored, then the basic facilities of PSD can be summarised very briefly (Figure 6.10).

The PSD facilities provide a standardised framework that can be applied to all records on all systems and which can quickly be learnt by both users and designers.

Even for skilled-users the additional features which need to be mastered are minimal (Figure 6.11).

AT MENU SELECTION		
'N'	-	(A number) selects an option from a menu
*	-	Causes an exit to the next highest menu
OFF	-	Causes log-off
AT DATA ENTRY		
*	-	In the 1st data field, causes an exit to the calling menu.
	-	In any other field, returns to the start of the entry.
@	-	Terminates repetitive data input
AT FOOT OF SCREEN		
*	-	Aborts entry
D	-	Prompts for new display key
C	-	Confirms print required
E	-	Confirms record to be erased
F	-	Files a record
N	-	Displays next screen
P	-	Displays previous screen
'N'	-	(A number) Directs the cursor to a field, for corrections.

Figure 6.10 Summary of PSD Features.

> AT MODULE MENU SELECTION:
>
> 'N' is the number of the Module to be selected
>
> NC   -   Selects the Module in Create Mode.
>
> NA   -   Selects the Module in Amend Mode.
>
> NE   -   Selects the Module in Erase Mode.
>
> ND   -   Selects the Module in Display Mode.
>
> NP   -   Selects the Module in Print Mode.
>
> NRD -   Selects the Report Display Menu for the Module.
>
> NRP -   Selects the Report Print Menu for the Module.
>
> Alternatively the format 'N+M' may be used where 'M' is the menu selection number of the appropriate Function.

Figure 6.11 Options available to skilled users at Module Menu Selection

Chapter 7

Report Display and Prints

Introduction

Up to this point the main subject has been the processing of single records in a standardised way.

Once records have been established on files the task of reporting on them, either in the form of displays or prints, cannot be standardised. The reports required and their formats will vary significantly from system to system

There are a number of ways in which the production of reports can be improved. In particular, the importance of the swing away from 'central' printing on large printers must be recognised.

Today the availability of cheap A4 printers means that a great deal of printing, formerly done centrally, can now be done locally. For short reports on-the-spot printing is a considerable advantage to users.

Generally, provision should be made for most reports to be both displayed and printed. Except where otherwise stated, the term 'print' should be taken to imply that there will be a corresponding display facility.

Secondary Processing

In the context of PSD the term 'Report' covers any processing which cannot be handled by the basic PSD Functions, anything which involves across-record processing is regarded as a secondary process and included on the Report Menus. The term 'Report Menu' is used because most of the items on these menus will be reports (Figure 7.1) and this is easier for users to grasp than Secondary Menus.

Thus a particular selection from a Reports Menu may simply result in a series of records being erased, and the only report would be a message to say that the task had been completed. Similarly, a report may consist of a single complex document, such as an Invoice, or it may involve listing many pages of details from files. It is with these latter aspects which this chapter is primarily concerned.

```
16.35 12/04/86            ABC SYSTEM           B01+01+02+6
ABC SUB-SYSTEM                              ACTIONS MODULE
                     REPORT DISPLAYS MENU.
              ENTER SELECTION NUMBER ...?[ ]

1. Overdue Actions, by Action on.

2. Overdue Actions, by Action type/Location code.

3. All Actions, by Action on

4. All Actions, by ABC No.

5. Actions without due dates.

6. Erase all completed/minuted actions.
```

Figure 7.1 Typical Report Menu. Includes any features that are not covered by the basic PSD Functions.

Report Format - Displays

In general, the same basic principles as those applied to records must be applied to the design of reports. Wherever possible the standard screen format already described (Figure 6.2) must also be used for report displays.

In particular the Screen Header (Figure 7.2) must be shown. At first sight it may seem 'wasteful' to restrict what can be displayed to 16 lines at a time, particularly for long reports, but the cost of this is negligible compared with the benefits.

```
16:36 12/04/86           ABC SYSTEM           B01+01+02+6+03
ABC SUB-SYSTEM                              ACTIONS MODULE
                      REPORT DISPLAYS
              ALL ACTIONS, BY ACTION ON.    PAGE 1.
```

Figure 7.2 Typical Header details for reports.

During reporting users still need to know precisely where they are in a system. So the Header is essential, and as it is standard no design effort is involved.

Users must also be told what they can and cannot do. So, provision for error messages and FOS routines is still essential.

Once the concept that all displays will show 16 lines of data has been established standard routines can be developed to handle this and users will quickly become accustomed to the displays.

Report Formats - Prints

Wherever possible the same basic format must be used for both Displays and Prints. This not only helps users to learn where to look for a particular piece of information, it also saves time on design and development.

As before, printed reports should, wherever possible, be designed to be output onto A4 paper. The 70 character line length must therefore be observed. As with records, the header and three screens of data can conveniently be fitted onto one printed page.

After the first page, many reports will not require the header details to be repeated. In this case four screens of data and the page number will fit onto a printed page (Figure 7.3).

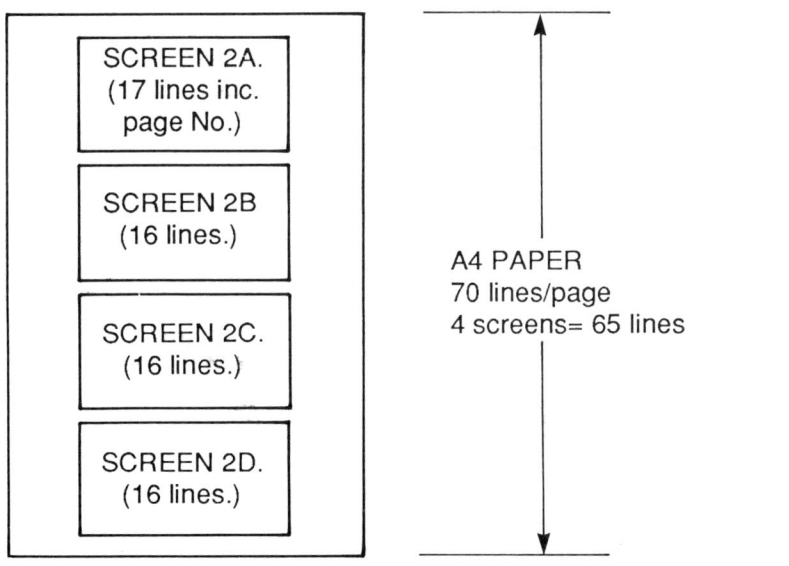

Figure 7.3 Report Prints. After the first page, leaving out Header Details will just allow 4 screens to be printed on a page of A4.

However, four screens per page is on the tight side, as it only leaves two-and-a-half lines at the top and bottom of each page. There is therefore insufficient space for top-filing and many printers cannot cope with single sheets with less than six lines at the top.

If there is any doubt about importance of saving paper or about the ability to cope with 4 screens/page, designers must stick to 3 screens/page. The spare lines can the be used to make simple reports easier to scan (Figure 7.4).

Allowing for 19 lines per data screen, as shown, three screens and a four line Header will take up 61 lines of printing. This leaves a total of nine lines to spare for filing and the possibility of misalignment.

After the first page, if no Header is required, three more spare lines can be used to split the middle six lines on each screen (Figure 7.5). As before, the page numbers on the actual VDU screen should be suffixed with letters, so that the numeric part corresponds to the printed page number (Figure 7.3).

Using these techniques will ensure that users can readily scan reports and compare what is on the screen with what is printed out.

16 LINES OF DATA PER SCREEN

```
Blank line.
X------------------------------------------------X
X                                                 X
X                 1st five lines of data          X
X                                                 X
X------------------------------------------------X
Blank line.
X------------------------------------------------X
X                                                 X
X                 Next six lines of data          X
X                                                 X
X                                                 X
X------------------------------------------------X
Blank line
X------------------------------------------------X
X                                                 X
X                 Next five lines of data         X
X                                                 X
X------------------------------------------------X
```

Figure 7.4 Report Prints. Showing the insertion of blank lines to improve user scanning. Split is 5-6-5 giving a total of 19 print lines, including blank lines.

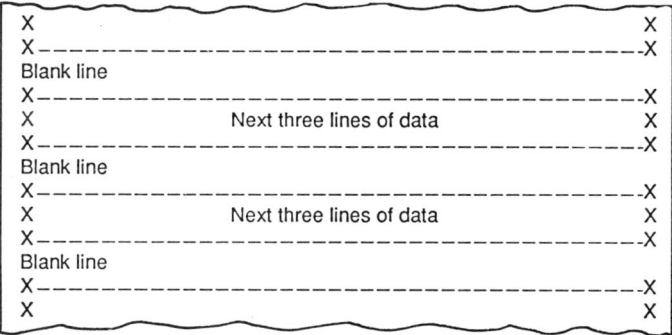

Figure 7.5 Report Prints. The middle six lines of screen data can be split into threes when Header details do not have to be printed, apart from the page number. The enhanced layout is of the form 5-3-3-5 and requires a total of 20 lines/screen.

In some cases, particularly where documents are for external use (eg. Invoices), it will be undesirable for Header Details to be printed on a document. But designers must make sure that such departures from the standard are essential. Departures from standards are costly in terms of design costs and user familiarisation.

Where printing has to be output onto a special form, such as paper with the company letter-head on it, efforts should still be made to ensure that displays and prints are as similar as possible.

So serious consideration should be given to ensuring that company logos and address details are limited to the top-filing space plus four lines. If this is done then these details can simply replace the Screen Header on print-out.

Local v Central Printing

As has been suggested, the availability of cheap printers has resulted in a swing away from central printing, to local printing.

Although the speed and quality of small local printers may not match the performance of bigger printers, local printing has many advantages:

*   Printing takes place when and where it is required.

*   Delays in transporting prints to users are eliminated.

*   Printers can be permanently loaded with special stationery for special applications.

*   Output can be checked immediately and re-printed if necessary.

*   The user is in total control and can determine priorities.

Wherever possible users should be given the opportunity to decide whether reports should be printed locally or centrally - at the time when the report is called for.

This can readily be achieved by prefacing the report run with a question on theVDU:

' Is Local printing required (Y) or (N) ... ?[Y] '

The abbreviations 'Y' and 'N' are commonly used for Yes and No. Entering 'N' will of course result in central printing. Note that for ease of use a default response of 'Y' is displayed.

Note also that once the form of the question has been determined, it must be strictly adhered to. Users will inevitably make mistakes if the next report poses the same question in a different way. In other words, if the question is next posed as:

' Is Central printing required (Y) or (N) ... ?[Y] '

The question could be posed in a variety of different ways. For example;

' Enter (L) for Local printing, (C) for Central ... ?[L] '

This eliminates the problem of reversing the implications of a 'Yes' response, but it calls for greater familiarity with the keyboard. Users will quickly become skilled at locating commonly used letters, such as 'Y' and 'N', but to become skilled at typing other letters will take time.

Another alternative is to use the menu approach (Figure 7.6). Since this only requires the use of the numeric key-pad, it appears to be the best method.

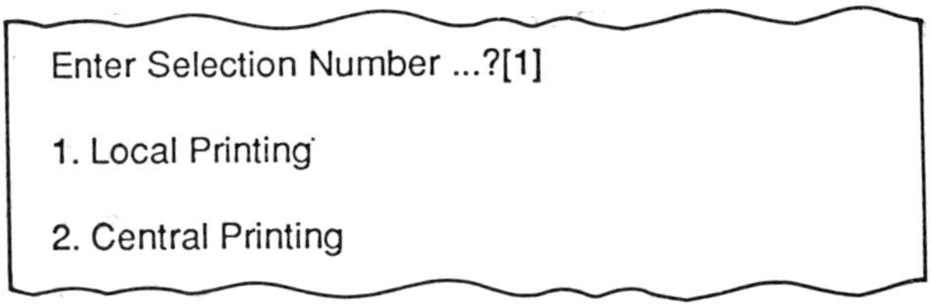

```
Enter Selection Number ...?[1]

1. Local Printing

2. Central Printing
```

Figure 7.6 Selecting Print Options - The Menu Approach. Eliminates the need for typing skills.

In many cases, local printers are loaded with continuous stationery of the same width as A4. Often however, the output will have to be copied and filed. It is therefore best to treat the stationery as a series of A4 sheets.

Note that this is what is called A4 Portrait, as opposed to A4 Landscape (Figure 7.7). Small printers cannot normally handle A4 Landscape. On the other hand, most 'central' printers are designed to run with the larger A3 stationery, or some intermediate size such as 11in. by 13in. Landscape.

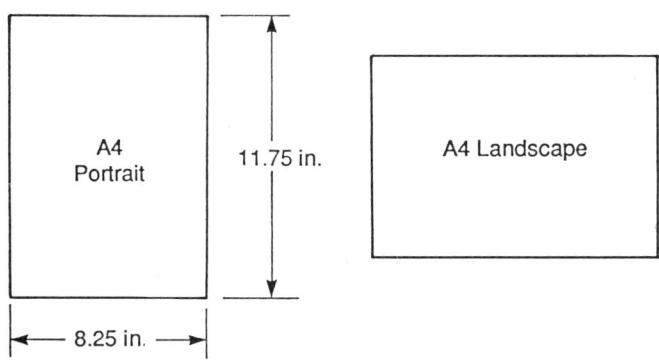

Figure 7.7 A4 Paper Sizes. Local printers will often only be capable of handling A4 portrait. (The measurements shown are approximations to the metric sizes).

So if reports are designed for Central printing, problems will normally arise when the need for Local printing is recognised.

Designing for A4 Paper

A4 is now the most commonly used paper size and is generally accepted as standard in the UK. The half and double sized sheets, A5 and A3 (Figure 7.8), are also widely used.

It has taken many years for the benefits of the A-Series of paper sizes to be recognised and for them to become established as standards. Computer produced documents should not negate this progress.

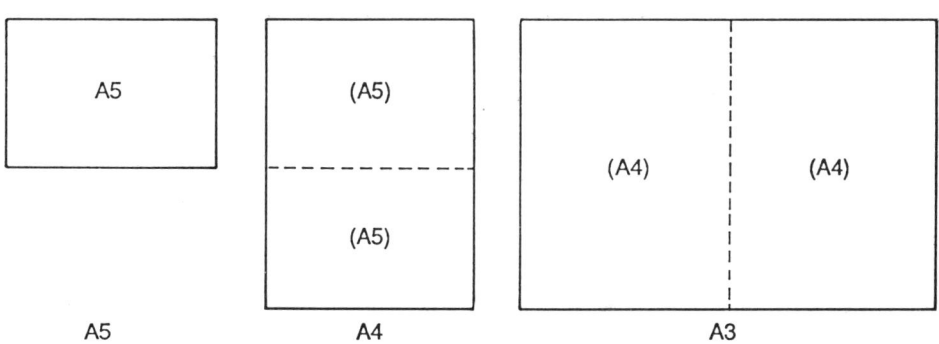

Figure 7.8 Paper sizes in most common use.

Because of the restrictions imposed by local printing the target must be to design reports to fit onto A4 Portrait, or smaller A-series sizes of paper.

At present, many reports are generated in a wide variety of sizes and it would app that a large number wouldn't fit onto A4, mainly because of the 70 character limitation (Figure 7.9).

SALESMAN	TERRITORY	SALES/MONTH FOR 12 MONTHS.
(20 chrs.)	(20 Chrs.)	(8 characters times 12.)

Assuming that the above include provision for a space between columns, this would require 136 characters per line.

Figure 7.9 A Report which appears to need more than 70 characters per line.

However, there are a variety of ways in which reports can be re-arranged to fit onto At first sight, some of the resulting layouts may not appear to be as aesthetic pleasing as before, but the benefits are such that changes must be made.

The following illustrate some of the many ways in which reductions can be achieve

*   Eliminate unnecessary details (eg. is it necessary to show both salesman territory?)

*   Put descriptive data on a separate line (Figure 7.10).

SALES/MONTH					
JAN.	FEB.	MAR.	APL.	MAY.	JUN.
Smith J.		North West			
1000.50	2242.60	1876.91	500.04	800.12	1001.73
Jones T.		North East			
2004.51	3072.86	4770.91	5000.14	6012.42	7094.84
etc.					

Figure 7.10 Putting descriptive data on separate lines can narrow the width of reports.

* Use two or more printed lines for each line of data (Figure 7.11).

SALES/MONTH					
JAN.	FEB.	MAR.	APR.	MAY.	JUN.
JUL.	AUG.	SEP.	OCT.	NOV.	DEC.
Smith J.		North West			
1000.50	2242.60	1876.92	500.04	800.12	1001.73
809.68	1067.50	987.07	1089.89	987.67	1200.82
Jones T.		North East			
2004.51	3072.86	4770.91	5000.14	6012.42	7094.84
6875.79	5674.98	3456.98	6000.78	5000.78	5677.98
ETC.					

Figure 7.11 Lines can be shortened by putting data on two or more lines.

* Report fewer columns per page (eg., report 6 months/page).

* Change units so that fewer characters per column are required (Figure 7.12).

SALES/MONTH (In £'s only)									
JAN.	FEB.	MAR.	APR.	MAY.	JUN.	JUL.	AUG.	SEP.	etc.
Smith, J.			North West						
1000	2242	1876	500	800	1001	809	1067	987	
Jones, T.			North East						
2004	3072	4770	5000	6012	7094	6875	5674	3456	
etc.									

Figure 7.12 Column widths can be reduced by changing units.

* Transpose rows and columns (Figure 7.13).

Figure 7.13 is on the next page

SALES/MONTH				
MONTH	NORTH WEST.	NORTH EAST.	SOUTH WEST	etc.
Jan.	1000.50	2004.51	6567.78	
Feb.	2242.60	3072.86	4532.90	
Mar.	1876.92	4770.91	2389.76	
Apr. Etc.	500.04	5000.14	3519.75	

Figure 7.13 Transposing rows and columns may fit reports onto A4.

Designing reports to fit onto A4, doesn't necessarily mean that they must always be printed onto A4. In fact, the productivity of a large printer can be doubled by printing two A4 pages at the same time, side by side on A3.

Another alternative, where data has been split into two lines for local printing, is to re-format the data on one line for central printing.

Bigger local printers can, of course, be installed, but this will normally result in a significant increase in cost and should be avoided wherever possible. Designers should also be aware of the fact that printer noise can be a source of irritation and suitable sound-proofing must be used.

Other Type Sizes

Up to this point screen formats have been restricted to 70 characters per line, to allow printing onto A4 in Pica type (10 characters/inch). This is because Pica is the largest typeface in common use.

Elite type (12 characters/inch) is also very popular. With Elite, a full screenline of 80 characters will occupy 6.7in., which fits conveniently onto A4.

It would appear therefore that Elite will in future provide a convenient standard, although it is not quite as legible as Pica. However, until such time as this is accepted as the standard the safest policy is to stick to 70 characters which can be output in either Pica or Elite.

This is not, of course, true if output has to be printed onto pre-printed paper. In this case the typeface to be used must be determined before the form is designed, so that boxes of the right size are used.

The Type-size to be used must be established before pre-printed forms are designed.

Printers which can print more than 12 characters per inch are now common. But smaller characters do present legibility problems, particularly under adverse conditions.

Where the typeface is small enough to allow more than 80 characters to be printed per line, this also introduces a new problem. In this case the screen becomes the limiting factor, because most of the VDU's currently available cannot readily display more than 80 characters per line. So there is a problem when one tries to maintain a one to one correspondence between what is displayed on the VDU and what is printed out.

Again designing systems to use a 'special' printer is not in general a good policy, mainly because it can restrict the use of a system to users who have 'special' printers; ('special' usually means expensive).

The converse of this is also true, in that users with special printers may well find that they cannot use standard packages. All in all, the safest and simplest approach at the moment appears to be to allow for Pica to be used - and to hope that in the not too distant future standards will be established.

Design for Ease of Use

Very large reports were a characteristic of most early computer systems. Frequently, these would take the form of full-file listings, and more often than not, they would be produced '...in-case they were required'. Often early reports were so big and difficult to handle that users never in-fact used them. Today, particularly with rectangular files, it is very much easier to ensure that reports are only produced when they are required and that they only show what is required in a form in which it can most readily be digested.

Generally, the reports associated with a module should, as far as possible, always be in the same format. In this way users will quickly become familiar with the format and designers only have one format to work out. For example, in the case of the Action File mentioned earlier, whether all outstanding actions or overdue actions are to be reported, the same format should be used (Figure 7.14).

There are a number of ways in which the size of a report can be restricted, to the advantage of users. Where dates are involved one of the simplest ways is to use an 'Effectivity Date'. This is a method whereby a system will call for a date to be entered prior to the printing of a report. The report is then produced, assuming that the 'Effectivity Date' entered is the current date.

If, for example, there are a very large number of overdue actions on an action file, it is probably pointless to list them all. By using an Effectivity Date of some months or weeks back only the oldest overdues would be reported as being overdue.

```
ABC   ACT  LOCN  ACT    DATE      ACTION     DUE       DATE
No.   No.  CODE  TYPE   ENTERED   ON         DATE      COMPLETED
XXXX  XXX  XXX   XX     XX/XX/XX  XXXXXXX    XX/XX/XX  XX/XX/XX
      X----------------------------------------------------------X
      X                         (ACTION)                         X
      X----------------------------------------------------------X
XXXX Etc.
```

Figure 7.14 Draft of typical report format. The same format must be used as far as possible for all reports from a module.

The same technique can also be used in the opposite way. By using an Effectivity Date of next week or next month what should happen next week or next month can be reported.

This approach can be implemented in a similar way to the ways first suggested for local/central printing. In other words, by prefacing the report run with a question:

' Enter Effectivity Date 'DD/MM/YY' ... ?[12/11/86] '

Note that the format of the respose expected is shown. The use of 'quotes' indicates that this shows the form of the response rather than what must actually be typed.

Another way of limiting output is to use a From/To technique (Figure 7.15).

```
1. List 'From' Action Number .....? [ _   ]

2. List 'To' Action Number ....[     ]
```

Figure 7.15 From/To Questions. Can be used to limit the length of reports.

There are a number of ways in which the user-friendliness of the From/To screen can be improved by displaying default values corresponding to the first and last values on the file. Thus:

* Leaving the 'From' field unchanged will result in reporting from the start of the numbers.

* Leaving the 'To' field unchanged will result in a listing ending with the last number on the file.

* Leaving both fields unchanged will result in a full-file listing.

To get a report on a single record, the same value must be entered in the From and To fields. This is somewhat tedious, but single records will normally be output using the Print function, rather than Report. Similar techniques can be used to limit reports to records with a particular parameter (Figure 7.16).

```
1. Action-on code to limit report to one person....?[ALL ]
```

Figure 7.16 Miscellaneous Restrictions. Where appropriate these can be used to limit the scope of a report.

In this case, entering a code would restrict the report to the staff identified. Again the default value of 'ALL' would result in all values being considered.

Although for simplicity the techniques shown above have been illustrated separately, they can be used in combination. But users should not be expected to answer a long list of questions before they can get a report. This can be avoided by ensuring that the Report Menu directs users to the facility which will offer the limited number of options required (Figure 7.17).

```
              REPORT DISPLAY MENU
            Enter Selection number ...?[ _ ]

   1. Overdue Actions, by Action On.

   2. Overdue Actions, by Action Type/Location Code.

   3. All Actions, by Action On.

   4. All Actions, by ABC No.
   Etc.
```

Figure 7.17 Typical Report Menu. A compromise between menu-options and options within the reporting program.

Note that selection 1 allows users to limit the report to overdue actions without the need for a question later, such as 'Do you require all or just overdue actions?. This would have been necessary if only selection 3 and 4 were shown. At the same time, however, efforts must be made to ensure that user are not presented with a bewildering array of report selections.

The designers aim must be to secure an equitable compromise between the number of report selections on each menu and the options presented within the report programs.

Copies of Reports

The instant availability of displays of reports, coupled with the more positive paging techniques recommended, will help to reduce the need for printed reports.

Similarly, the more widespread use of centralised computers, and the networking of data from one computer to another will help to reduce the need for multiple copies of printed reports. But the problem of how to handle requirements for multiple copies of reports will remain for some time to come.

On many systems multiple copies are still produced using carbon paper. But this is expensive in terms of the cost of the stationery and the time spent decollating copies. Also many printer cannot produce good carbon copies and a great deal of time can be wasted changing to stationery with the right number of copies. As a general rule therefore the aim of the designer must be to limit printing to one copy and then to either repeat the print or to produce further copies by photocopying.

Stopping a Print

Finally, one miscellaneous and often neglected point. It is not uncommon for users to realise that the wrong report has been selected after printing has started. Or parameters which are going to give an excessively long report may have been entered.

Users must not therefore be locked into a report program. Provision must be included to abort a print run at any time.

Chapter 8

Password Control, Record Keys & Codes

Introduction

This chapter looks first at the problem of ensuring the security of systems from the point of view of unauthorised access. It is achieved primarily by means of passwords. The term password control has therefore been used to distinguish this aspect from the operational aspect of assuring the availability and integrity of data in a system.

Any system of any consequence must be protected by password control.

On many systems this can be a source of considerable irritation to users. In the main, this occurs when users have to remember and enter a variety of passwords as they progress through a system.

On some systems this is even taken down to Field level. In which case, even when users have accessed a record, they may have to enter a variety of passwords before they can change fields. This type of irritation can and must be avoided.

From the users point of view, password control should be taken care of once and for all at log-on time.

Log-on

It may seem to be a bit late to introduce the subject of Log-on at this stage, but a clear understanding of the PSD Structure is necessary to enable the essential simplicity of password control to be appreciated.

The log-on process will be the user's first contact with a system and it is essential that this should be friendly. A short welcoming message is a nice touch.

Users should not, however, be presented with a bewildering array of useless details. On the other hand, they must not be left with a blank screen or a cryptic prompt. It must be quite clear what the user should do next. The entry of a single password is all that is normally necessary to protect a system, but on most systems it is most convenient to use a two-tier security system (Figure 8.1).

```
┌─────────────────────────────────────────────────┐
│           WELCOME TO THE XYZ SYSTEM             │
│              To Log-on please enter;            │
│   1. Your User Identification....?[        ]    │
│                                                 │
│   2. Your Password.....  [         ]            │
└─────────────────────────────────────────────────┘
```

Figure 8.1 Typical Log-on Screen.

Usually this will be in the form of:

* A User Identification (User I/D). Normally this should be kept as short as possible, whilst allowing a unique I/D for each user.

* A Password. Provision for passwords of up to six characters should be sufficient in most cases.

Both of the fields should be typed 'blind'. In other words, what is typed should not be displayed on the screen, thus protecting the confidentiality of the codes. The details entered will be checked against a User/Password File (Figure 8.2) and users will not be allowed past the log-on screen until authentic values have been entered.

On major systems, where operations staff are on hand, provision should normally be made to prevent speculative entries. This will usually take the form of locking-out a terminal after two or three invalid attempts to log-on.

USER I/D	PASSWORD
A001	SX99TR
A009	246
A024	954TP
A034	TXXXT
Etc.	

Figure 8.2 Schematic of User/Password File.

Once an authentic match has been found on the User/Password File, the User I/D will be noted for subsequent checking and the Main System Menu will be displayed. On exceptionally large systems, where it may be desirable to have more than one Main

System Menu, the one which is required can conveniently be identified by prefacing User I/D's with a letter to select the system required.

Levels of Authority

In addition to holding the User I/D's, the main security files must hold details of the level of authority of each user (Figure 8.3).

USER I/D	SUB-SYSTEM NO. 01+01 01+01 01+03....			NN+NN
A001	6	6	6	6
A009	3	3	2	1
A024	4	4	3	2
A034	1	1	1	1
Etc.				

Menu selection numbers

Figure 8.3 Schematic of Security Files showing Levels of Authority of users.

This part of the system is transparent as far as users are concerned and a variety of different levels can be used. It is recommended that six levels should be used, with one being the lowest and six the highest.

The file allows the authority level of each user to be shown for each sub-system. The numbers along the top identify each sub-system by the menu selection numbers required to reach it. The file could be targetted at a lower level, that is, to allow the authority of a user to be shown for each Module. This would then allow a user to have different levels of authority for different modules in a sub-system, but this would result in a much bigger file being required. It would also require more effort to set it up and to maintain it. Normally this level of control should be avoided.

Function Levels of Authority

The Level of Authority of Users is used in conjunction with a file of Function Authority Levels (Figure 8.4) to determine what users can and cannot do.

The Function Authority Levels show the minimum level of authority necessary to allow a user to perform each Function for each Module on each system.

Again each module is identified by the selection numbers required to call up the module. Similarly, along the top of the illustration the Basic Functions (Create, Amend, etc.) and Reports are identified by their menu-selection numbers.

MODULE No.	BASIC FUNCTIONS 1 2 3 4 5	REPORT DISPLAYS 1 2 3 4 etc	REPORT PRINTS 1 2 3 4 etc
1+1+1	6 6 6 1 1	2 2 2 2	3 3 3 3
1+1+2	3 3 3 1 1	2 2 2 2	2 2 4 2
1+1+3	4 2 4 1 1	3 3 2 2	3 3 2 2 Etc.

Figure 8.4 Function Levels of Authority. Schematic of file.

So by comparing the level of authority of a user with the level of authority required to perform a particular Function or Report the system can readily determine whether or not to allow a user to access the facility.

In the case illustrated in the Sub-system 01+01 user A034 has a very low authority level of 1 (Figure 8.3). So only the basic Functions 4 and 5, Display and Print can be accessed (Figure 8.4). On the other hand, user A001 has a rating of 6 and can access all of the Functions and Reports.

Where appropriate the matrix showing the Function Levels of Authority can be limited to the five Basic Functions and the two Report selections. But this would not allow the system to be selective about which reports can be run by a particular user.

In many cases, particularly where very long reports are possible, it will be desirable to be selective about which reports a user can run. To achieve this a matrix of the form show in Figure 8.4 is required and provision must be made for the maximum number of each type of report selection. With the approach described, users only need to be able to remember their User I/D and their Password to access any authorised parts of a system.

Effort is obviously required to set-up and maintain the security files. But this is small in comparison to the problems which are created for users when their progress is continually blocked by demands for passwords.

Limiting the number of passwords also helps to make systems more, rather than less, secure.

Where users have large numbers of passwords to contend with they will normally write them down - often in their User Guide. This clearly makes systems vulnerable. At the same time, the way in which the two security files are structured means that the effort required to maintain the files is minimal.

When a new user has to be authorised, apart from allocating an I/D and Password, all that needs to be done is to determine what sub-systems he or she should be authorised to use and at what level. Similarly, when a new Module is introduced, only the authority required to run the module has to be entered. The question of who can use the module is then taken care of automatically.

Using the recommended approach, security is based at Record rather than Field level. In other words, if users can change any field on a record, they can change all the fields that can be changed.

At first sight this may appear to pose a problem, particularly if a record includes sensitive data such as salaries or profits. In fact the approach does exactly the opposite. Far from creating a problem it shows designers how to design records. In other words, in addition to searching for Rectangular Files, designers must consider whether or not the same level of security is appropriate for all the fields on the record.

Where different levels of authorisation are required for different fields on a record, the record must be split to form the subject of two modules (Figure 8.5).

Now what is perhaps most remarkable about this from the HCI point of view is that we suddenly find that computer systems begin to look more and more like the manual systems with which users are already familiar.

On manual systems users don't have to enter a password to be able alter details on a record and if salaries are confidential we don't put them on the same record as other freely available details.

| MODULE A. | WORKS I/D | SURNAME | FORENAMES | ADDRESS | SALARY/MTH |

Level of authority required is not consistent. Split to 2

| MODULE A. | WORKS I/D | SURNAME | FORENAMES | ADDRESS |

| MODULE B | WORKS I/D | SALARY/MTH |

Figure 8.5 Record split to facilitate security.

The recommended approach produces systems of a familiar nature to which users can readily relate.

Once again the approach which has been recommended is simple, and above all easy to use. But the key to the simplicity of the security system lies outside what has been described. In fact the viability of the approach lies in the highly structured nature of PSD.

Security considerations are a vital part of the design of a system. PSD enables security to be achieved and security makes PSD systems secure.

For most commercial systems the measures described above will be sufficient. Further measures can be taken, such as requiring users to insert a security key (like a cash card) or by restricting users to particular terminals.

Similarly, on a dial-in system provision can be made for the computer to dial-back to ensure that the dial-in is from an authorised terminal. Care must also be taken to ensure that the security files themselves are totally secure.

However, additional features usually cost money and may in many cases prove to be too restrictive. Care must once more be taken, to ensure that any additional measures which are contemplated are necessary.

Finally on this topic, one further point. There is a school of thought which suggests that only the selections which a user is entitled to use should be displayed on menus. The main argument behind this thinking is that it is wrong to offer selections to users and then to tell them that they are not authorised to run the option.

Looked at from a simplistic point of view this sounds reasonable. On the other hand, we do not try to insist that shops should only display the goods that customers can afford. And if we did which customer should determine what is displayed and would we expect what is displayed to be changed for each customer?

Clearly things could get very complicated and the same applies to the idea of restricted menus. There are in fact all kinds of practical problems, not the least of which is the problem of producing a variety of different User Guides for each system - and then ensuring that each user gets the right one.

There is also the problem of whether to renumber the selections when some are left off a menu or whether to simply leave gaps. And senior staff will find it difficult to help junior staff if they have different menus for a module.

One possible compromise would be to stick with the one-system concept, but to dim the options on each menu where the users authority level is not high enough to allow selection. In this way, particularly as far as the all important Functions Menu is concerned, the standard pattern of the system can be preserved, whilst indicating to users what they can and cannot do. On balance, however, the simpler cheaper alternative is preferred.

Record Keys

As has already been stressed, all PSD Records must have a Key which will uniquely identify each record.

The task of determining what to use as the key to a series of records may appear to be fairly trivial. But on most systems the task of entering record keys is the one which users will most frequently be called upon to perform:

* To Amend, Erase, Display or Print a particular record, users must enter the key.

* To add an item to a customer's order, users must enter the key (the product code number) of the item.

* To display or print a particular Order or Invoice, users must enter a key, in this case the Order or Invoice number. And so on.

Since Record Keys have to be used a great deal by users they play an important role in HCI.

Because keys have to be typed repeatedly (or fed in by some other means) it is clearly desirable that they should be short.

Thus, for example, on a system holding details of the Members of a Club, although the name of each member could be used as the key, it is normally more convenient to allocate a Membership Number to each member. This can then be used as a key. Apart from the fact that this minimises the amount of typing required to access a record, keeping keys short has other advantages. In particular, short keys can be stored and sorted by computers more efficiently than longer keys.

From the programming and computer processing angle, the simplest way of handling keys is to just number records from one to however many there are.

Again, however, as has been stressed, it is inappropriate to allow any one aspect to dominate the designer's thinking and this applies, in particular, as far as processing efficiencies are concerned.

One of the main problems with purely numeric coding is common to both manual and computer systems i.e. if all keys look alike, they can readily be confused. Thus, for example, suppose that a Wholesaler has 500 Customers (coded 1 to 500), 200 Suppliers (coded 1 to 200) and 2000 Stocked Items (coded 1 to 2000). Without further clarification, it is not possible to determine whether '122' is a Customer, a Supplier or a commodity. It is not difficult to see that under these circumstances the keys, and indeed order numbers and quantities, can readily become transposed.

On manual systems therefore one will normally find that this problem has been avoided by giving each key a unique format. For example:

    S136 - Supplier 136
    C024 - Customer 024
    103-042 - Product 103042
    X11029 - Customers Order No., 11029
    P4069 - Purchase Order 4069.

Although it is not easy to quantify the benefits of what one may call 'requisite variety', it is considered to be highly desirable that this should be retained on computer systems. The primary consideration in devising formats for keys must therefore be the usability of the keys.

Record keys must be short, so that excessive typing is avoided. But where appropriate they should also be distinctive to limit the possibility of confusion.

Keeping keys short also has the advantage that there is less chance of a typing error being made. The greater the number of characters in a key, the greater the chance that one will be typed incorrectly.

Some years ago, to my horror, I received a letter which asked for the following reference to be quoted:
    'R/DQ45/25942/67/8D/G4665'
Fortunately, since then commonsense has largely prevailed.

The reference does, however, illustrate one of the most common mistakes in devising keys, namely the inclusion of excessive descriptive data.

The primary purpose of a record key is to uniquely identify a record. Descriptive data should not normally be included in the key, it should be held in the record.

Returning to the example of Membership Records, the way in which this would normally be handled would be to have a record of the form shown in Figure 8.6.

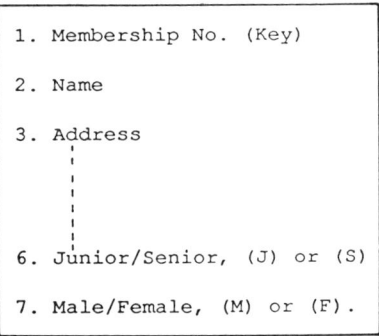

Figure 8.6 Details on Specimen Membership Record.

In this case a purely numeric membership number would normally be used. However, an alternative would be to include details of fields 6 & 7 in the key. For example, 'JM50' would be a Junior/Male member.

At first sight it may appear that the more complex key could have advantages. For example, if records are stored in membership number sequence, then a straight listing of the file would ensure that all junior/male members would be listed together.

However, this would mean that the file would have to be re-sorted whenever a new member joined. Similarly, although the chances of a sex-change are small, problems will arise when a Junior member becomes a Senior. In this case therefore, as in most cases, it is much simpler to hold records in the sequence in which they are entered, to use a simple non-descriptive key, and to devise suitable reporting programs to provide classified listings. Having said that, however, the example does illustrate one of the main problems with simple keys. This is the problem that if users don't know someone's key (Membership No.) they cannot go directly to the required record.

This is not an insurmountable problem in that any bona fide system must have reporting facilities which will readily enable keys to be established. In this case this could simply take the form of an alphabetic display of all names and membership numbers.

Ensuring that the right key is used can also be a problem with simple keys. But this should normally be taken care of by ensuring that sufficient detail is displayed (on line 21, if necessary) to enable a key to be verified visually. For example, if the membership system is extended to allow payment of subscriptions to be recorded, it is important that the name of the member should be displayed when a key is entered. The key can then be verified.

In some circumstances this approach is not feasible. Under these conditions additional security can be obtained by introducing a 'Check-digit' at the end of each code. The modulus 11 system is the most common check-digit system, the check-digit being the remainder after dividing the key by 11. Introducing a check-digit is particularly useful where keys are to be read by light-pens etc., as it enables the system to check immediately whether a key has been read correctly or not.

Although it is not generally recommended for on-line systems, additional security can be obtained by incorporating abbreviated identifying details into keys. For example;

    WS14B   -   Womens Skirt, Size 14, Blue.

    MTXLG   -   Mens Trousers, Size XL, Grey.

This approach has advantages where only a limited number of attributes are necessary to uniquely identify a product and users can readily deduce the keys. It also has the advantage that a straight sort on the keys will result in similar items being listed together.

Clearly, as the number of attributes required increases the length of the key required will also increase. The benefits of having a key that can be deduced will then be off-set by more effort being required to type keys.

It is difficult to know where to draw the line between when to use identifying keys and when not. But, since keys can readily be looked-up, identifying keys should only be used when the advantages are clear, and when the approach will not lead to excessively long keys.

The question as to what is an 'excessively long key' is again one where there is no clear cut answer, although experience suggests that purely numeric keys of more than six to eights digits create problems.

A useful compromise in some circumstances is to include a generic identifying code in the key. For example, 'S904' where 'S' indicates 'Skirt'.

From what has been said it will be apparent that the task of devising keys is not an exact science and more research in this field would be useful. At the same time the task will frequently be complicated by the fact that users may already be using keys on their manual systems.

Where keys are already used to identify Customers, Parts or Catalogue Items etc., the prospect of having to change these may be quite daunting for users. Under these circumstance designers may have to accept the fact that inefficient keys must be retained. Alternatively, users can be weaned off inefficient keys by introducing a 'short-key' and allowing users to use either key. In other cases complex keys may be thrust upon users in the form of National Insurance or Vehicle Registration Numbers and so on. The two examples quoted in fact lend themselves to examination of the ways in which this problem can be handled.

In the case of NI Numbers most companies treat this as descriptive data and allocate an Employee or Clock Number to identify each employee. Apart from the fact that the latter is normally much shorter, it also has the advantage that establishing a record won't be delayed, because new employees cannot remember their NI Number. On the other hand, most Fleet Owners will normally use the Vehicle Registration Number as a key, rather than allocate a shorter number of their own. Although there is very little that the average systems designer can do about Vehicle Registration Numbers, they do illustrate a number of interesting facettes of the design of keys.

Until fairly recently vehicles were registered locally and each Licensing Authority was identified by a series of up to three letters. So by putting these letters in front of each number each Authority could issue its own numbers independently.

As so often happens on systems, however, the fact that circumstances have now changed seems to have been overlooked and registration numbers still include the irrelevant area code.

As a result large numbers of potential codes were 'locked away' and it became necessary for another digit to be added to the numbers. At this point someone had a brilliant idea and decided that this should be a letter which would indicate when the car was registered - descriptive data.

With a little imagination, it is not difficult to see that the registration number could have been extended further to indicate the number of wheels on the vehicle, the horsepower, colour and so on. Fortunately, this has not happened. But proposals are now in hand to include a code to show the month of registration to eliminate the sales peak which the current system generates each year.

As was suggested, there isn't much that a humble systems designer can do about this problem. However, it is hoped that it will serve as a warning to all to think carefully before deviating from simple numeric or alpha-numeric keys.

One final point on this topic. Many overseas countries seem to have avoided this problem on their vehicles. So again this illustrates another important aspect of systems design.

Always look around and see what others have done or are doing. Even if their ideas are not as good as yours it may still help you to improve your own designs.

Codes

The use of codes in record keys has already been mentioned. In this section the subject of coding other details within a record is considered. Codes, or abbreviations, are commonly used in everyday life. Some typical examples are;

£	-	Pounds.
Kg	-	Kilograms.
10	-	A Shoe size.
XL	-	An Extra Large garment size.
L37 3LF	-	A Post Code.

Some of the codes used are somewhat specialised, but their appearance on computer records or reports should not present users with any difficulties. Even so, particularly where units of measure are concerned, it is advisable to ensure that a system will check that what is entered is a valid code.

Normally this check will consist of simply checking that the code is in a 'Table of Valid Codes'. In the case of the Post Code, however, most private systems would not check the code or would merely check the format of the code. Common codes of this nature will be stored and printed as they stand without the need for further clarification and should not present any problems.

What this section is mainly concerned with therefore is what may be called 'uncommon codes'. That is codes which are derived for the convenience of computing.

The need for uncommon coding will normally become apparent when there are only a limited number of alternative responses that can be put into a particular descriptive field. For example, suppose that a company divides up the country into eight Sales Territories;

> North, North East, East, South East, South, South West, West and North West.

As each Sales Order is processed, one could type in the appropriate region for subsequent analysis - if one was not thinking clearly! A region is an attribute of a Customer, not a Sales Order. So by putting the region on each customer's record it only has to be entered once, rather than every time a customer places another order. Even so, if there are several hundred customers, then the task of typing the full description of each region is obviously wasteful. The alternative is to limit what has to be typed by coding.

The simplest form of coding would be to number the regions from 1 to 8. But usability must be considered. In this case, although the benefits are difficult to quantify, it should be apparent that users will more readily relate to codes of the form, N, NE, E, SE, S and so on.

Using codes in this way will save on storage space in the computer. However, it must be stressed that this must not be a primary consideration. Thus the fact that a two character alpha code will take up a few more bits of storage space than a numeric code is a trivial detail on all but massive files.

Use codes to reduce the amount of typing of repetitive descriptive data. Wherever possible use codes which are meaningful.

Using meaningful codes also has a significant advantage as far as reporting is concerned. If what has to be reported on can be output directly from a single file, this is very easy to handle. If codes must be interpreted and their meaning must be shown on reports, this will clearly add to the complexity of the reporting program. This is not a difficult task, but each report will require a special program to be written. As a general rule therefore if descriptive data has to be reported in full, designers must realise that using coding to simplify input will make reporting more complex.

There are other alternatives. It is possible, for example, to arrange for a system to extend a code at the time when a record is being created. In other words, when a user types in a code, the system will interpret it and display and store the full description.

Taken in isolation this may appear to be quite a useful user-friendly idea, but it is not recommended. The essence of PSD is that systems must not play clever tricks on what users put into records.

A fundamental principle of PSD is that what users type into a record is what will appear on the record, and is what will subsequently be stored on the record.

Providing that this concept is applied throughout, users will readily understand systems and will therefore readily relate to them.

One final point. Where codes are used on records these should be stored in place of, rather than in addition to the full description. To store what amounts to the same information twice on a record is clearly not good practise.

Chapter 9

Miscellaneous Features

Introduction

What has been described so far covers all the basic features of PSD as applied to conventional general purpose EDP systems. In this chapter the advantages and disadvantages of alternatives to conventional keyboard systems are considered.

Colour

VDU's capable of displaying details in colour are readily available. But the general concensus of opinion appears to be ... that colour should be used with discretion.

For normal EDP colour is not necessary. In fact the introduction of colour on menus and input screens will normally prove to be distracting.

Colour adds significantly to the cost of VDU's. In many cases it can increase hardware costs by as much as 30%. What isn't so obvious, but equally important, is that it also increases the cost of virtually every other aspect of the development of a system. Designs take longer, programmes are bigger and more complex, printers are more expensive and limited, and the production of User Guides is more difficult and costly.

PSD does not require the additional expense of colour, the use of which should be avoided, unless a particular application clearly demands it.

For graphical displays or computer-aided design, for example, colour may be highly desirable. But such applications should be treated as 'specials', so that colour is not allowed to permeate through to other applications and only special-users have to have colour VDU's.

Mice, Joysticks and Roller-Balls

Many systems now have facilities to allow the cursor to be moved around the screen by means of a special device, other than the keyboard. The most common of these devices is called a Mouse (Figure 9.1). Moving the Mouse to and fro on a flat surface produces a corresponding movement of the cursor.

The same effect can be achieved with a Joystick or by rotating a Roller-Ball. The latter is simply a ball in a holder, which allows the ball to rotate freely.

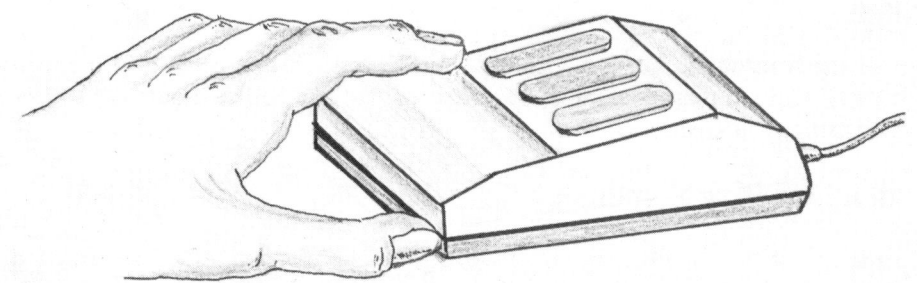

Figure 9.1 A Computer 'Mouse'. Not recommended for EDP.

Once again there are special applications where devices of this nature are invaluable. Unfortunately, there are also a great many applications where the use of devices of this nature is totally inappropriate.

The main problem with devices of this nature is that operators only have two hands. To operate the device users must move a hand away from the keyboard to reach for the device. To a skilled typist, in particular, this is an anathema.

At the same time cursor manipulation is a task at which very few people are skilled. It can also be extremely difficult if the buffering on a computer introduces a time lag between the device being moved and the cursor actually moving.

So using PSD the need for cursor manipulation has been reduced to a minimum and devices such as mice should generally be avoided.

Having said that, it should be made clear that there are circumstances where the availability of a Mouse is extremely useful. For example, in design work if a user needs to 'point' to a particular part of a design to call for it to be enlarged.

Similarly, on some systems, the computer can actually sense the position of the Mouse. This is obviously a vital feature for systems where details of complex shapes have to be captured, a process known as Digitising. But this process is also frequently misused. The most common mistake is to use the facility for menu selection. On systems of this nature, users are provided with a squared-board, on which all the menu options are inscribed. Users can then select an option by moving the Mouse to the appropriate square, and pressing a button on the Mouse. This introduces a number of unnecessary problems. The first problem is where to put the menu board, in relation to the keyboard. If the keyboard is conveniently positioned, the menu board will be difficult to read and reach, and vice versa.

The approach also makes it difficult to introduce changes, because menu boards have to be re-inscribed. It also tends to lead to cryptic menus. A variation on this approach is to just have a squared board and to display the selection titles, in corresponding squares on the VDU.

This tends to result in menus which are more cryptic than ever. It also highlights another problem in that the number of selections that can be fitted onto a board or a screen is strictly limited.

Touch Sensitive Screens

Instead of the cursor having to be directed to a particular part of a screen, some systems allow the user to indicate a particular position by touching the VDU screen.

This is particularly useful for computer aided design and similar applications, but it has similar problems to the menu board in that, if the keyboard is conveniently situated for typing, the screen cannot be conveniently placed for touching.

On some systems menu selection and the equivalent of FOS processing are also performed by touching illuminated boxes along the bottom of the screen.

Normally, this severely restricts the number of selections that can be made available and whilst it may appeal to unskilled users, a skilled typist will find it a strain. It also leads to very cryptic labels which are often displayed at only half the normal illumination.

Obviously, PSD can be fully implemented on systems of this type, by simply ignoring the touch facility. Unless an application clearly requires 'touching', it is recommended that the facility should be ignored.

Automatic Data Capture

The task of actually typing data into a computer can be avoided in a number of ways, the most common of which is Bar Coding (Figure 9.2). In some cases all the data necessary to create a Record may be captured automatically. In others, only part of the data may be captured and the remainder must be keyed in.

Figure 9.2 Bar Coding. A quick and easy way to get data into a computer, if the circumstances are right.

In both cases significant savings in time and additional security can be achieved with automatic data capture, without deviating from the basic principles of PSD.

Effectively, automatic data capture merely provides an alternative to typing and provision should normally be made for either alternative to be used. In this way, problems with codes that cannot be read can be circumvented.

There are a wide variety of devices that can be used to read Bar Codes, ranging from hand held pen-like devices to motor driven machines. The type which is most suitable will depend on the nature of the application.

Optical Character Recognition (OCR) is very similar in principle to Bar Coding. But it has the advantage that the code can also be read by users. The disadvantage of this is that the machine readability of OCR is not normally as consistent as with Bar Coding.

For normal commercial purposes therefore, except where space is at a premium, Bar Coding with an interpretation of the code is currently the most reliable. However, this may change as a limited number of sophisticated OCR readers can already read conventional text.

Magnetic Ink Character Recognition (MICR) is similar to OCR, but the characters are printed in magnetic ink (Figure 9.3). This makes the printing more expensive, but it is more difficult for details to be altered. MICR is therefore used mainly for security purposes, on applications such as Cheque Coding.

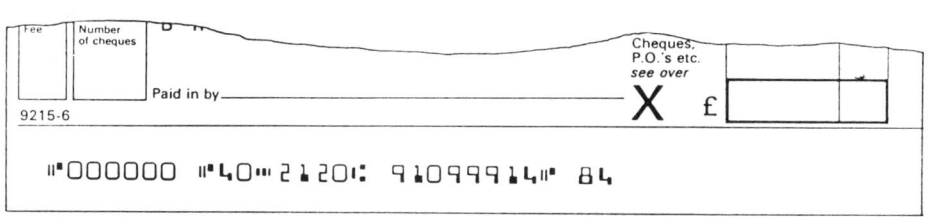

Figure 9.3 Magnetic Ink Character Recognition (MICR). Used primarily for security purposes.

The next step up is to provide a magnetic strip on which larger amounts of data can be stored. The data cannot be read without a reader and cannot readily be altered by users. So magnetic strips are used extensively for security purposes on Cash Point Cards and Time Booking Systems.

The final stage in the progression is to provide cards with more tape and to allow data to be stored on and read back from the tape. These cards usually serve as labels onto which details of a series of operations can be recorded as an item progresses.

Special Keys

The importance of ensuring that systems can run on a wide variety of computers has already been pointed out. And to this end the benefits of designing systems around standard typewriter keys have been stressed.

At the same time the need for special keys was identified to perform tasks which are not standard typewriter-tasks. To insert and delete characters and to enter data, for example.

For Word-processing (WP), as will be seen later, a number of additional features are required. However, for normal EDP only one other special key needs to be considered. This is the <HELP> key. Pressing <HELP> at any time will take users out of whatever is being done and cause guiding notes to be displayed.

The nature of PSD is such that very little guidance should be required and simply providing a User Guide should be sufficient.

Special applications may call for specially designed keyboards or printers. But particular care must be taken to ensure that the basic principles of PSD are retained as far as possible and that any deviations are absolutely essential.

One of the main benefits of PSD is flexibility and, in particular, the ease with which systems can be changed in order to meet ever changing requirements.

Deviations from the basic PSD methodology can quickly lead to systems which rapidly become obsolete because of their restrictiveness and difficulties in program maintenance. This is particularly so when special input panels are used.

The design of Cash Dispensers for Banks is a typical example of this. The design is examined in more detail later. So for the moment, suffice it to say that the early designs provided a classic example of the sort of problems that can arise. The main problems arose because menu selection was achieved by means of buttons along the side of the screen - and only six buttons were provided. Therefore once the need for more than six selections was identified, problems were inevitable. Modern Cash Points now have a bewildering array of selection buttons, but as will be seen later, this still hasn't solved the problem as effectively as it could have been resolved.

Word Processing (WP)

WP is one of the most common and rewarding forms of modern computing. Although WP may appear to be essentially the same as EDP, it is not. EDP systems are highly structured and restricted. In WP what is processed can take an infinite variety of forms and may be anything from a short letter to a whole book or library.

It is beyond the scope of this book to look in detail at the way in which WP systems should be designed. So what follows is merely intended to show how WP and EDP should be related.

For WP a variety of special facilities are required to allow text to be manipulated, and these facilities cannot be provided by means of the conventional typewriter keys. On some systems this problem is overcome by introducing a special shift-key, which is normally called the Control Key or <CTRL>. Special WP functions (Figure 9.4) can then be invoked by holding down <CTRL> and pressing conventional keys.

```
* CUT      Allows a highlighted section of text to be removed
* COPY     Copies a highlighted section of text
* PASTE    Inserts copied text
* FIND     Finds a specified word(s) in a text
* EXCH.    Exchanges one word for another word/words
* PAGE     Displays the next page of text
* DOC.     Displays the end of a document
* PARA.    Moves the cursor forward one paragraph.
```

Figure 9.4 Sample of Typical WP Special Facilities

This has the advantage that a large number of special functions can be included with only one special key being added to keyboards. The main problem with this is that the keys don't normally have 'special' labels, so users have to look up or remember which key does what.

Unskilled users also tend to have problems, because they fail to fully depress <CTRL> before striking a letter-key. Where a terminal is to be used for WP therefore it is desirable that special keys should be provided and that these should be labelled.

The wide variety of WP packages currently available is such that most systems designers should not have to design WP system, but it is important that the package selected should be user-friendly.

It is also important that the same computer or terminal should be used for both WP and EDP. There are systems on the market that are designed purely for WP. Often they have many excellent features, such as VDU's which allow a full page of A4 text to be displayed. If it is absolutely clear that a free-standing dedicated Word-processor is what is required, then a special WP computer may be justified. This can, however, create a great many problems. Requirements frequently change, and the stage can soon be reached where each user needs two VDU's, one for WP and one for EDP. Problems can also arise when the need to move data from one computer to another is recognised or when the decision to move to electronic mail is taken.

Wherever possible the same type of computer, or one that is fully compatible, should be used for all WP and EDP systems.

Voice Input And Output

Some observers seem to believe that voice input is the answer to what is often described as 'keyboard phobia'. In fact it is badly designed systems that are the real problem, not keyboards. And voice input simply introduces more problems.

As has already been stressed, people are exceptionally good at pattern recognition and this facility is used extensively in conversation. Even so misunderstandings can and frequently do occur, particularly when a variety of different dialects are involved.

The human voice is not a very positive way of communication. Thus, whilst a few simple systems and toys may be driven by a limited number of commands, it is unlikely that voice input will ever replace more positive forms of input for EDP.

Voice output has been used successfully, to confirm what has been dialed on telephones and to transmit emergency messages. The technique has also been applied to give users short instructions on the way to use simple devices, such as Pay-phones

However, even users with limited skill will quickly tire, of being told what they have typed or what to do next by a robot-voice. So voice output is not likely to figure to any significant extent in EDP systems.

On the other hand, as far as WP is concerned, the prospect of being able to dictate a letter directly into a computer is attractive. It is conceivable therefore that such systems may become commercially viable within a few years, although the problems involved are considerable.

Keyboards

Keyboards vary considerably in terms of the number of special keys and their functions. This is not helpful to users and it is important that all concerned should press for standards to be established.

Chapter 10

Designing Records and Normalisation

Introduction

Now that all the basic concepts of PSD have been described, the methodology for actually defining records can be summarised. This chapter covers this by comparing the algorithms developed for PSD with an alternative, namely Normalisation.

Normalisation is a methodology which was first formalised by E. F. Codd (CODD, 1970). The methodology is limited in that it is concerned primarily with the problem of how to divide fields between records. It also introduces a great deal of obscure terminology.

Normalisation has, however, attracted a large number of enthusiasts, and has the distinction of being the first serious attempt to rationalise the design process. The approach is very different from PSD although, since the underlying concepts are the same, the results obtained should be the same in both cases.

This chapter will therefore serve to allow the two approaches to be compared; to reinforce the basic concepts of this aspect of PSD and/or to present designers with an alternative.

Terminology

One of the main problems that many people will find with most descriptions of the process of Normalisation is the terminology which must be absorbed.

Records are usually described as Entities and Fields are called Attributes, whilst Files tend to be described as Data Sets.

As with PSD, the main aim of normalisation is to develop Rectangular (two-dimensional) Files. But for reasons which aren't clear, instead of referring to Records and Fields on Files, two further terms are introduced.

The new terms are Tuples and Domains. Tuples are the equivalent of Records and Domains consist of occurences of a particular field on successive records. A simpler alternative would be to describe these as rows and columns respectively (Figure 10.1), although even this may cause confusion in the minds of some users.

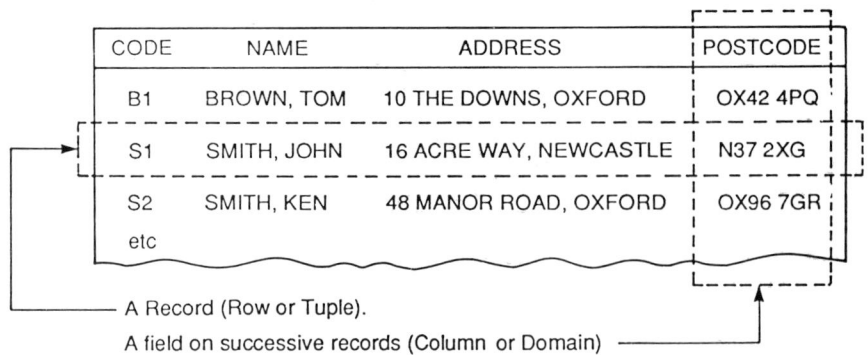

Figure 10.1 A File illustrating Tuples and Domains.

As has been stressed throughout in describing PSD, the introduction of new or unfamiliar terms is not helpful. So, what follows has been translated as far as possible into terms which will hopefully prove to be more acceptable.

Normalisation

The process of Normalisation consists of three steps which it is suggested should be carried out in sequence to produce what are called First, Second and Third Normal Forms.

The process will be illustrated by reference to a simplified file of students on 'Open University' type Courses. Each student lives in a particular Region, which has a Code, and students may take a number of Courses.

Courses are also coded and the Grade which a student has reached is to be recorded. In its unnormalised form, the data would set out as in Figure 10.2.

STUDENT No.	NAME	REGION CODE	REGION NAME	COURSE CODE	COURSE NAME	COURSE GRADE
B1	T. BROWN	O	OXFORD	30	HISTORY	3
				40	GEOGRAPHY	3
S1	J. SMITH	N	NEWCASTLE	30	HISTORY	4
S2	K. SMITH	O	OXFORD	40	GEOGRAPHY	4

Figure 10.2 Data in its Unnormalised Form (UNF).

First Normal Form (FNF)

To convert data into FNF '...all repeating groups must be removed'.

In this case, since students can attend more than one Course, the Course details are an example of a repeating group. To convert the data into FNF, therefore, two separate files must be created (Figure 10.3).

STUDENT FILE

STUDENT No.	NAME	REGION CODE	REGION NAME
B1	T. BROWN	O	OXFORD
S1	J. SMITH	N	NEWCASTLE
S2	K. SMITH	O	OXFORD

STUDENT/COURSE FILE

STUDENT No.	COURSE CODE	COURSE NAME	COURSE GRADE
B1	30	HISTORY	3
B1	40	GEOGRAPHY	3
S1	30	HISTORY	4
S2	40	GEOGRAPHY	4

Figure 10.3 Data in First Normal Form (FNF).

Second Normal Form (SNF)

To convert the data into SNF '...all non-key fields must be dependent on the whole key and not just part of it'.

The key to the first file in Figure 10.3 is Student No. and all the details in the file are clearly related to the key.

However, in the Student/Course File, there is a multi-part key since Student No. on its own does not uniquely identify a record. The key, is of course, Student No. plus Course Code.

At the same time, the Course Name is clearly not an attribute of this key. It is related to Course Code rather than Student No./Course Code. So the second file must be divided into two further files (Figure 10.4).

STUDENT/COURSE FILE

STUDENT No.	COURSE CODE	COURSE GRADE
B1	30	3
B1	40	3
S1	30	4
S2	40	4

COURSE NAME FILE

COURSE CODE	COURSE NAME
30	HISTORY
40	GEOGRAPHY

Figure 10.4 Data in Second Normal Form (SNF). The Student File remains as in Figure 10.3.

Third Normal Form (TNF)

Finally, to convert the data into TNF '... non-key fields, which are dependent on other non-key fields must be removed'.

In this example on the Students File (Figure 10.3) the Region Name is clearly directly related to the Region Code, and so the Student File must be split into two (Figure 10.5).

STUDENT FILE

STUDENT No.	NAME	REGION CODE
B1	T. BROWN	O
S1	J. SMITH	N
S2	K. SMITH	O

REGION NAME FILE

REGION CODE	REGION NAME
N	NEWCASTLE
O	OXFORD

Figure 10.5 Data in Third Normal Form (TNF). Other files remain as in Figure 10.4.

So the TNF will consist of four files (Figure 10.6). The key to each record is underlined.

```
┌─────────────────────────────────────┐
│  STUDENT FILE                       │
│                                     │
│  Student No., Name, Region code.    │
│                                     │
│  STUDENT/COURSE FILE                │
│                                     │
│  Student No./Course Code, Grade     │
│                                     │
│  COURSE NAME FILE.                  │
│                                     │
│  Course Code, Course Name.          │
│                                     │
│  REGION NAME FILE.                  │
│                                     │
│  Region Code, Region Name.          │
└─────────────────────────────────────┘
```

Figure 10.6 Summary of files generated by Normalisation.

Comparison With PSD

As has already been suggested, the results obtained above are the same as one would expect to find from using PSD, although there are subtle differences in the way in which the results would have been obtained.

From the point of view of the practitioner the most striking thing about most descriptions of the process of normalisation is that they seem to suggest that what exists should be ignored. In other words, the first step appears to be to create chaos out of order by lumping as much as possible into one file in the form of unnormalised data.

There would appear to be little value in doing this, particularly where a manual system already exists and one would expect to find that the records in use were rational ones.

Thus for instance, in the case of the example shown, an astute designer would probably discover that the manual records being used were already in the form shown in Figure 10.6. In other words, already in 'Third Normal Form'

Under these circumstances therefore the concept of varying levels of normalisation becomes somewhat irrelevant. In PSD the first step is more positive:

Determine what records are necessary to support the required system and put these into Rectangular Files, with a unique key for each record.

In many cases, reference to the records currently used on manual systems will enable a solution to be found immediately. In some cases, however, the following step may be necessary.

Where a complex file is encountered, convert this to two Rectangular Files by putting Header Details in one file and Item Details into another.

This is, of course, equivalent to the process of producing FNF (ie. eliminating repeating groups). The main point, however, is that repeating groups should not have been entertained in the initial design. Similarly:

Ensure that all fields included in a record are directly related to its unique key.

This is equivalent to the step of producing the SNF (ie. '...all non-key fields must be dependent on the whole key...'), but again the PSD approach is more positive. It should be clear that whether the unique key to a record is a single or multi-field key the whole of the key must be considered when assigning fields to records. Again therefore fields which do not satisfy the required conditions must not be allocated to a record.

Where descriptive details in one or more fields may be repeated on a number of records on a file, consider coding these details to save time on repetitive entry.

The details will then be entered once and held on a separate file, together with the identifying code. Only the code will then be entered into and held on the original file.

This corresponds to the step of producing the TNF (ie. '...non-key fields which are dependent on other non-key fields should be removed...').Again, however, it should be apparent that once the details relating to a code have been entered (eg. Region Code 'O', Region Name 'Oxford') only the code should be entered on any other files.

Appraisal

From what has been said, it should be apparent that PSD offers a more direct approach to systems design than normalisation. It is therefore likely to produce results faster. But many designers may find it helpful to use the more methodical step by step approach offered by normalisation.

Since skilled designers may be expected to arrive at the same results, whichever of the two approaches they use, the choice of method is perhaps not all that important.

It is important, however, that the wider aspects of PSD should not be ignored, whichever method is used. In particular, the wider implications of each record must be fully considered.

One of the main dangers with normalisation is that it tends to create the impression that systems design is a purely mechanical process, which it is not.

Normalisation will undoubtedly help aspiring designers to master the art of recognising how data should appear in records. But they must realise that this is only a small part of the design process.

Whatever approach is adopted, there is no substitute for getting 'out into the field' to establish what is required from a system.

Normalisation will not prevent confidential fields, such as Salaries or Examination Marks etc., from being included on records which can be displayed by large numbers of people. Similarly, it will not force designers to think at each stage about the effects which the five basic functions will have on a record (ie. Create, Amend, Erase, etc.).

It would therefore be easy in the example shown earlier to forget to make provision to ensure that a Student cannot be erased from the Students File, whilst he or she is still on a course.

So to avoid these problems PSD includes a step for which there is no equivalent in normalisation. Namely:

In determining what fields are to be included on a record, consider the implications of the five Basic Functions, that is Create, Amend, Erase, Display and Print Record.

There is, of course, no reason why this step cannot be performed after arriving at a TNF, but experience suggests that the five basic functions play a vital role in the formulation of effective designs. Somehow, being constantly aware of these five Basic Functions seems to help to concentrate the thinking of designers, particularly thinking about 'What records must be Created' and 'What will be the effects of Erase'.

This will also help to ensure that another common error is avoided:

Data of a transient nature must not be included on records holding data of a more permanent nature.

The main reason for this constraint is that if the two types of data are put into one record, then one cannot readily erase the transient data without also erasing the permanent data.

For example, suppose that a College wishes to keep a permanent record of its students, past and present. Suppose also that a record of 'digs' addresses is also to be held. If both the home address and digs address are put into one file, then the digs address cannot be Erased when the student leaves. Two files are clearly required, even though the key to both will be the same.

The ability of PSD to concentrate the thinking of designers is clearly important, particularly in the early stages of the development of a system. At this stage designers will frequently find themselves dismayed by a bewildering array of new faces, strange forms and unusual processing requirements.

At times starting to develop a new system can be rather like wandering around in a thick fog where one can see a few yards of path at a time, but not where the path is leading. Clearly, anything that can help to dispell this fog as quickly as possible is vital.

Chapter 11

Design Phases

Introduction

In the earlier chapters all the basic principles of systems design have been covered. In this chapter the basic steps of the actual design process are considered.

Normally, the most difficult part of a systems designers job is the task of deciding what a system should do. The second most difficult part is to ensure that a new system isn't designed if a suitable system already exists. There are a great many systems (usually called Packages) which are already available. Using one of these will often save a great deal of time and money.

Where an established Package has to be evaluated, the task of the systems designer is somewhat different from that of developing a new system from scratch:

* In the case of a new system, the designer must start by determining the needs of the business and then decide how best to satisfy these needs.

* In the case of a package, it is normally simpler to determine what the package does and then to consider how well it satisfies the user's needs, and what must be done to make it acceptable.

In both cases the techniques used are very similar. As this guide is primarily aimed at systems design, it is assumed from here on that a 'new' system is required. It is also assumed that the system is being developed for a commercial organisation where formal approval for expenditure is required.

Project Initiation

Before too much time and effort is expended on a project, it is essential that a brief Project Initiation Report should be prepared and formally authorised.

The report must describe what exists, what is proposed, and what it is likely to cost and save. It must also contain clear terms of reference, together with estimated time-scales and expected costs for the next phase of the project.

To be able to complete this report the designer must have a fairly good understanding of what the system is going to do.

In the case of a small free-standing system, what the system should do will normally be fairly obvious. However, in most commercial organisations there are very few free-standing systems. Nearly all systems are linked in some way or another, which poses a problem.

In the 1960s, when commercial EDP began to spread, the term IDP (Integrated Data Processing) suddenly became the vogue. The philosophy of IDP was that, because systems were linked, they shouldn't be programmed in isolation but as one fully integrated system.

Many organisations then spent very large sums of money attempting to chart all the complexities of their business. It took nearly two years before people began to realise that, although they had produced lots of charts, they hadn't actually produced any programs.

The situation was also made more difficult by the continually changing nature of commerce and industry. As a result of this the stage was quickly reached where charts were going out of date faster than new charts could be completed. Almost as quickly as it had appeared, IDP was replaced by the philosophy of '... let's at least get something programmed and running'. So small isolated systems were then developed and as time has progressed the experience gained has enabled these systems to be expanded and integrated.

Somewhat surprisingly, although the name IDP has fallen into disuse, there are still a number of advocates of this approach. Theoretically, the approach is right, but, in practice, it is a recipe for disaster on a grand scale.

The practical solution is a modular approach, coupled with easy-to-modify programs.

Clearly, long-term development plans must not be ignored, particularly as far as the choice of the computer itself is concerned, but as far as detailed evaluation is concerned the designer must take a short-term view.

For detailed examinations, the designers aim must be to identify the smallest part of any system that can be implemented with advantage.

Working in this way may not appeal to the purists. But, it has many real advantages:

* The task of the designer is considerably simplified, by being able to concentrate on a limited part of a system.

* It is easier for users to grasp the implications of what is proposed.

* Fewer users will need to be satisfied that what is proposed is viable.

* Development times will be shorter.

* Implementation is easier for all concerned.

* Experience gained from implementation will almost certainly have a favourable influence on subsequent developments.

* Systems will be up and running faster.

The last point is particularly important. At present, many systems have a very limited life and protracted development times can result in systems being obsolete before they are implemented.

Project Identification

In determining what is suitable for EDP the main criteria is normally savings. Generally, these will be tangible savings, resulting from reductions in clerical effort or lower stock levels and so on.

However, intangible saving can be just as important. It is often very difficult to put a value on features, such as the more timely production of accounts, or to estimate the effect of fewer stock-outs on customer goodwill, but these intangible savings must not be overlooked.

To a large extent the task of identifying suitable projects is intuitive and some designers will prove to be better at it than others.

At this stage therefore it is important to ensure that the best brains available are employed, as it is difficult to recover a project after a bad start.

Essentially what the designer will normally be looking for is:

* Activities involving a lot of clerical effort, eg., Accounting.

* Activities which are already mechanised, eg., Typing.

* Areas where a variety of people need access to the same data, eg., Stock Records.

* Aspects where more timely information could lead to better control, eg., Share Prices.

* Areas where more sophisticated calculations may provide benefits, eg., Sales Forecasting.

* Places where different people maintain records of the same information, eg., Employee Details.

* Systems which involve sorting data and reporting on it in different ways, eg., Stock Accounting.

Feasibility Study

The primary aim of the systems designer is to produce a System Specification. In the case of a minor project it is possible to move directly to this stage. But in most cases an intermediate stage is desirable. In other words a Feasibility Study.

The objective of the feasibility study is to provide all concerned with a more detailed idea of how the system will work, what it will cost to develop, what it is likely to save, and likely time scales for subsequent work.

The basic aim of the feasibility study is to secure approval for more detailed work to be done, to produce a definitive specification. The Feasibility Report which is produced should normally show:

* *Introduction.* Giving details of the background and purpose of the study.

* *Management Summary.* Briefly outlining the main conclusions of the study and presenting the terms of reference for the next phase. A summary of costs and benefits must be included.

* *Existing System.* Where what exists at the moment is briefly described.

* *Proposed System.* In which what is proposed is outlined, together with possible alternatives.

* *Development Plans.* Identifying resources and expected time-scales.

In most cases, the first task of the designer must be to obtain a clear but concise view of the existing system. Where job descriptions and/or detailed task instructions already exist, these will serve as useful background information.

But background information must not be regarded as a substitute for actually seeing what exists and what is done.

Seeing staff actually performing a task will not only help to fix it in the designers mind, it will also help to ensure that the designer discovers what actually happens, rather than what is supposed to happen.

An organisation chart is essential and at each stage a copy of any forms or reports, which are used or issued, must be secured. Completed forms are much more helpful than blank ones.

A note book is useful, so that vital facts and figures can be jotted down for subsequent digestion. Wherever possible details should be double checked. Organisation charts quickly become out of date and it is not uncommon to find that two people, sitting side by side, use the same form in different ways.

A Column Flow Chart (Figure 11.1) is a convenient way of recording what happens when a variety of forms and people are involved. Small sections of the chart can be recorded in rough as the designer collects information. These can then be consolidated onto larger sheets later. In some cases a large sheet of cartridge paper may be required to provide a comprehensive view of a system.

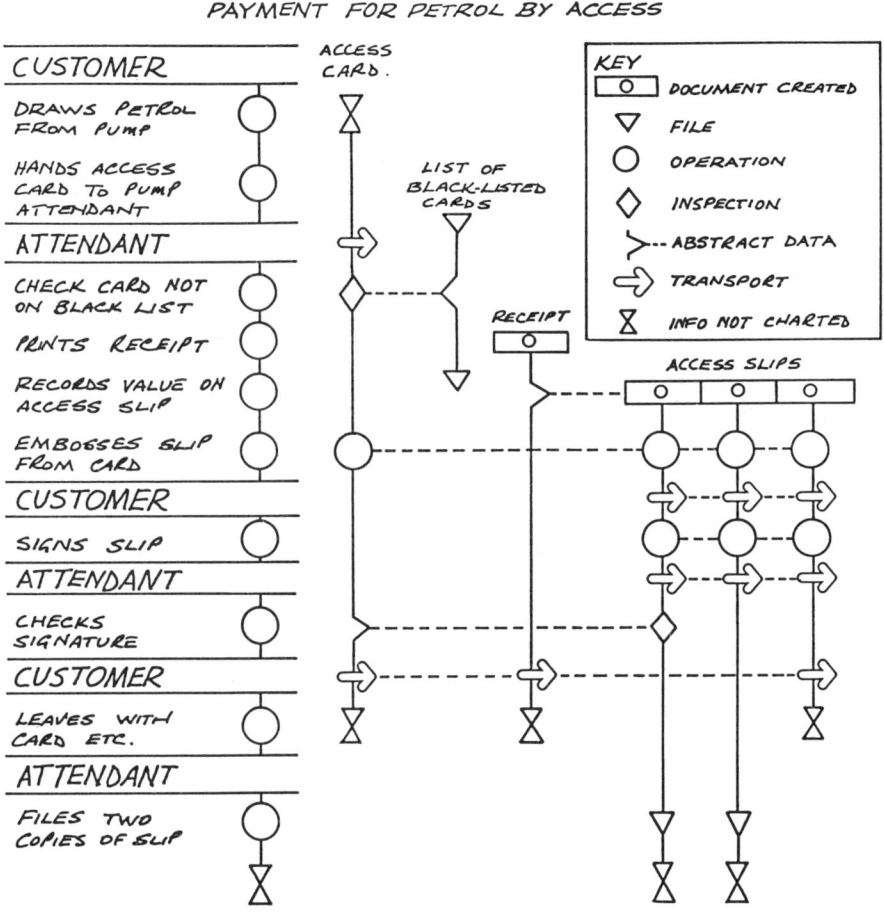

Figure 11.1 A Column Flow Chart. Ideal for recording complex transactions.

The comprehensive view is intended primarily for the benefit of the designer. What is included in the Feasibility Report should be a lot simpler, but illustrations should be used whenever possible to show existing and proposed methods (Figure 11.2).

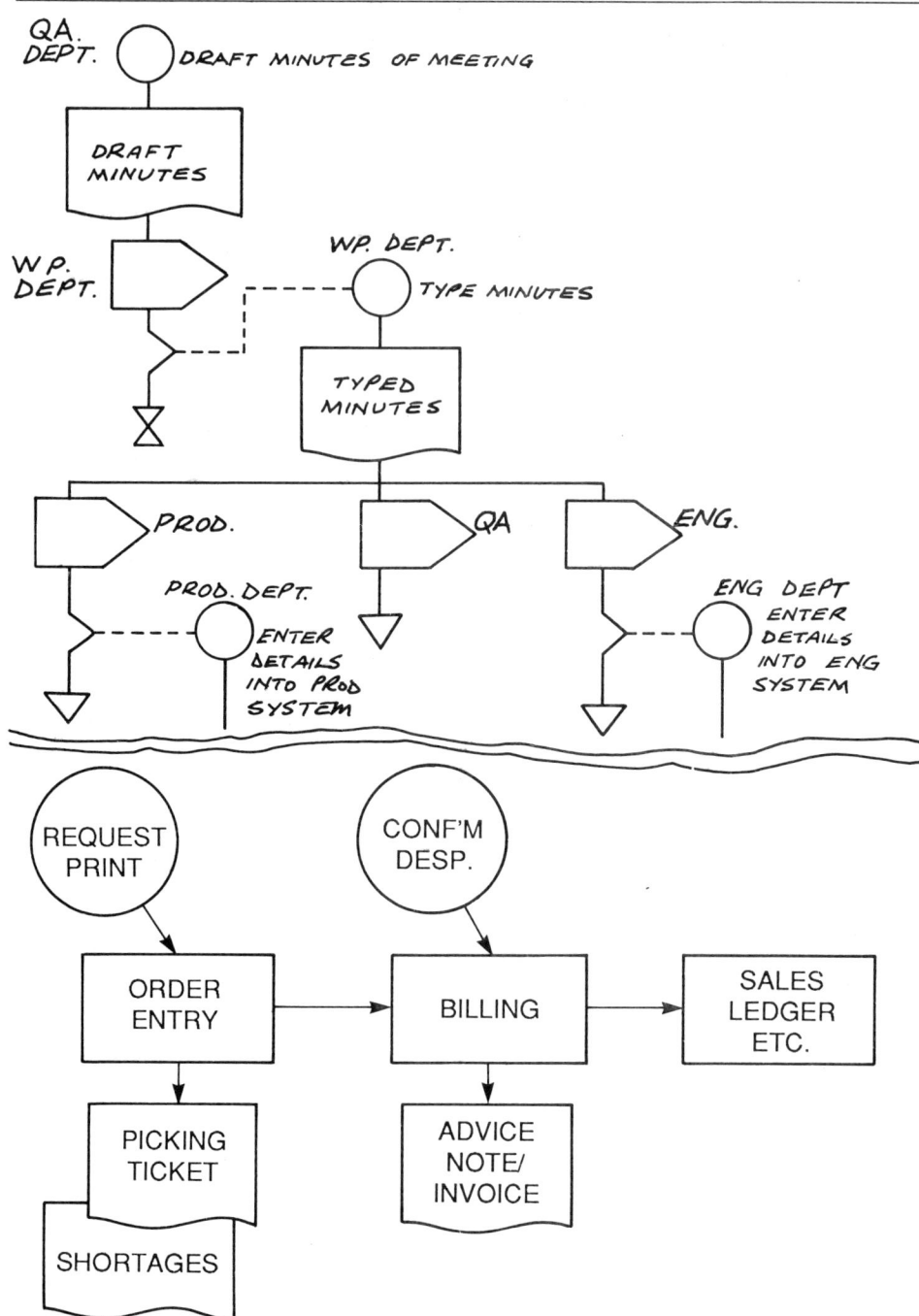

Figure 11.2 Illustrations help to clarify proposals.

At this stage, the Modules of the proposed system should be identified, but little else will have been done in terms of defining fields, report formats and so on.

Apart from allowing a decision to be made as to whether or not to continue, the Feasibility Report serves three other purposes. Firstly, writing it helps the designer to gain a better understanding. Secondly, it enables users to see whether or not the designer has understood their problems. Finally, it allows all concerned to comment on the development proposals.

The System Specification

Once a feasibilty report has been approved, the next step is to produce a System Specification.

A System Specification should normally consist of two main parts: a descriptive part, which will summarise the system and tell management what they need to know; and a detailed part, which will serve primarily to tell programmers precisely what is required.

The descriptive part will include a description of the log-on procedures and will show the menus for the system (Figure 11.3).

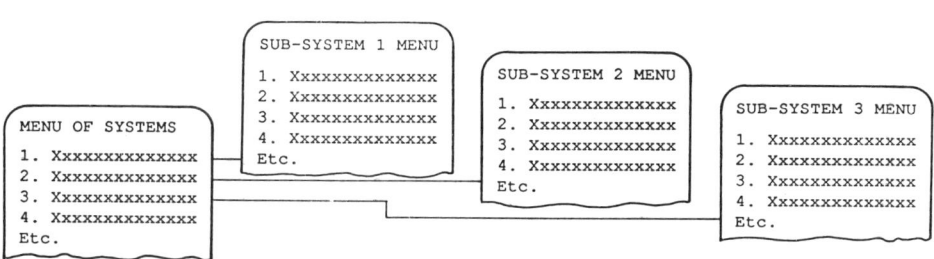

Figure 11.3 Menu Structure. Only the top level is shown. Lower levels would be shown on separate pages, repeating the calling menu.

Thereafter details of each module must be described in turn. A fuller examination of this aspect is shown in Chapter 14. For the moment suffice it to say that the specification of each module will consist essentially of the following:

*   A brief description of the purpose of the module.

*   A definition of the Fields on the Record.

*   Field validation rules.

*   Record processing rules.

*   Details of Reports and report processing.

Once all the modules have been specified details of File Sizes must be estimated (Figure 11.4). Estimates of File access frequencies and proposed security levels must also be included (Figures 11.5 and 11.6).

ESTIMATED FILE SIZES			
RECORD TYPE	CHARACTERS /RECORD	NO. OF RECORDS	TOTAL CHARACTERS
ABC HEADER	113	2000	226,000
ABC DETAILS	1263	600	757,800
LOCATION IMPL.	48	600	28,800
ACTIONS	200	1200	240,000
AGENDA/ MINUTE ITEMS	374	60	22,440
MINUTE FILES (3)			191,520
		TOTAL	1,466,560 *

* Approximately 1½ Megabytes. Allow for 3mb. to cover overhead and contingencies.

Figure 11.4 Estimated File Sizes. Typical example.

Armed with this information the systems designer, in conjunction with programming and hardware experts, can then firm up on the details necessary to complete part one of the specification. In other words to determine details of hardware requirements, costs, benefits and development plans.

Fuller details of the actual design process are described in the next chapter. But it should be noted that it will normally be most convenient to complete part two of the specification before attempting part one.

FILE ACCESS FREQUENCIES - ACCESSES/WEEK

MODULES	CREATE	AMEND	ERASE	DISPLAY	PRINT	REPORT DISP	REPORT PRINTS	REPORT, DISPLAYS										REPORT, PRINTS									
	1	2	3	4	5	6	7	1	2	3	4	5	6	7	8	9	10	1	2	3	4	5	6	7	8	9	10
1. ABC HEADER	5	1	-	20	5	-	-	10	5	1	1	1	½	-	-	-	-	5	½	½	½	½	-	-	-	-	-
2. ABC DETAILS	5	1	5	150	10	-	-	5	5	-	-	-	-	-	-	-	-	5	5	-	-	-	-	-	-	-	-
3. ABC IMPLEMENTATIONS	10	40	10	100	10	-	-	5	5	-	-	-	-	-	-	-	-	5	5	-	-	-	-	-	-	-	-
4. ACTIONS	50	50	50	100	20	-	-	5	15	1	1	1	-	-	-	-	-	5	15	1	1	1	-	-	-	-	-
5. AGENDA/MINUTE ITEMS	20	1	½	1	½	-	-	1	1	1	½	5	5	½	½	-	-	1	1	½	2	1	½	½	½	-	-

Figure 11.5 File Access Frequencies. Typical example.

SECURITY LEVELS

ABC SUB-SYSTEM
MODULES
01-05

	CREATE	AMEND	ERASE	DISPLAY	PRINT	REPORT DISP	REPORT PRINTS
	1	2	3	4	5	6	7
01. ABC HEADER	6	6	6	/	/	/	/
02. ABC DETAILS	6	6	6	/	/	/	/
03. ABC IMPLEMENTATIONS	6	6	6	/	/	/	/
04. ACTIONS	6	6	6	/	/	/	/
05. AGENDA/MINUTE ITEMS	6	6	6	/	/	/	/

REPORT, DISPLAYS

1	2	3	4	5	6	7	8	9	10
/	/	/	/	/	/	*	*	*	*
/	*	*	*	*	*	*	*	*	*
/	*	*	*	*	*	*	*	*	*
/	/	/	/	/	6	/	*	*	*
6	6	/	6	/	/	6	6	*	*

REPORT, PRINTS

1	2	3	4	5	6	7	8	9	10
/	/	/	/	/	/	*	*	*	*
/	*	*	*	*	*	*	*	*	*
/	*	*	*	*	*	*	*	*	*
/	/	/	/	/	6	/	*	*	*
6	6	/	6	/	/	6	6	*	*

Figure 11.6 Security Levels Typical example.

System Testing

Once the system specification has been approved the next stage is to actually program the system. In some cases the designer may also program the system, but this is not recommended. Normally therefore the next stage at which the designer will be required will be at system testing.

Rigorous testing of systems is essential if costly problems are to be avoided. Programs can readily be changed during the development phase, but changes to live programs can create problems for both users and programmers.

One solution that has been proposed is that Prototype Systems should be developed (JONES, 1985), but using PSD this is neither necessary nor desirable.

Once users have become familiar with the essential simplicity of PSD, they quickly become able to judge whether or not what is proposed is what they require. The main problem at the testing stage therefore is to determine whether or not the programs will actually work as per the specification.

So the primary task of the systems designer at this stage is to confirm that the system conforms to the specification. Using PSD this task is also simplified. Large parts of any PSD system will consist of standard parameter-driven routines and once these have been tested only cursory attention is required.

It is not possible to generalise the rules for system testing, other than to say that in addition to handling bona fida data correctly, the system must handle invalid data or responses equally correctly.

Once any obvious 'bugs' (program faults) have been removed, a useful ploy is to get a user or someone who knows little or nothing about computer systems to help with the testing.

An untrained user will frequently press keys or do other things which a professional would never dream of doing, and a system must be robust enough to cope with this.

The final stage of testing must of course include testing and acceptance of the system by the user.

User Guides And Procedures

The system designer will normally be responsible for producing user guides, and possibly procedures. The procedures will describe how the system will fit in with other events and who should do what and when.

Initially, a general guide to the structure of PSD and the basic way in which it works must be produced. Once this has been done, it should be common to all systems which are developed using PSD, which should be all systems.

The task of producing user guides for any subsequent PSD system is therefore minimal. In most cases the system outline, taken from the specification together with details of each module, should be sufficient to tell users all that they need to know.

If further clarification is required, the details in the specification should be expanded on a module by module basis. In this way, users who only require access to a limited number of modules can readily be provided with just the details that they require.

Implementation

Implementation, or 'going live', is a phase which usually requires very careful thought and planning. A progressive approach whereby data is taken on as the need arises is by far the simplest way, although it suffers from the draw-back that remnants of manual systems may persist for some time.

In many cases, a progressive approach is not possible and implementation must be prefaced by a file building (or file transfer) exercise. This can be a major task and must not be under-estimated, particularly where existing manual systems may have to be frozen for some time.

'Annual Holidays' often provide a convenient time to implement major systems. In all cases, however, implementation must be arranged so that the freeze-period is as short as possible. Generally, this can be achieved by ensuring that masterfiles, such as records of customers, names and addresses, parts lists and so on, are built up prior to going live.

Care must be taken to ensure that adequate provision has been made for existing data to be taken on, particularly where the computer will in future be numbering documents automatically. If existing documents are to be taken on, provision must be included to over-write the automatic numbering.

As has already been suggested, the modular nature of PSD will normally enable systems to be implemented bit by bit, thus reducing the pressure on both systems staff and users. Anything else that can be done to ensure a smooth and efficient implementation, must be done.

The first few days in the life of a system can create attitudes which will take a long time to change. A successful implementation usually means a successful system.

Maintenance

No matter how well a system is designed, changes will inevitably be required. Managers will realise that they require additional information, organisations will be split or merged, or new technology will open up new opportunities.

The modular and standardised nature of PSD, coupled with the concept of designing for flexibility, will help to minimise the problems associated with making changes. It also makes it easier to see where changes are required in programs and easier to disseminate revisions to user guides and so on.

PSD will limit the number of programs that have to be written and will help to ensure that they are structured in a standardised manner, thus making it easy for them to be maintained - even when the original programmer has moved on.

It is still essential that programs should be adequately documented. But PSD will significantly reduce the amount of documentation required, thus making the vital task of keeping it up to date that much easier.

Appraisal

Designers who haven't used PSD may feel that some of the aspects of what has been described have been over simplified. In particular, the concept of producing a definitive specification and then testing the system against this may seem to be treating users as second-class citizens. This is certainly not what is intended and as always in real life there must be a willingness to make last minute changes.

Based on many years experience, however, the production of a definitive specification is essential:

*   Without a definitive specification users will continually change their minds about what a system should do and programmers will be in the unenviable position of continually trying to hit a moving target.

*   A great deal of wasted programming can be saved if what is actually required is determined before programming starts.

*   Generally, users are better able to absorb the implications of being talked through a specification rather than a rough demonstration. (This is similar to the problem of spotting errors in typescript. For reasons which aren't clear, errors can be detected more readily on hardcopy than on a VDU screen.)

*   Whatever advanced programming language is used a badly specified system will still result in a bad system.

So what is in fact being advocated is that users' needs must be considered in great detail at the design stage and before programming starts. Where a totally new system is to be introduced, then it is clearly not possible to learn from how users currently handle their problems. Under these circumstances, however, there is a greater rather than a lesser need for designers to talk at length with potential users.

Unfortunately, many techniques which are currently being advocated tend to encourage designers to become desk-bound. It is not surprising therefore that many systems that are produced still fail to satisfy users.

Chapter 12

The Methodology of Design - The Rough Design Phase

Introduction

This chapter is concerned with the fundamental problem of trying to decide how to break down a system into Modules and what fields to include in each module. The phase is called the 'Rough Design Phase', because subsequent phases will normally lead to the need for revision.

As has been suggested, the process is to some extent intuitive. In general, it is also an iterative process where the systems designer must be prepared to explore a number of alternatives before deciding on the best.

Before entering this phase the systems designer must have obtained a thorough understanding of the current system, or system requirements, on the lines suggested in the previous chapter.

The process is illustrated by means of a case study. The case study has been simplified very considerably, but it should serve to illustrate the basic methodology.

Background To Case Study

A small Insurance firm comprises two Agents, two Secretarial staff and two Clerks. The Agents sell only two types of policies, Life and Household insurance policies. Business is so good that all the staff have to work excessively long hours to cope and there is no room in the office for more staff.

The two Secretarial staff spend most of their time typing letters, policies and renewal notices. The two Clerks work mainly on addressing envelopes, filing and retrieving customers files.

About 50% of the file retrieval is done on a routine basis by reference to a Renewal-Date Book, which lists customers and policy numbers by their renewal date. The rest of the retrieving is to answer miscellaneous queries and for new policies or claims.

A copy of each renewal notice is filed in date order until payment is received. It is then filed in the customer's file and brief details are recorded on a Contents Record at the front of the file. Late renewals are expedited after two weeks.

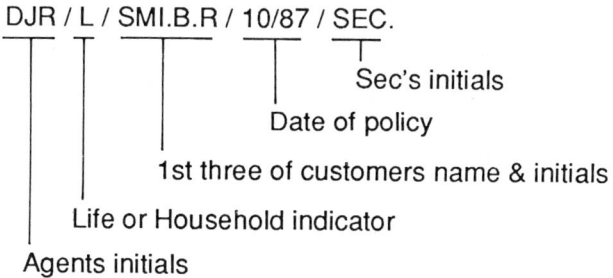

Figure 12.1 Case Study - Policy reference number format.

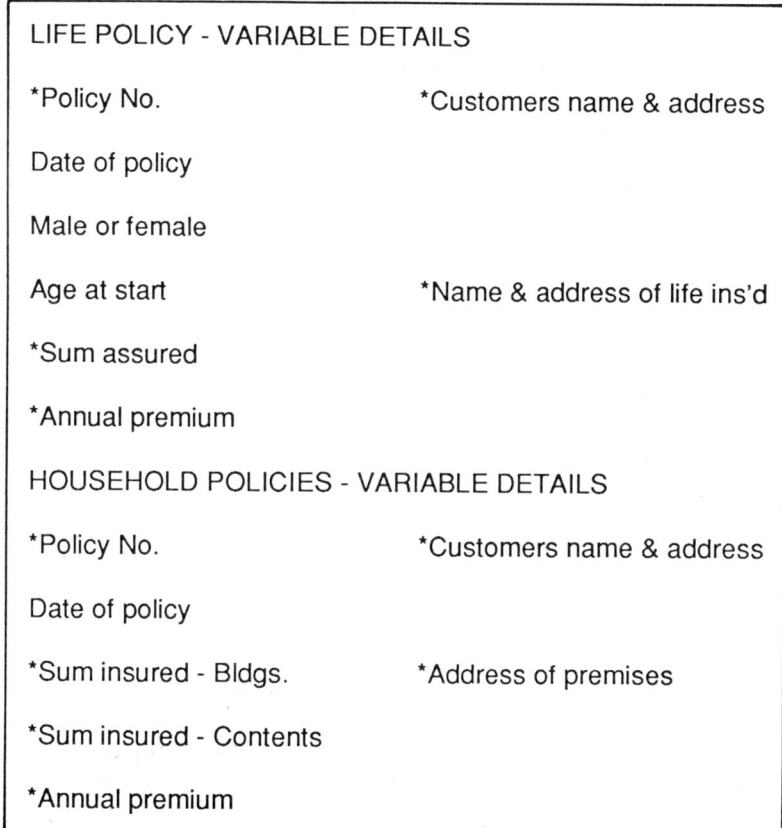

Figure 12.2 Case Study - Key details of policies. Items marked with an asterisk must be printed on renewal notices.

The two Agents draw 5% commission on all premiums received for policies which they have sold. To facilitate this each policy is given a reference number of the form shown in Figure 12.1.

The key details relating to each type of policy are shown in Figure 12.2. Sums insured and premium rates will change from time to time, but other complications will be ignored.

The senior Agent has recently attended a seminar at the local Chamber of Commerce and believes that a computer would help him with the boring task of Payroll and Accounting.

Appraisal Of Existing System

The first step after noting what exists is to appraise what is being done at present and to consider whether or not it is sensible. The customer is not always right - at first.

If what exists or what is proposed doesn't make sense, the systems designer must tactfully suggest alternatives in order to establish what is really required.

In the case study the senior Agent may only spend an hour a week on Payroll and Accounting; hardly enough to justify a computer and certainly not enough to resolve the problem of over-worked staff. On the other hand, the task of processing policies has all the characteristics of an ideal computer application:

*   A significant secretarial/clerical content.

*   The need for repetitive printing of similar details.

*   Routine calculations.

*   The need for numbers of people to file and retrieve specific information in a limited number of forms.

From here on, it is assumed that the agent is amenable to the suggestion and that the task of mechanising the processing of policies is the main task. It is also assumed that no suitable package already exists. This does not mean that the possibility of adding a Payroll Package at a later date has been ruled out. Similarly, the use of WP to speed up the task of typing letters may also be considered later. However, at this stage these must be dismissed as they are not part of the main problem.

Systems designers must concentrate their attention initially on the smallest viable part of a system.

The importance of this approach may become clearer if one considers that the proposed system may well eliminate the need for many of the letters which are currently typed. It is also vital, of course, to concentrate the designers thinking.

The first step in the designer's thinking must now be to discover the underlying nature of the system by eliminating features which are necessary purely because the system is a manual system.

For example, the fact that there is a Contents Record on each customer's file may suggest that the computer system should produce a similar record. This will not be the case.

Similarly, the method of coding, or the absence of coding, for key data must be critically reviewed. For example, the method used to code policies is extremely tenuous. To have to key in over 20 characters to identify a policy would be extremely tedious, time consuming and error prone.

Unless there is a very good reason for doing otherwise, use straight numeric coding to identify records. Descriptive details can then be shown in the body of the record.

Using a straight numeric coding, for example, five digits would allow 100,000 policies to be uniquely identified.

Search for Modules

Once the systems designer has got a feel for what is required, the next stage is to search for Modules.

The key to searching for Modules is to think in terms of what are the main records that must be Created to allow the system to function.

It is also helpful to remember that each module that is established will also introduce facilities to perform all the other basic Functions (ie. Amend, Erase, Display and Print).

It must also be remembered that Records must fit into Rectangular Files.

To help with this task a large sheet of cartridge paper is invaluable. This will allow details of each record to be shown graphically as the system is being developed step by step.

Start with the main activity and work logically through it, before going on to consider other activities.

In the case study assume that Life policies predominate, and that a customer is the start of the system. There are obviously certain basic details which must be recorded, such as the name and address of the customer.

Having identified the need for a series of records, the next step is to determine what is to be the unique key for the records.

The customer's name and initials could be used, but this would be rather long in most cases and prone to spelling mistakes. A decision must therefore be made as to how to code customers. In this case, since customers cannot be expected to remember their code, a purely numeric key is not very helpful.

An easier form of key would be provided by say the first three letters of the customer's name and up to three initials (Figure 12.3). Note that provision has been made for a number to be added at the end of the key to distinguish between people with the same name and initials.

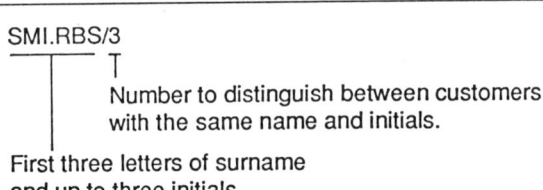

SMI.RBS/3

Number to distinguish between customers with the same name and initials.

First three letters of surname and up to three initials.

Figure 12.3 Case study - Customer Code.

So details of the basic fields required for the Customer Record can now be pencilled in on the large sheet of paper (Figure 12.4).

CUSTOMER RECORD

CUST CODE	SURNAME	FORENAMES	STREET ADDRESS	TOWN	DIST	POST CODE	PHONE No.
SMI.BRS/ N.							

Figure 12.4 Case study - '1st Rough' of Customer Record.

It is helpful to include a sample line of data in the '1st Rough'. Where it is possible to determine the logical sequence in which records should appear to be held it is also helpful to show two or three keys to illustrate this. In this case, the logical sequence is obviously alphabetic.

At this stage the systems designer is not concerned with field sizes or other minor details, but with the basic structure of the system.

In doing so the main task is to identify what data is directly related to the chosen keys.

It will almost invariably be necessary to return to the 1st Rough, to add or to change details. So it is better to establish the overall framework before worrying too much about details.

The Next Module - Life Policies

The next logical step is to think about policies. There are two basic types of policies. They do have certain features in common, but the differences are such that they should be considered separately, at least initially.

Consider Life policies first. Again before a record can be roughed-out a key must be determined. Bearing in mind the fact that the use of existing policy numbers has been discounted, there are a number of alternatives that could be adopted, but the simplest appears to be a straight numeric, prefaced by an 'L' for Life.

Where there is doubt about the merits of using a complex key, opt for a simple one and see how it works out.

The details which must be held for Life policies are essentially the same as those previously shown (Figure 12.2), but in arriving at the form of the Record (Figure 12.5), a number of features have been taken into account.

First, provision has already been made for details of the customers name and address to be stored. So only the customer code needs to be held here.

Details held on one file should not normally be repeated on another file. Only the key to the data should be repeated.

LIFE POLICY RECORD

POLICY No	DATE OF POLICY	CUST. CODE	PERSON INSURED CODE	SUM ASSUR'D	TERM	ANNUAL PREMIUM	
L10016							

Figure 12.5 Case study - 1st Rough of Life policy record.

Note that a code, of the same form as the customer code, has been used instead of the 'Name and address of Life insured'. This is because it is clear that the details required are essentially the same. In fact the customer and the life-insured will often be one and the same. So the same file can be used for both purposes.

Look for ways in which new data can be accommodated in existing files, or where duplication of data can be avoided.

There are, as always, alternatives. The people insured could have been put on a separate file. This would allow users to distinguish between customers and people insured. But this would result in a great deal of duplication.

This duplication can readily be avoided by adding two marker fields to the customer record (Figure 12.6). These markers can automatically be set to 'Y' when a particular customer code is entered into either part of a policy. This is not infact the best solution, but it will suffice for now.

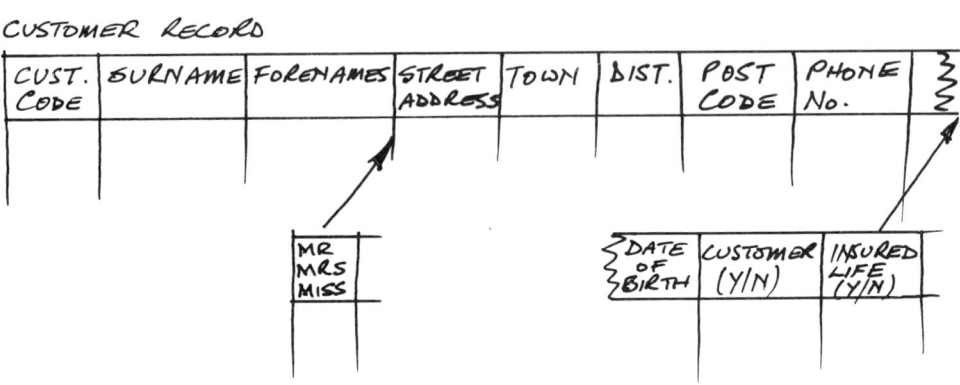

Figure 12.6 Case study - 2nd Rough of Customer Record, with markers added.

Explore the alternatives at each stage and select the best.

Two other changes have been introduced on the revised customer record. Part of the information required to calculate the premium for a Life policy is the Sex of the person insured. This could have been achieved by making provision for a Male or Female field (M or F).

Another alternative, shown above, is to provide a field for the title of the person to be recorded (ie., Mr, Mrs, Ms, Sir etc.). This has the advantage that it will allow letters to be correctly addressed, and the computer could readily be programmed to know that 'Mr' is male and so on.

This again is not the complete answer and readers may like to consider how to handle a Major - in the Women's Royal Army Corps. A solution is suggested at the end of the chapter.

Ensure that fields are put into the record to whose key they are truly related. For example, Sex is an attribute of a person not a policy, so details must go on the customer record.

Another factor which determines premiums is the age of the Life insured on the date when the policy is taken out. At first sight this may appear to be related to the policy. But the problem can be viewed from a different angle. If the customer's date of birth is held, clearly related to customer, the computer can readily calculate the age of the customer whenever a policy is taken out.

Age therefore needn't be held on file. So instead of having to enter it for each policy, the date of birth is entered once. This has another advantage in that the computer will not make a mistake in calculating a person's age.

Look for ways in which the need for a field can be eliminated, particularly if it may have to be entered a number of times. If any calculations have to be done, make sure that the computer does them. Always aim to input basic rather than calculated data.

There is scope for thought about whether or not the premium needs to be stored. Certainly, the computer must calculate premiums automatically. However, it has been assumed that rates may change from time to time, but existing premiums will not be affected. Hence the need to store the premium.

Again there are ways round this. A code could have been stored to indicate which rates had been used to calculate the premium and so on. But doing this would merely save a few characters of storage and would add significantly to the complexity of the system. So it doesn't seem to be worth pursuing.

Always aim for simplicity and flexibility. Avoid the temptation to try to 'save' a few characters of storage space, particularly if this is going to introduce complexity.

Household Insurance Policies

Household policies obviously have many similarities with Life policies and the first question that arises is whether or not the same customer record file can be used.

Some of the details on the file, such as Sex and Date of Birth, are irrelevant as far as household insurance is concerned. It may also be desirable to distinguish between clients who have Life and those who have Household policies.

If customers normally have only one type of policy, then two separate files could be considered. In this case, however, since customers are likely to have both types of policy, it will be most economical to use one file. Again a simple marker system can be used to show which customers have which policies.

Avoid duplication of data by using existing files wherever possible.

It is not difficult to see that as far as the records for Household policies are concerned a similar key to Life policies can be used, but prefaced with 'H'.

However, the data held for Household policies is very different, so a new module must be developed. The logic for developing the record is essentially the same as before and the results are shown in Figure 12.7.

HOUSEHOLD POLICY RECORD

POLICY No	DATE	CUSTOMER CODE	ADDRESS OF PREM. CODE	BLDG. VALUE	CONTENTS VALUE	PREMIUM
H00136						

Figure 12.7 Case study - 1st Rough of Household Policy Record.

The Address of Premises Insured presents a new problem. In most cases, it will be the same as that of the customer. Looking to the future, it can be assumed that this is the case if this field is left blank on the Household record. The key problem is not this, but where to hold the actual details of the address

Once more, there are a number of ways in which the address details could be handled. If there was only one possible Premises Address for each customer, the customer record could be extended to show this, but this would be wasteful and is not applicable in this case.

Similarly, it would be wasteful and confusing to treat each Premises Address as another customer, with a different code and no surname etc. However, this does suggest an alternative.

Be prepared to review what has been done and consider alternatives.

If the actual address part of the Customer Record was replaced by a code, pointing to an Address Record (Figure 12.8), then all addresses could be held on one big file.

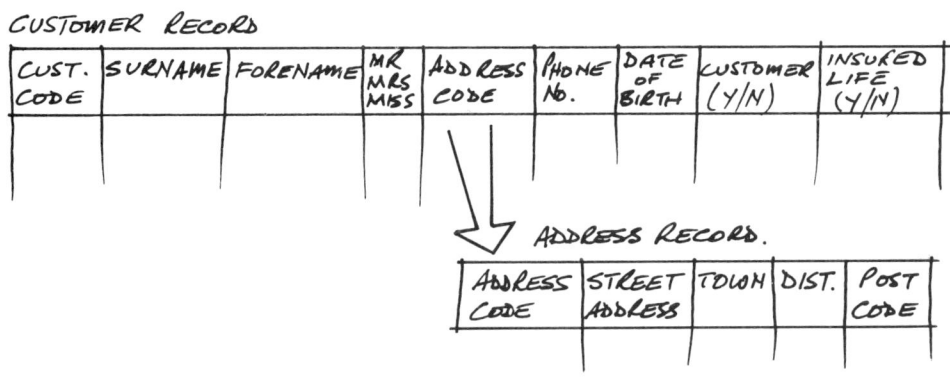

Figure 12.8 Case study - Customer Record, another alternative.

But working in this way would mean that two Modules would have to be provided and each of these would have to be accessed to create a 'full customer record'.

A simpler solution is to establish an Insured Premises Address Module (Figure 12.9), which would only need to be accessed when the need arises.

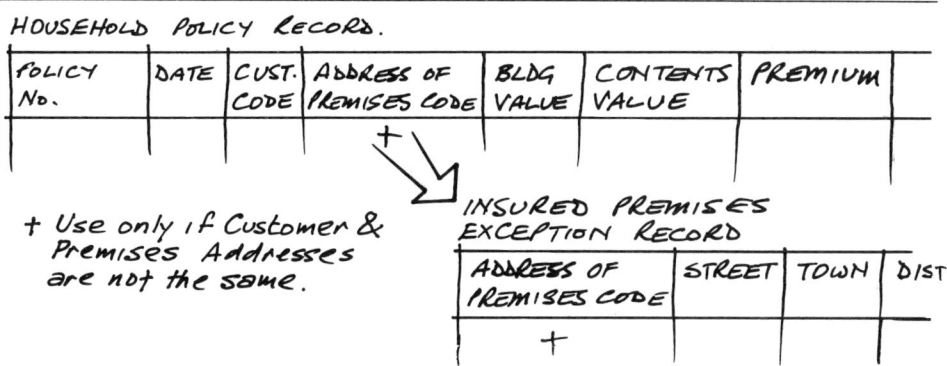

Figure 12.9 Case study - Household policies with Insured Premises file.

Avoid unnecessary fragmentation, which will destroy the basic logic of a system and will call for more modules than necessary to be accessed.

Again the premium will be calculated automatically by the system and again the option chosen is to store it. There is one additional aspect to actually storing the premium. Treating it as a field means that the value can be changed arbitrarily in exceptional circumstances. This can be both an advantage and a disadvantage depending on security considerations.

Decide whether a detail needs to be stored or should be calculated when required.

This completes the Rough Design Phase. The next stage is to refine the design in the light of what the system is required to do.

Solution To Problem Of Major In WRAC

Some years ago this problem would probably have been solved in a very different way from the way that it should be handled today. Before looking at the recommended solution it is useful to consider an alternative, so that the advantages and disadvantages of the two can be compared.

One alternative would be to make provision for a Table of Titles to be held (Figure 12.10). The titles would be numbered and would show whether the title was for a Male or Female, when a customer has an unusual title, instead of Mr or Mrs etc., the appropriate number must be entered on the customer record. Suitable programs to pick up the full title must then be provided, when output is required.

This sounds reasonably simple, but in fact it leads to endless complications. To start with, users must have a look-up table to find out what number to put in. Thereafter, to make sense any display or print programs must also incorporate a look-up-table program.

Title No.	Title	M/F
1	Pte.	M
2	Pte.	F
3	Cpl.	M
4	Cpl.	F
.		
.		
.		
10	Mjr.	M
11	Mjr.	F
Etc.		

Figure 12.10 Possible solution to the WRAC Major problem.

Again therefore the approach which is recommended is to go for the simplest way and that is to make provision on the Customer Record for any title to be entered, and for Sex to be indicated as it was initially (ie. M/F).

Where a record is likely to be used for a variety of purposes ensure, as far as it is practicable, that all the data on the record is in a form that can be reported upon directly.

Chapter 13

The Methodology Of Design - Refining The Rough Design

Introduction

At this stage the rough design is far from complete. But by now the process of drawing out the details of the main modules of the system should have given the designer a real feel for the shape of the system.

Unfortunately, the details have had to be presented here bit by bit. It should be emphasised therefore that, in practice, they should all be shown together on a large sheet of paper. In this way the designer can see the whole of the emerging system at a glance.

So far the modules that have been identified are:

* The Customer Record Module.

* The Life Policy Module.

* The Household Policy Module.

* The Insured Premises Address Module.

The main task now is to consider each module in turn, to establish what Reports are required and to refine the records where necessary.

Rough details of the reports, which are identified, can be added to the large sheet of paper in a similar way to the way in which Records were sketched in.

There are clearly a large number of reports that could be produced from the four modules, so what follows has been restricted. Only enough reports to illustrate the basic principles are considered.

In all cases provision must be made for a full listing of all the data held on file for each module.

It is surprising how often this simple facility is overlooked, and users are left in the situation where they cannot be sure what is or is not on file. The provision should include the 'From/To' feature described earlier, so that selective listings can be obtained.

Generally, provision must be made for all reports to be both printed and displayed, and the same basic format should be used wherever possible. However, at this stage, designers must not allow themselves to be distracted by concern about formats. These can be worked-out later. At this point only the reports required and the fields to be shown need to be established.

So, the prime task of the designer at this stage is to consider what reports are required from the system. In the main, this will involve considering, what major activities take place in relation to each module. And, whether or not the system can perform these activities with the data on file.

Consider the Customer's Record first. This serves primarily to hold details for use by other modules. But it does have full details of the names and addresses of customers, and as was suggested earlier, a significant amount of time is spent on addressing envelopes. A facility to address envelopes would therefore be useful. The best way of doing this on computer-produced documents is to use window-envelopes. This saves having to print addresses on both a letter and an envelope, and it eliminates the possibility of a letter being put into an envelope addressed to somebody else.

However, if a lot of circulars or standard non-personalised mail has to be addressed, then a label printing facility would be required. The fields to be included in the label printing should be self-apparent. Similarly, since only a single label may be required, the facility should include From/To features. Provision to limit printing to either Life or Household customers would also probably be desirable.

Since telephone numbers are also shown on the customer's record, this could be used to provide a convenient directory, or on more sophisticated systems direct dialling, so a menu of the form shown in Figure 13.1 seems likely.

```
REPORTS   MENU

1. File listing (From/To)

2. Label printing (From/To) - All customers

3.   "        "       "     - Life customers

4.   "        "       "     - Household customers

5. Phone numbers (From/To)
```

Figure 13.1 Case study - Menu of Reports for Customer Record.

Identify the reports required to satisfy the users needs.

At this point in time, if not before, it may become apparent that it would be more useful if the file listing showed not just whether a customer had Life or Household policies, but how many of each.

So on the customer's record, instead of storing 'Y' or 'N', the actual number of each type of policy must be stored (Figure 13.2). This also has other advantages. Clearly, a customer's record must not be erased from the system whilst the customer still has a policy, so these counters will enable the system to take care of this.

Review the contents of each module to ensure that reports can be produced in the most helpful form.

CUSTOMER RECORD

CUST. CODE			DATE OF BIRTH	CUST. (Y/N)	No. OF LIFE POLICIES	No. OF HOUSE'D POLICIES	

Figure 13.2 Case study - Customer Record, with policy counters.

The Phone Number report allows another useful way of working to be illustrated. Clearly, if a user has to remember the key to a customer's record to get a phone number, this is not very helpful.

A technique which is commonly used in reporting therefore is to allow codes to be truncated. The fact that the code is truncated is indicated by an asterisk. For example, entering a 'From' code of 'SMI.***' would result in a listing from the first customer whose name starts with SMI. The customer's full name and address must, of course, be included in the report, so that the correct client can be identified.

Note that the way that the customer code is designed, should normally allow users to narrow or widen the search. For example, 'S**.***' would result in a wide search, whilst from 'SMI.B**' to 'SMI.B**' would result in a very limited report.

Life Policy Reports

Again, there are a wide variety of reports which could be required - to provide details of what policies are due to mature next month and so on.

As in the case of all reports, the details shown in the report can be taken from any number of modules. For example, on most reports it would be desirable, if not essential, to show the actual name of the customer, rather than just the code.

Similarly, reports may call for calculations to be performed, as part of the reporting process. For example, to total the value of the policies due to mature next month. None of these features should present any special difficulties.

The two main parts of the Life Policy processing will be concerned with producing policies initially, and then with producing renewal notices. In both cases, the aim must be to try to ensure that details do not have to be output onto special pre-printed stationery. Apart from the cost of the stationery, the task of changing stationery in a printer and lining it up is tedious, time consuming and wasteful.

Significant benefits can be achieved, if details can be output onto plain paper. Where appropriate the output can then be attached to a covering document, that shows standard clauses and conditions and so on.

In some cases, the standard form of display for PSD Records may be all that is required and the Print function is all that is required. Where a different format is required this must be called for via the Reports Print Menu.

Since a Policy will almost invariably need to be printed after it has been created, designers may be tempted to try to save users' time by going directly to the 'Policy Print' after Create. This must be avoided at all costs.

The temptation to deviate from the basic PSD structure must be avoided as it will destroy the basic pattern of the system and leave users confused.

However, there is one way in which the task of users can be simplified in such cases. We can retain the key of the record Created and pass this to the reporting program. In other words, the reporting program will assume that the last policy created (or amended) is to be printed, unless it is told otherwise.

For the sake of completeness it should perhaps be pointed out that if special stationery has to be loaded users would not normally want to do 'one-off' prints. In other words, it would normally be best to wait until the end of the day and then to do a print-run, assuming that this delay is acceptable. In this case, a marker or similar device would be required to show which policies were awaiting printing. Again a check must be made to ensure that all the details which the designer wants to report on are either on file or can be deduced from what is on file.

Alternatively, most modern systems now have facilities for output for printing to be 'Spooled'. Spooling is a very useful feature which allows output to be stored until such time as it is convenient for it to be printed. Clearly this will involve users in additional processing. But the flexibility which this provides is often vital if unacceptable delays, caused by protracted print runs, are to be avoided.

Ensure that users can readily switch from one task to another as and when the need arises.

Failure to recognise that on-line systems must be as flexible as, if not more, than manual systems is probably the most common problem with small systems. If, for example, customers require immediate service, it is no good allowing the computer to be tied up on an hour long print-run.

Turning now to the task of producing Renewal Notices, this illustrates a number of important concepts. It is obviously a report function and the details required have already been illustrated (Figure 12.2). In this case, however, users would not call for a particular policy or range of policy numbers to be reported. The system must sort through the file and select those that are due for renewal.

The system could be designed to print details for all policies due for renewal in, say, two weeks from the current date. But a more flexible approach would be to use the principle of an Effectivity Date. The renewal notice print program would first ask for a date and would then print all those due for renewal by that date. In this way, the need for earlier posting at Xmas or staff holidays can be anticipated.

It would seem to be advisable for the system to query dates which are a long way ahead, so that a slip-up doesn't result in renewal notices for a whole year being printed.

The printing poses a number of other problems which are typical of this sort of dynamic situation. For simplicity, assume that all premiums are paid annually, then:

* Normally, a Renewal Notice must only be printed once a year.

* Provision must be made for re-printing in special circumstances (eg. notice lost in the post).

* Overdue premiums must be identified and expedited.

* It should be possible for payments to be recorded.

* What is paid may not always be the correct amount.

* Ideally the system should work out the commission due to each Agent.

So what at first looked like the need for a fairly simple report has suddenly turned into something quite complicated. This cannot be avoided and the only solution is to work through each of the problems in turn.

Again a variety of solutions are possible. One approach which seems reasonable is as follows. Firstly, the Renewal Notice Print program must set a marker against each policy when a notice has been printed satisfactorily. This will inhibit further printing of Notices, using the normal program. Note that the term 'printed satisfactorily' is used. In many cases, a computer may think that it has printed a report, when in fact the ribbon on the printer has broken or the stationery is badly misaligned. In circumstances like this, printing must not be inhibited until the user confirms that a satisfactory print has been obtained.

A second report program, which ignores the 'print-inhibitor' may also be required. Similarly, a program will be needed to initialise the inhibitors each year. The latter is not strictly a report program, but it would be run via the Reports Menus.

The subject of payments is always a sensitive one, where careful consideration of the security of a system is essential. The simplest approach here is to establish another module to take care of this, a Payments Due/Received Module (Figure 13.3). Records can then be deleted when the correct payment is received.

Unfortunately, what is received isn't always what is expected and provision must be made for this.

PAYMENTS DUE/RECEIVED

PAYMENT No.	POLICY No.	AMOUNT DUE	DUE DATE

Figure 13.3 Case study - Payments Due/Received Module.

Without going into this aspect in too much detail, it should be clear that making provision for a Balance Owing field (Figure 13.4) will enable this problem to be resolved. As many people have found to their cost, however, this is an aspect that needs very thorough testing.

PAYMENTS DUE/RECEIVED

PAYMENT No.	POLICY No.	PREMIUM	BALANCE OWING	DATE DUE

Figure 13.4 Case study - More flexible Payments Due/ReceivedRecord.

Looking at the Payments Due/Received Record immediately suggests the need for a number of reports. For example, an Arrears Report, where the system would look at each record and would list details of the policy, if a premium, or part of a premium, is overdue. Whilst this is being done it is probably better to produce a three part report covering all exceptions. In other words to list Policies:

a) Where the full premium is in arrears.

b) Where part of the premium is in arrears.

c) Where too much has been paid.

At this stage it is a bit early in the development process for a designer to actually work out the logic for producing such a report. But whilst it is still fresh in the reader's mind it provides a chance to show how complex logic should eventually be documented by using a flow chart (Figure 13.5).

After the exceptions listed on a report have been checked, then a logical follow-up would be to consider providing facilities to print Reminder Notices and/or Credit Notes. Again there is scope for further thought, but this is far enough for the purpose of this exercise.

There is one further facet that is worth examination, the calculation of the commission due to each agent. Assume for the sake of simplicity that it is a straight percentage of the premiums paid and that it is paid annually, at the end of each year.

One fact that should become apparent is that by changing the way in which policies are coded the facility to identify which agent should get the commission has been destroyed. This must be corrected by making provision for an Agent Code to be shown on each policy record (Figure 13.6).

The two Agents could have been coded simply as agents 1 and 2. But it is obviously important that the correct code should be used. To limit the possibility of errors, provision has been made for a slightly longer, but more positive code in the form of the agents' initials.

Ensure that provision is made to limit the possibility of serious errors being made.

The actual value of the percentage to be paid as commission must be held somewhere. This could be built into a program, but would call for a program-change if the Agents decide to change the rate.

A much more flexible approach would be to develop another module, a Control Module. The Control Module can then be used to hold any parameters associated with the system, if these are likely to require changing. So, in addition to the Agents percentage, details of any factors used to calculate premiums can also be stored.

Design for flexibility by having a Control Record, which will allow system parameters to be changed, without calling for program changes.

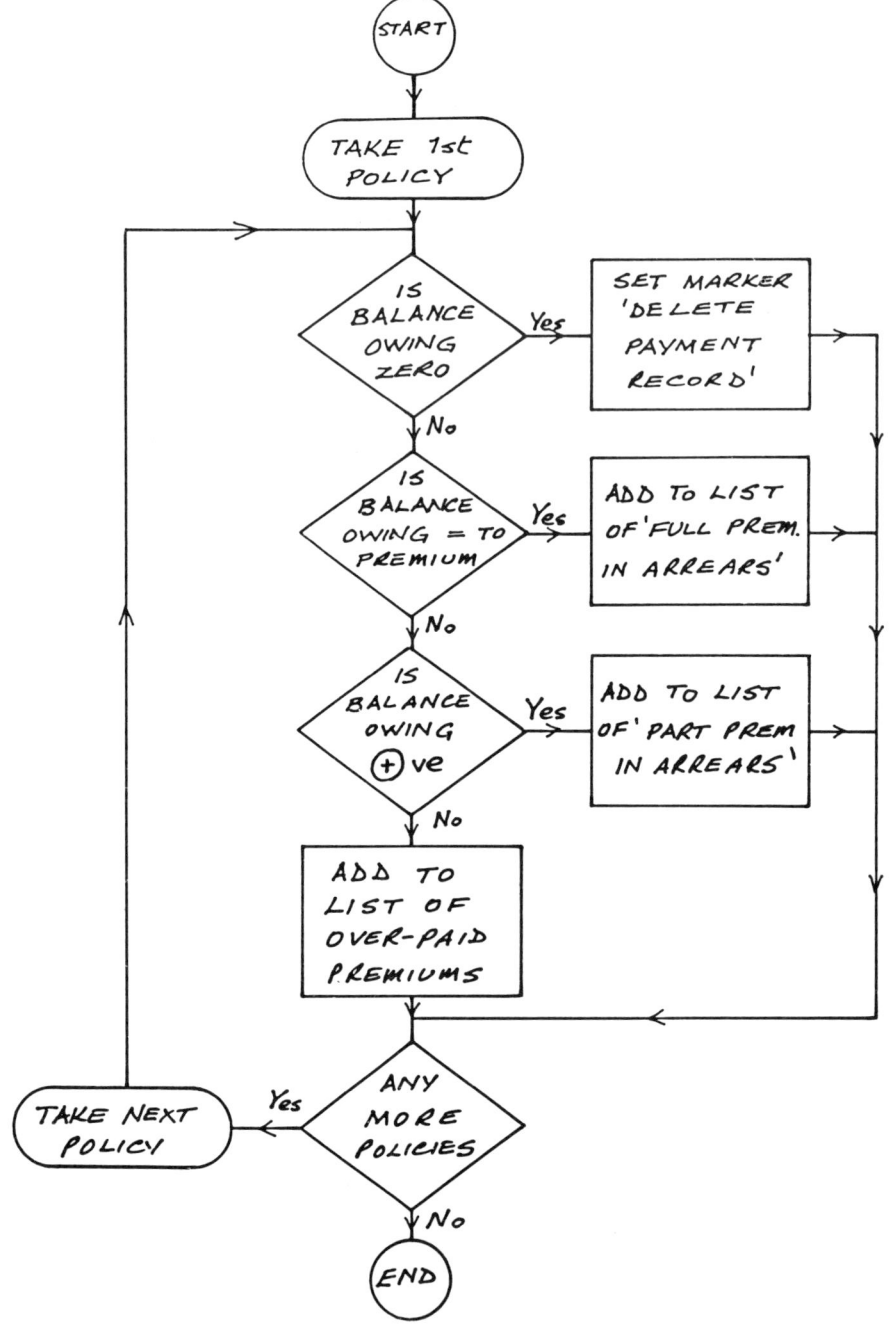

Figure 13.5 Flow Chart. Used to clarify complex logic.

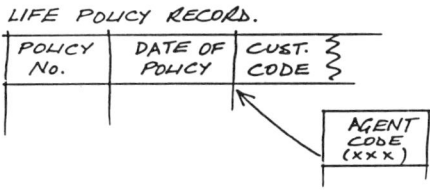

Figure 13.6 Case Study - Amended LIfe Policy Record.

The Control Module will obviously need to have a very high level of security associated with it. It is therefore a logical place to arrange for details of the Commission due to Agents to be displayed.

This raises two important issues, both of which are often difficult to resolve. Firstly, consider the actual calculation of the commission. If, as each premium is paid, the commission due to an agent is calculated, this can readily be accumulated in two 'Commission' fields, one for each Agent (Figure 13.7a).

But it would be simpler to use the fields to accumulate the total values of the premiums paid, and then to only calculate the commission at year-end, or when a report is called for (Figure 13.7b). Working in this way would not be satisfactory, however, if the percentage can be changed mid-term and the change must only apply to subsequent premiums.

On the other hand, if when the percentage is changed, it must apply to all premiums paid, the first alternative (a), makes things more difficult.

In this particular case, the solution would appear to be to make provision for both the commission and the total premiums to be accumulated (Figure 13.7c). Since the calculation of a straight percentage for two numbers is a trivial task that could be done manually, this allows all the options to be covered.

Designers must be quite clear about exactly what is required, and should not attempt to save storage space or processing time, if this is at the expense of simplicity and flexibility.

The second problem is whether or not to treat these totals as 'Fields' of the Control Module record. If they are treated as fields, then by definition they can be altered by anyone who has authority to Create or Amend the Control Record.

Working in this way does have advantages in that values can be adjusted manually to take into account any exceptional circumstances. But on a system of this nature there shouldn't be exceptional circumstances which cannot be handled by the system, rather than by manual adjustments.

% Commission	ACCUMULATED COMMISSION	
	AGENT 1	AGENT 2

a) Provision for commission to be calculated as each premium is paid.

% Commission	ACCUMULATED PREMIUMS	
	AGENT 1	AGENT 2

b) Provision for commission to be calculated at year-end.

% Commission	AGENT 1		AGENT 2	
	ACC^m COMM.	ACC^m PREMIUMS	ACC^m COMM.	ACC^m PREMIUMS

c) Provision for both of the above alternatives

Figure 13.7 Case study - Alternative ways of calculating Commission.

The alternative is to treat the totals as Counters. These will automatically be updated by the system, but can only be reported upon.

Determine whether accumulators are to be treated as Fields of a Module, or as Counters. Fields can be freely amended by authorised users. Counters can only be amended by the system.

Summarising the Design

Once all the facets associated with Life policies have been determined, these can be summarised by drawing up the corresponding menus. The menus together with the rough design on the large sheet of paper should be sufficient to give the designer an in-depth feeling for this part of the system.

The next stage is to work through each of the other modules in turn, in the same way:

* Identifying the Reports that are required.

* Checking that all the fields necessary to produce the reports are available, or can be added.

* Determining what counters are required and how these should be handled.

The problems presented by the other modules in the Case Study do not differ greatly from those already described and should be handled in exactly the same way.

When all the modules have been completed, a review of the overall design may suggest certain other Counters that could usefully be added. For example, Number of Life and Household Policies on file, Total Values and perhaps number of Customers.

Once this task has been completed, the details, coupled with estimates of rates, file sizes and costs, should be sufficient to enable a feasibility report to be completed.

Once this has been approved the next stage is to finalise the design in the form of a system specification. This process is described in the next chapter.

In conclusion, it is perhaps appropriate to mention that there are a number of computerised systems, which can be used to formalise Flow Charts and so on. But in the early stages of the design these must not be regarded as substitutes for a pencil, an eraser and a large sheet of paper.

Chapter 14

Finalising the Design

Introduction

The final stage of the design process is essentially a matter of converting the rough design into a formal specification. Details of the suggested content of the specification have already been described (Chapter 10).

This chapter is therefore restricted to considering the documentation of the design of the actual system. It is assumed throughout that PSD will be used and that users will already be familiar with the basic principles of PSD, so the need for further documentation is minimal.

By now the designer should be in a position where sufficient is known about the system to enable the overall menu structure to be determined. This is essentially a matter of grouping modules into logical sub-systems, and deciding what to call these and the system.

The menus will serve as a useful check-list, on which each module can be ticked off as it is completed. Each module must again be considered in turn, and will involve the designer in the following tasks:

* Describing briefly the purpose of the module.

* Confirming the fields on each record and defining field sizes and validation rules.

* Formalising rules for processing and filing records.

* Establishing formats for reports, and processing rules.

* Defining what Counters and Tables are required.

Once the detail of all the modules has been worked-out, the following must also be confirmed:

* Authority Levels for both modules and staff.

* File sizes.

* Access frequencies.

To a large extent this is a routine task. But at each stage the robustness of the system must be reviewed and in particular the question 'What if ... ?' must be asked.

What If.. ?

A key factor in ensuring that the final designs are robust, is to ask this question - and to assume the worst.

The Case Study provides a good example of the type of situation common to many systems where failure to consider all the options can result in problems. In the rough design phase it was assumed that the agent's commission would be calculated on the basis of premiums paid.

What if - a client only pays part of a premium, or pays too much, or if a refund is demanded? Clearly, all these possibilities are likely to occur and the system must be designed to handle them.

Year-end or Month-end processing, or any process which involves re-setting markers or counters, is usually an area where there is scope for a large number of 'What if ...' questions.

Similarly, if a system is expecting a particular event to occur, the fact that this may not occur as planned must be anticipated. For example:

> A customer orders 100 items, but there are only 20 in stock.
>
> A client is invoiced for £500, but only sends £300.
>
> A discount for prompt payment may be claimed.

There is no single solution to these problems. It is up to the designer to resolve each problem according to the circumstances. In all cases, the first step is to make sure that the existence of potential problems is recognised. At first sight some of these problems may appear to be somewhat daunting and the largest part of most systems will be concerned with handling 'exceptions'.

However, these problems will have already been solved with manual systems, so solving them with a computer should not be difficult.

The main thing is to isolate each problem and solve each one in turn in an iterative way, as described in the previous chapter.

If the resulting system appears to be complex, this is almost invariably a sign that the designer has not tackled the problem correctly. The only solution then is to re-work the design from a different angle.

Documenting Modules

As the problems associated with each module are resolved the specification of each module can be completed (Figure 14.1). Note that the header boxes correspond to what will eventually be shown on the VDU screen. The Screen I/D also serves as a Section (page) Number to facilitate rapid cross-reference between Screens and the Specification.

Following the description of the purpose of the module, basic details of each field are shown:

Field Number.

Description or name of the field.

Number of characters.

Alpha or Numeric (A/N).

Optional or Mandatory (O/M).

Validation rules and notes.

A standard pro-forma for the Module Specification is useful. Where this is provided it is most convenient to provide for 16 fields per page, so that each page corresponds to a screen. The primary key fields can be indicated in the Notes or by underlining.

In some cases, it is helpful to add an example of the type of data that will be entered, or to show the structure of a field more graphically, as 'AAA.NNNX', for example. But this should only be necessary where complex tests are to be applied to a field, or where the programming language to be used demands this level of detail.

The other details shown for each field should be self-apparent, apart from Optional/Mandatory. This indicates whether a field can be left blank or whether it is mandatory that something should be put in the field. On a Customer Record, for example, it would not make sense to have a customer without a Name. On the other hand the client's Post Code may not be known.

When a field is 'skipped' there are several possible options as to what is to be stored or displayed. With numeric data, in particular, should 'skipping' result in a zero being displayed? This is largely a programming problem and consistency is the main need of users and designers. All field sizes must, of course, be designed to accommodate the maximum anticipated number of characters. Designers should always err on the side of flexibility. Only specify that a field is mandatory if it is essential and allow for alpha characters if there is any doubt about data being numeric.

	System title. ABC SYSTEM	Screen I/D. 01+01+02
Sub-system title. ABC ADMIN	Module title. ACTIONS MODULE	

Description of Module.

Allows Actions to be entered for subsequent minuting and progressing. Permits reporting in a variety of different ways as shown over-leaf, 01+01+02+6 & 7

Fields on Record

No.	Description	Chrs.	A/N	O/M	Validation rules & notes
1	ABC No.	4	N	M	Must be 4 chrs. See note 1.
2	ACTION No.	3	N	M	See Note 2.
3	LOCATION CODE.	3	A	O	Must be in Locations Table.
4	ACTION TYPE	2	A	M	Must be valid type - Note 3

Record processing rules & notes

Note 1. In Create mode, number must be on ABC Header File.

Note 2. In Create mode, number must be generated automatically within ABC No.

Note 3. Valid action types are;

       AM- Miscellaneous Actions.

Figure 14.1 System Specification. Module spec. sheet.

Input Formats

Generally, it will not be necessary to show the input format for a record, because it will be implicit once the Module Specification Sheet has been completed.

The only time when attention is required is when large fields are involved, where the number of fields per screen may have to be less than 16. It may also be desirable to avoid splitting a large field (Figure 14.2).

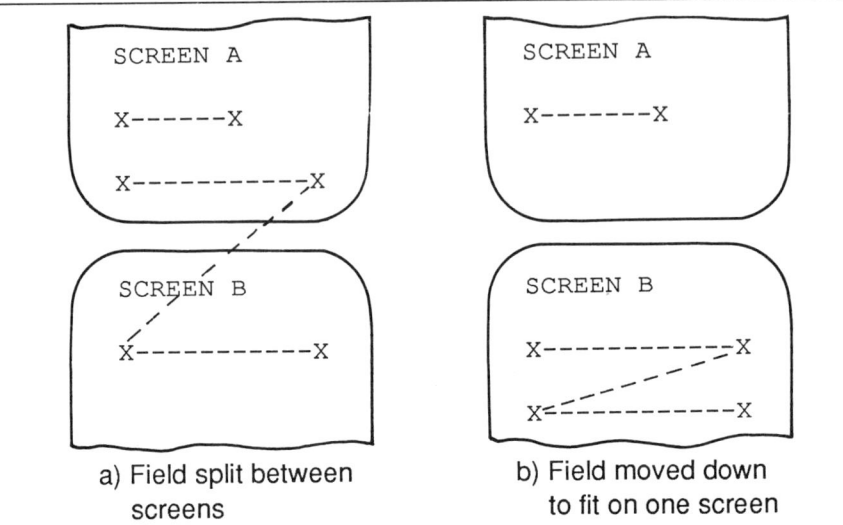

a) Field split between screens

b) Field moved down to fit on one screen

Figure 14.2 Input Screen Design. Normally only required when large fields are split between screens.

Field Validation

During record creation the first test normally applied is that a record with the same key does not already exist on a file. This test should ideally be written into the PSD Standards and will not then need to be referred to again.

In all the basic modes, other than Create, a record with the appropriate key must exist for processing to continue. Again the test should be written into the Standards and not need to be specified each time a new module is developed.

Generally, it should be assumed that data consisting of less than the specified number of characters is acceptable input. Where this is not the case the rule that a particular field must consist of a particular number of characters must be specified. Similarly, if only particular letters or a range of values are valid, this must be shown, but only if these restrictions improve the system.

Record Processing

Once the validation rules for each field have been specified, the processing to be done on the record when it is filed must be defined. This may involve checking through the fields to ensure that what has been entered is consistent, performing calculations and/or adjusting Counters and so on. Where complex logic is involved a Flow-chart should be included to make the process clear and unambiguous.

Normally, when a record has been processed systems should return to the start of the particular function to allow another record to be processed in the same way. In other words, if a user has just created a Customer Record, the system should assume that the user wishes to continue creating Customer Records.

Designers should think very carefully if they are tempted to depart from this standard. What may be a slick innovation as far the designer is concerned will often prove to be quite bewildering for users. But if a departure from the standard is unavoidable, it must be specified at this stage.

Specifying Reports

The reports required and their contents will have been pencilled-in at the rough design stage. The main task now is to determine the actual formats to be used. Every effort must be made to ensure that the same format is used for as many reports as possible, and that it is the same as the print format. Most computer systems now have facilities to enable screen formats to be generated on the VDU, but the advantages of such systems are not at all clear.

Where such facilities are not used, the task can be performed quite adequately by manual means. For this a pro-forma of the VDU screen is required, like the one already shown in Figure 6.2. For reports which cannot be contained within the constraints of the VDU screen larger sheets are available. But again the introduction of non-standard sizes for reports should be avoided. In addition to the format for reports, details of 'From/To' and Central/Local printing options must be specified when these are required. The sequence in which records must appear on reports must also be shown.

The use of pre-printed stationery must be avoided as far as possible. Where this is not possible, provision must be included for test-text to be printed to allow forms to be lined up.

Where a system can 'free' a terminal during printing, a decision must be taken as to whether or not this is desirable. Alternatively, any progress messages which are to be displayed during printing must also be defined. Provision may also be necessary for unsatisfactory copy to be reprinted.

Re-Appraising Designs

During the process of finalising the design, it is quite common for points to be dicovered, which have previously been overlooked. Any changes that are required must be entered onto the rough design and the process of finalising the design must be repeated.

As the details of each module are worked out, it is helpful to talk through the details with users. In this way, any changes that are required can hopefully be spotted, before the final Specification is published.

Even at this late stage a casual remark from a user may mean that the designer must be prepared to return to the rough design stage and make quite drastic changes. Typical of the sort of remarks which cause problems are comments such as '...and we have decided to introduce another type of Life Policy', or '...we are taking on another Agent and going to open another office'.

Businesses change all the time and at the stage where designs are being finalised systems designers must be particularly aware of this and of the importance of ensuring that systems can readily adapt to changes.

The modular nature of PSD will help considerably to ensure that systems can readily be adapted to changes. But a great deal still depends on the ability of designers to anticipate areas in which changes are most likely.

Completing The Design

Once all the modules have been specified, details of File Sizes and Access Frequencies must be finalised and revised estimates of hardware requirements, further development costs and savings must be produced.

Providing the revised estimates still confirm that the system is viable, the System Specification can then be completed by adding the Management Summary. The Specification is then ready for approval by users.

Additional Details

Some designers find that constructing a Data Model of a system helps to clarify details of the design. These can vary considerably in the amount of detail shown (Figures 14.3 and 14.4), but they do not permit the same level of detail to be shown as the 'large sheet of paper'. Whilst Data Models can be used to summarise the detail of a design, experience suggests that they must not be regarded as a substitute for the Rough Design.

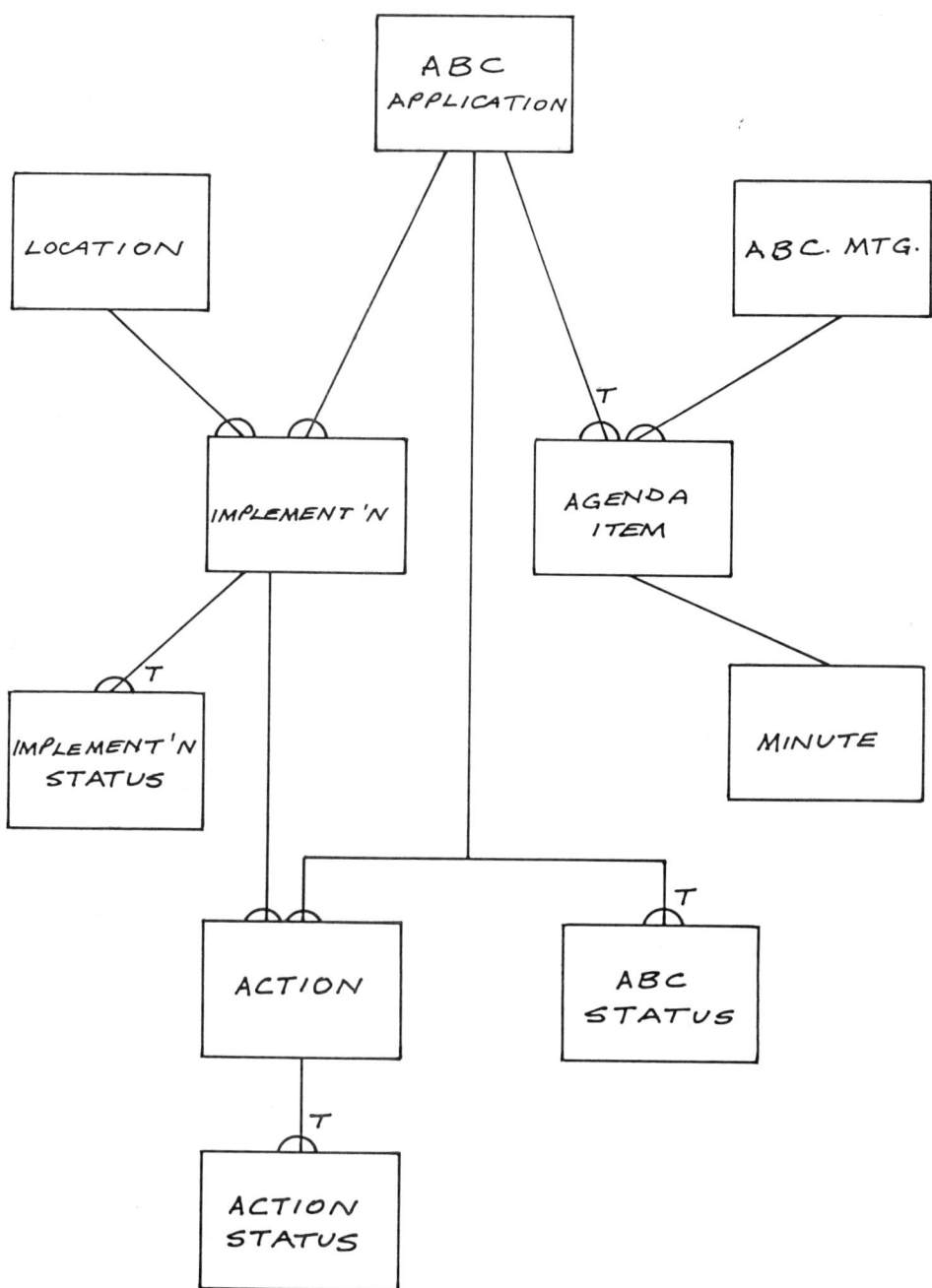

Figure 14.3 A simple Data Model.

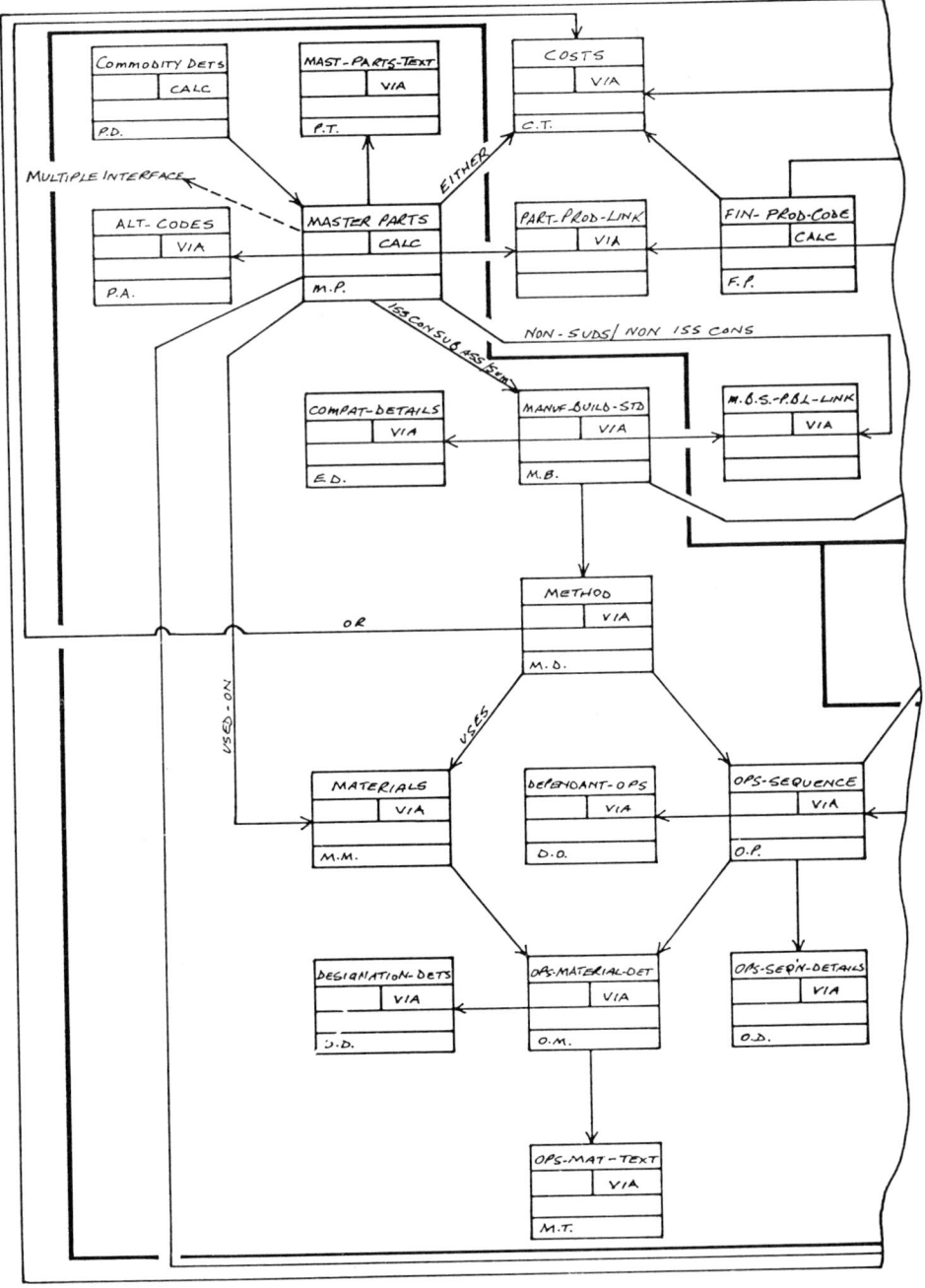

Figure 14.4 A more detailed Data Model. Must not be regarded as a substitute for the 'Rough Design'.

Chapter 15

Special Applications

Introduction

The main aim of PSD is to ensure that the vast majority of everyday EDP can readily be performed in a standardised way, using conventional computer facilities.

The methodology as it stands does not cover what may be called 'special applications'. Nevertheless, many of the concepts embodied in PSD can be applied to improving the design of special applications

The aim of this chapter is to suggest how this can be done by looking, in particular, at two such applications. Firstly, a bank cash-point and then at the word-processing facilities on the Amstrad PCW8256.

The first device should be familiar to most people and the latter, offering professional WP facilities for about £400, should be widely used. Clearly, the HCI of these devices is important.

Customised Devices

Special input panels could be designed for almost any EDP system. As a general rule the basic methodology of PSD is - don't. Using standard equipment has a great many advantages in terms of cost and flexibility.

Producing special input panels is costly. It also makes systems less flexible, and when enhancements are required, this may mean that hardware as well as software must be modified.

Having said this, there are clearly many applications where the use of a conventional computer terminal is inappropriate. Generally, these applications will be of limited scope, will involve special features, and must be capable of being operated by users with little or no training.

The bank cash-point is a good example of the need for a customised device. Conventional computers are not equipped to dispense cash, so something special is clearly required and for the general public the device must be simple to use and robust. But looking at some of the early designs shows very clearly the sort of problems that can arise.

Early Cash-Point Designs

Early Cash-Points were relatively simple devices designed primarily to dispense money and to allow users to view their balance (Figure 15.1).

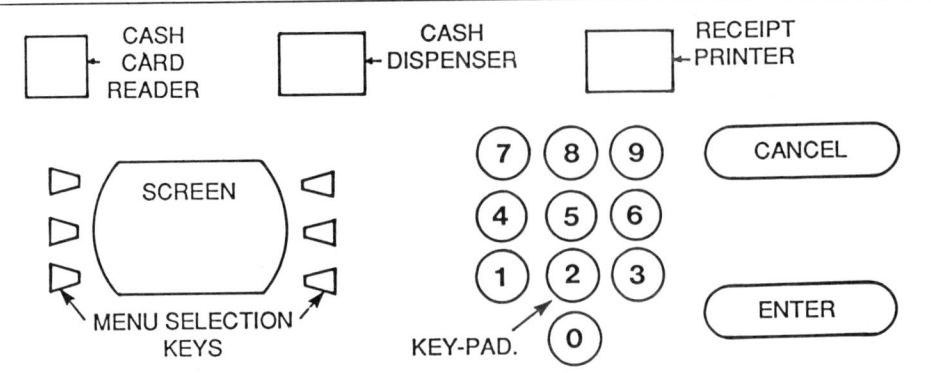

Figure 15.1 Early Bank Cash-Point - Schematic.

The concept of a magnetic-strip card to identify users is good, but on many systems what should be a simple, friendly process is far from it. So let's take a look at what can happen.

At times when systems are heavily loaded the first message that a user will get is 'Please take your card' - an instruction given to the previous user.

Then as you stand poised to insert your card the next message that appears is '... enquire in the bank about our new Super Savings Account ... '. With a growing queue of people behind you this can be very frustrating, especially when the bank is in fact closed.

At last the long awaited message arrives 'Next customer, please insert your card'. The designers could perhaps have left the 'please' out, because apart from that it is difficult to imagine a colder less welcoming message.

Then as you are left to contemplate the message you find that the system hasn't caught up with itself and still won't take your card. Eventually, after what seems to be an age, your card is sucked into the machine. Then the chances are that the machine will promptly eject the card. This is explained by a masterly pronouncement 'This is not a Bountiful Bank Card'.

At this point, the queue behind you usually doubles, and you may be inclined to panic. Don't, it is probably the computer that has got it wrong. What has probably happened is that you have inserted the card upside down or back to front.

If there was time, one would probably wonder at this stage why the problems had not been minimised by centralising the magnetic strip and arranging for it to be read in either direction. Unfortunately, since the cards are, quite rightly, also designed to be read by wiping through a reader by hand, this is not a feasible solution. On the other hand, it does not seem too much to expect to see 'TOP' and an arrow on the cards.

Once a card has been accepted, keying in your Personal Identity Number (PIN) doesn't normally present any problems, although at least one type of dispenser was programmed in such a way that pressing <CANCEL> at this stage resulted in the message 'Invalid PIN code'. The request for a PIN was then repeated and <CANCEL> had to be pressed three times before the card was returned.

Probably the worst feature of the early dispensers, from the HCI point of view, appears once a valid PIN has been accepted. This is the menu display (Figure 15.2). This allows users to select the option they require.

```
XXXXXXXXXXXXXXXXXXXXXXXXXXXXX
CASH              XX BALANCE
WITHDRAWAL        XX ENQUIRY
XXXXXXXXXXXXXXXXXXXXXXXXXXXXX
CASH              XX REQUEST
TRANSFER          XX STATEMENT
XXXXXXXXXXXXXXXXXXXXXXXXXXXXX
END               XX
PROCESSING        XX
XXXXXXXXXXXXXXXXXXXXXXXXXXXXX
```

Figure 15.2 Bank Cash-Point, Menu Display. Cluttered screen adds to selection difficulties.

The actual key-pressing is not difficult, but the distracting boxes on the screen make it difficult to locate the item required. Many banks also added to this difficulty by continually changing the facilities available.

The most serious limitation of the design, however, lies in the fact:

* That special keys are provided for menu selection.

* That there are only six of these keys.

Displaying a simple menu (Figure 15.3), would not only make it easier to read what options are available, it would also eliminate the need for the six special-keys. Removing the need for the special keys will, of course, reduce the complexity and hence the cost of Cash-points. But it also has another significant advantage, in allowing for more than six selections to be made.

```
Please key in selection number & press
the ENTER key

1. Cash withdrawal

2. Cash transfer

3. Balance enquiry

4. Request Statement

5. End processing
```

Figure 15.3 Bank Cash-Point. Simple-menu alternative.

On many modern Cash-points this restriction has been removed. The way in which it has been achieved is not by eliminating the need for special-keys, but by adding more and more special-keys. Those who have adopted this approach clearly have now recognised the need for more versatile Cash-points, with as many as twenty special-keys (Figure 15.4).

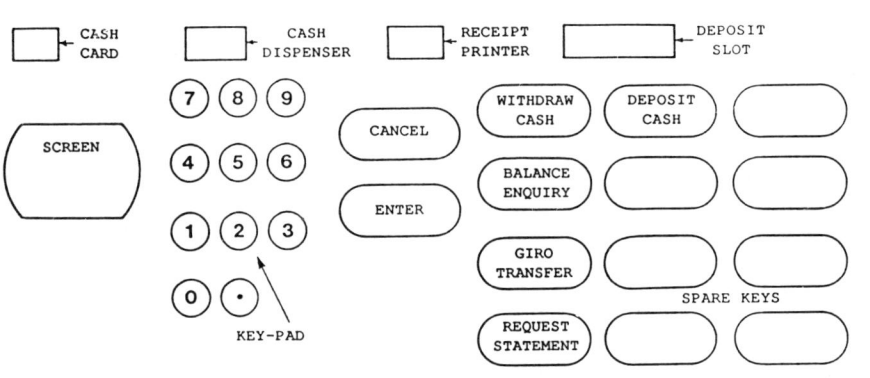

Figure 15.4 'Modern' Bank Cash-Point. Terminals must be modified to add new facilities.

One problem immediately apparent is that, because selections must be engraved on the special-keys, the detail shown must be cryptic and 20 is a lot to choose from. However, the fact that most of these keys are currently blank, presumably to allow for expansion, highlights the main problem with the approach - introducing enhancements.

Instead of an enhancement being a matter of introducing new software centrally, new keys must be engraved and then fitted to every terminal all over the country. Using the

PSD menu approach all of these problems can readily be avoided. Once the required selection has been made entering the amount of cash required via the simple numeric key-pad is straight forward. Note, however, that on the first design (Figure 15.1), there is no provision for a decimal point to be entered.

Where round numbers of £ notes are to be dispensed, there is no need for a decimal point, but looking to the future when the terminal could be required to do other things, like paying bills, this facility is going to be needed, so, it seems short-sighted for a simple facility not to be included, when it will pave the way for future developments. Finally, it shouldn't be too difficult to ensure that when the system displays 'Please take your card', the card is not still hidden inside the machine.

Appraisal

What has been achieved by the banks and building societies, in providing Cash-point facilities is quite remarkable and the concept of capturing details of a transaction at the time when it occurs, without the need for further clerical effort, is extremely powerful.

More recently, the design of some systems has improved considerably, although not all the developments make sense. One must, for example, seriously question the merits of a system that encourages users to juggle with three or more accounts in the same bank. What is worth noting, however, is that in almost every case where improvements have been made these have been achieved, albeit unwittingly, by applying the basic principles of PSD.

WP on the Amstrad PCW8256

Because of the added complexity of WP and greater user involvement, there is a great deal of scope for improving the HCI of most WP packages. Unfortunately, PSD, as it stands, is not capable of resolving some of the more complex problems which WP presents.

The primary aim of this section, is to highlight some of the problems, in the hope that it will stimulate further efforts to resolve the problems. What follows is based on the WP package 'LocoScript' supplied with the Amstrad. In considering this the following points should be noted:

*   This book was only made possible by the availability of the Amstrad PCW8256.

*   The analysis which follows is of necessity incomplete and is concerned mainly with the areas where there is scope for improvement, rather than with the multitude of commendable aspects of the system.

*   Notwithstanding the scope for improvement, I would not hesitate to recommend the Amstrad PCW 8256 as a WP system. It is, I believe, currently second to none in terms of value for money.

* The analysis is based on Loco Script 1.2, which has now been superceded by a much improved version 2.0.

The Keyboard

The keyboard (Figure 15.5) consists of a conventional QWERTY layout, with a block of 20 special keys on the right. These provide for function selection and invaluable WP features such as <PAGE>, <PARA>, <END OF LINE>, <CUT>, <PASTE> and so on.

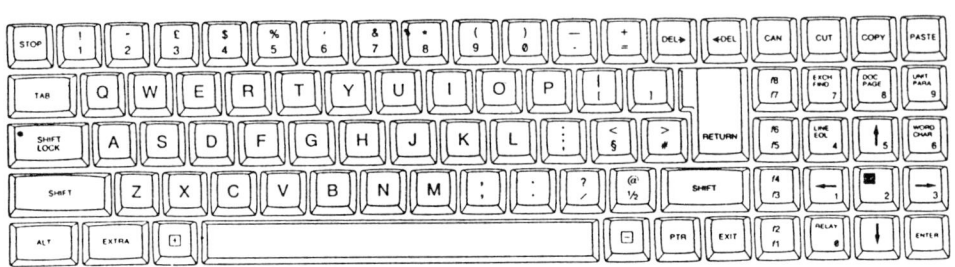

Figure 15.5 The Keyboard on the Amstrad PCW 8256.

There are also three Shift-keys, <SHIFT>, <ALT> and <EXTRA>. These serve primarily to allow a very wide range of Greek Characters, Accents and other special characters to be typed, such as ©. <ALT> is also used to reverse the implications of keys such as <PAGE>, i.e. to page back up a document.

None of the keys should present users with any serious problems, although reference to the manual is necessary to determine which key prints what in the extended character set.

At either end of the space bar there is a <+> key and a <-> key. The main purpose of these keys is to tick or remove ticks from menus etc. They can also be used to invoke menus of special features such as underlining or 'Bold'. More about this later.

There is also a <STOP> key which will stop documents during scrolling, but it won't stop printing or more complex processes such as layout changes.

The <CAN> key is more positive. In most cases, it simply cancels the last command, that is, until the computer gets into its stride, printing or scrolling etc., then it has no effect.

Again the <PTR> key doesn't, as one may expect, turn the printer on, although it will stop it. On the other hand <SHIFT><EXTRA><PTR> initiates a screen print (Figure 15.6).

```
                    Disc management.              Printer idle.  Using none.
   C=Create new document   E=Edit existing document   P=Print document   D=Direct printing
   f1=Disc change   f2=Inspect   f3=Copy   f4=Move   f5=Rename   f6=Erase   f7=Modes   f8=Options
Drive A:                        Drive B:       not fitted   Drive M:
127k used   46k free   25 files  0k used   0k free   0 files   2k used  100k free   2 files
████████████   group 4    0k                               LETTERS    1k   group 4   0k
SAMPLES    12k    group 5    0k                            SAMPLES    0k   group 5   0k
CONT        1k    group 6    0k                            CONT       1k   group 6   0k
TEMPLATE   17k    group 7    0k                            TEMPLATE   0k   group 7   0k
A:LETTERS    7  files  A:SAMPLES   5 files  A:CONT    1 files  A:TEMPLATE  12 files
  0 limbo files          0 limbo files       0 limbo files       0 limbo files
████████████████       ADVERT   .EG   1k    TEMPLATE.STD  1k    LET2PAGE.HDP   2k
READ    .ME   9k       DOCUMENT .EG   4k                         LET2PAGE.PLP   2k
TEMPLATE.STD  1k       LAYOUT   .EG   1k                         LETTER  .HDP   1k
  4 hidden   86k       QUOTE    .EG   3k                         LETTER  .PLP   1k
                       TEXT     .EG   3k                         MANUSCRP.      2k
                                                                 MEMO    .      2k
                                                                 PAGENUM .CEN   1k
                                                                 PAGENUM .PR    1k
                                                                 PAGENUM .RJ    1k
                                                                 PHRASES .LET   1k
                                                                 PHRASES .MUL   1k
                                                                 TEMPLATE.LAB   2k
```

Figure 15.6. Initial LocoScript Display - Normal Mode.

Screen prints are extremely useful for documenting systems and the illustrations which follow have been pro 'uced using this facility. The shaded areas are highlighted areas of the screen. Finally, there are two other important keys, <ENTER> and <EXIT>. These will again be examined in more detail later.

To sum up, the keyboard has a nice feel to it and shouldn't present new users with any major problems, providing that they are prepared to study the User Guide, but the fact that the keyboard has a variety of special keys which are not commonly found is not helpful.

Similarly, if users try to do something that the computer doesn't like, such as pressing an inappropriate key, the results can be quite disturbing. The error indicator on the Amstrad can't really be described as a 'Bell'. It is more of a loud 'Shriek'. In some cases, error messages are displayed when an illegal operation is attempted, such as trying to write to a disc which is 'Write-protected'. Generally, the 'Shriek' is the only indication that an error has been made.

If a more serious mistake is made, the machine doesn't just 'Shriek' once, it 'Shrieks' on and on. No indication of what is wrong is given nor is the way to stop it shrieking indicated.

This is not a condition which is commonly encountered. However, readers should note that pressing <CAN> will usually return the system to normality.

LocoScript 1.2

When users first switch on their Amstrad, they will be presented with a totally blank screen, but simply inserting the LocoScript disc galvanises the screen into action.

Whilst the disc is being read, the fact that something is happening is indicated by the screen being painted with a series of black lines. This is a useful indicator, but one would have thought that a more welcoming display could have been devised.

Once the disc has been read one of two screens will be displayed (Figures 15.6 or 15.7). At first sight these two screens may appear to be identical, which is a problem, but closer examination of lines two and three will reveal subtle differences.

These differences are the key to one of the most impressive features of the Amstrad. Namely, its ability to allow users to continue processing in the normal way, whilst simultaneously printing a document. A great time saver.

Loading a sheet of paper into the printer automatically switches the system into Printer Control Mode (Figure 15.7) and, because the screens differ by so little, this can cause confusion, although the word 'Printer' is displayed flashing.

```
                    Disc management             Printer idle  Using none
Printer: Online   at line: 28              Idle          High quality  Single sheet
f1=Options   f2=Paper   f3=Actions   f5=Document/Reprint   f7=Reset   f8=On/Off Line   EXIT
Drive A:                           Drive B:      not fitted  Drive M:
127k used  46k free  25 files      0k used   0k free  0 files  2k used 100k free  2 files
LETTERS     9k     group 4   0k                              LETTERS    1k   group 4   0k
SAMPLES    12k     group 5   0k                              SAMPLES    0k   group 5   0k
CONT        1k     group 6   0k                              CONT       1k   group 6   0k
TEMPLATE   17k     group 7   0k                              TEMPLATE   0k   group 7   0k
A:LETTERS   7 files  A:SAMPLES    5 files  A:CONT    1 files  A:TEMPLATE   12 files
 0 limbo files        0 limbo files         0 limbo files     0 limbo files
PHRASES.STD  1k       ADVERT  .EG  1k      TEMPLATE.STD 1k   LET2PAGE.HDP  2k
READ    .ME  9k       DOCUMENT.EG  4k                         LET2PAGE.PLP  2k
TEMPLATE.STD 1k       LAYOUT  .EG  1k                         LETTER  .HDP  1k
 4 hidden   86k       QUOTE   .EG  3k                         LETTER  .PLP  1k
                      TEXT    .EG  3k                         MANUSCRP.     2k
                                                              MEMO    .     2k
                                                              PAGENUM .CEN  1k
                                                              PAGENUM .PR   1k
                                                              PAGENUM .RJ   1k
                                                              PHRASES .LET  1k
                                                              PHRASES .NUL  1k
                                                              TEMPLATE.LAB  2k
```

Figure 15.7 Initial LocoScript Display - Printer Control Mode.

To return to the normal mode, Disc Management (Figure 15.6), <EXIT> must be pressed. If a document is in the process of being printed this will result in the printing continuing, which doesn't seem to be very logical.

However, to return to the initial screen. For new users to be confronted with this screen as their first point of contact with the system must be quite bewildering. Particularly, as no indication is given as to what to do next and cursor selection is required.

Most researchers seem to agree that 'cluttered' screens should be avoided. There is considerable scope for thought about the nature of this screen and indeed about how to structure the system, so that users can more readily relate to it.

The main problems with the screen lie in the top three lines into which a variety of status messages, function prompts and menu selections have all been crammed.

As a result, many of the menu selections are cryptic and there are inconsistencies. For example, 'C' is used to Create a new document, but to Erase a document <F6> must be pressed. Similarly, a variety of disc handling functions are also mixed in.

The same basic approach is used throughout the system, although a variety of facilities can also be invoked by the use of the <+> and <-> keys (Figure 15.8). The fact that cursor selection is a problem appears to have been recognised and skilled users can invoke the options by typing the letters shown in capitals.

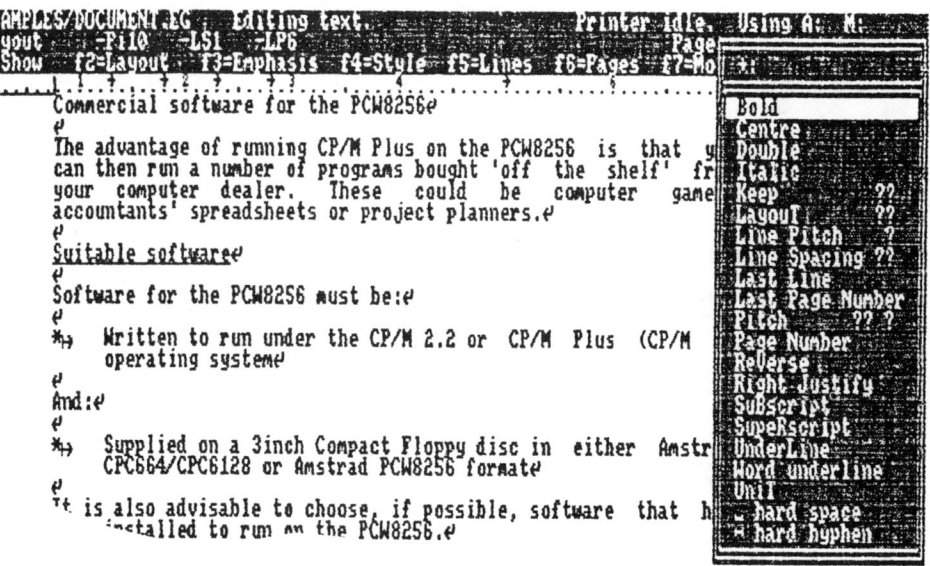

Figure 15.8 <+> key facilities menu.

Use of the function keys <f*> for menu selection from the main menus is not easy due to the cryptic prompts. What makes this more difficult is that many of the facilities are hidden under several layers of structuring, without any obvious logic to the structure. This is perhaps best illustrated by an example.

Suppose, for example, that a document has to be changed, so that broken paragraphs at the bottom of a page are not permitted. The operations involved would be as follows:

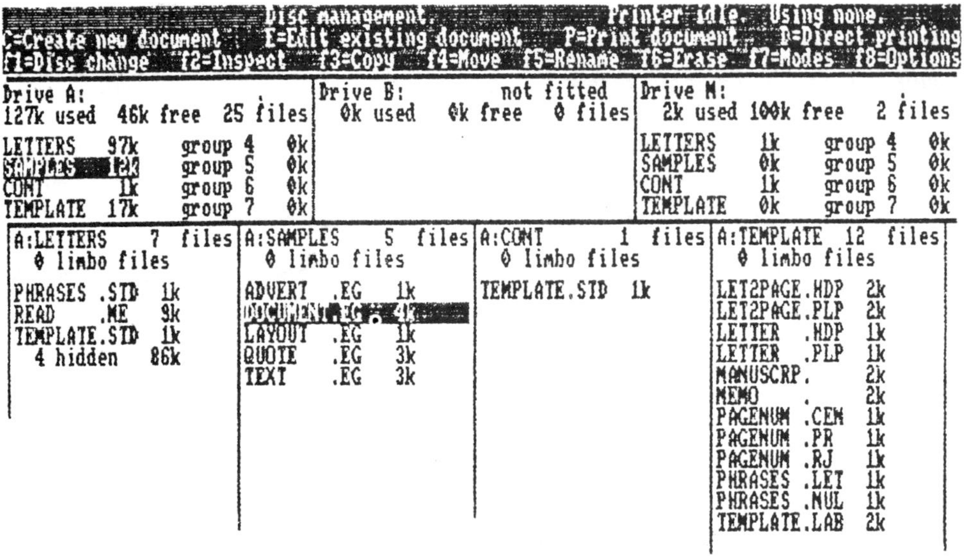

Figure 15.9 Operation 1. - Cursor to document to be edited.

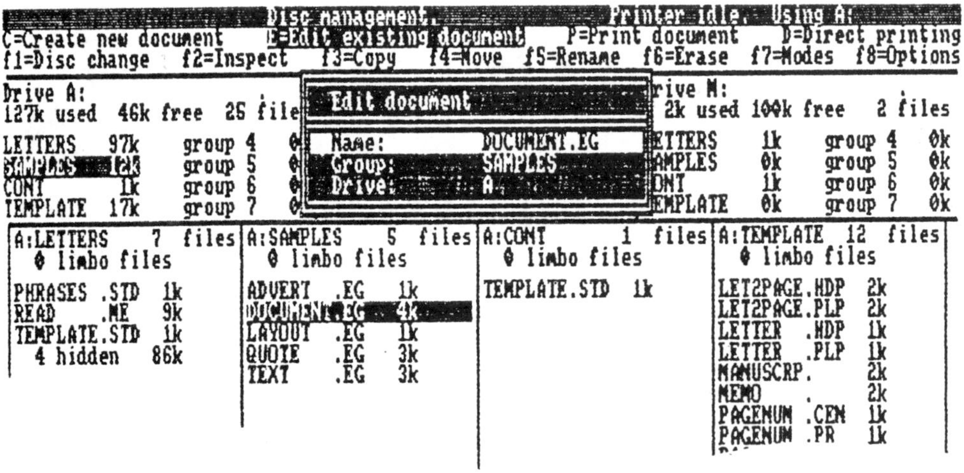

Figure 15.10 Operation 3. - The system prompts for confirmation of edit.

1. Cursor to required document (Figure 15.9).

2. Press <E> for Edit.

3. The system then displays what was already highlighted, but now in a highlighted window (Figure 15.10). Press <ENTER> to confirm that this is the document to be edited.

4. The first page of the document is then displayed. Press <f7> to select 'Modes'.

5. An Editor Sub-modes menu is then displayed (Figure 15.11). Select appropriate mode. In this case Edit Header and press <ENTER>.

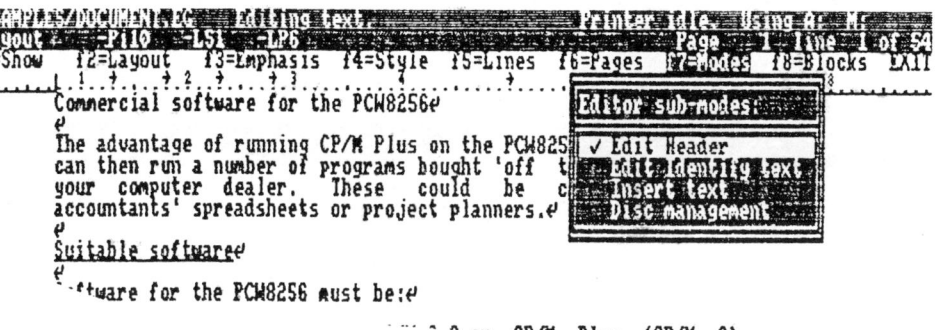

Figure 15.11 Operation 5. - Editor sub-modes menu.

6. Facilities to edit Headers and Footers are displayed (Figure 15.12). Note that the titles shown on the screen from here on do not correspond to the selections made. Press <f7> to select 'Options'.

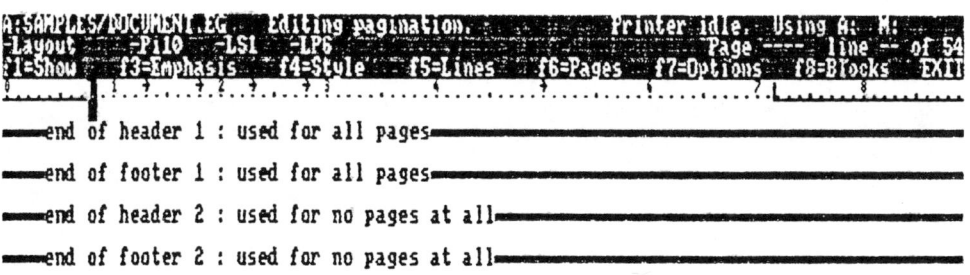

Figure 15.12 Operation 6. - Menu for further selection to be made.

7. More options are displayed (Figure 15.13). Press <f6> to select 'Breaks'.

Figure 15.13 Operation 7. - A further selection menu.

8. The 'Page breaks' menu is displayed (Figure 15.14). Cursor down to the appropriate option. Press the <+> key.

9. Although the display shows 'EXIT', press <ENTER> to return to the 'Options' menu (Figure 15.13).

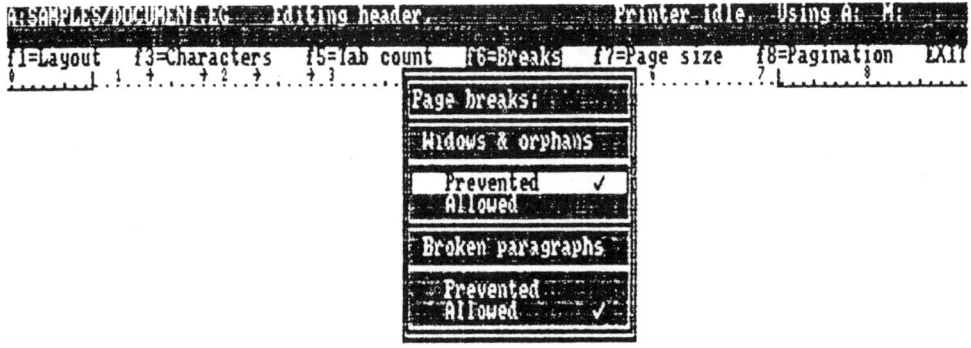

Figure 15.14 Operation 8. - The Page breaks menu.

10. Press <EXIT>. The system then asks for confirmation that you have finished (Figure 15.15).

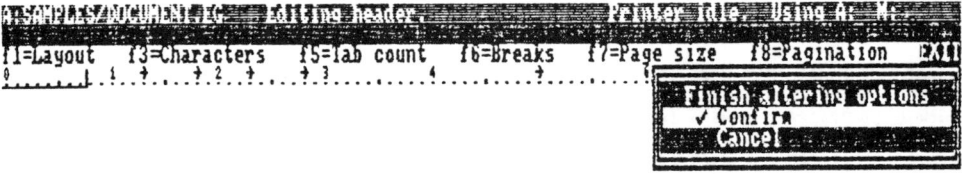

Figure 15.15 Operation 10. - Request for confirmation.

11. Press <ENTER>. The system returns to the facility to edit Headers and Footers (Figure 15.12).

12. Press <EXIT>. The system asks for confirmation that the edit is to be used (Figure 15.16).

13. Press <ENTER>. The system returns to the document display.

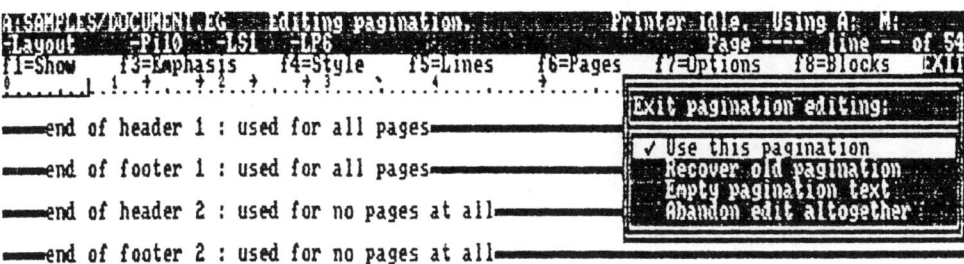

Figure 15.16 Operation 12. - Request for confirmation of edit.

14. Press <EXIT>. The system asks if you wish to finish editing etc. (Figure 15.17).

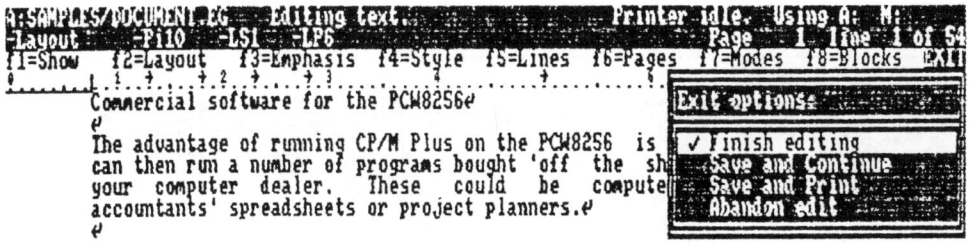

Figure 15.17 Operation 14. - Exit options.

15. Select the appropriate option and press <ENTER>. This completes the edit and the system returns to the main menu.

This example was deliberately chosen to illustrate one of the more difficult tasks. But, throughout the system, difficulties are created by uncertainty about whether it is necessary to use the <+> and <-> keys or simply to move the cursor to a selection and press <ENTER>.

A variety of other tasks have also been made unnecessarily difficult. For example, instead of just providing users with a series of layouts, which can be numbered, a Base Layout is introduced (Figure 15.18).

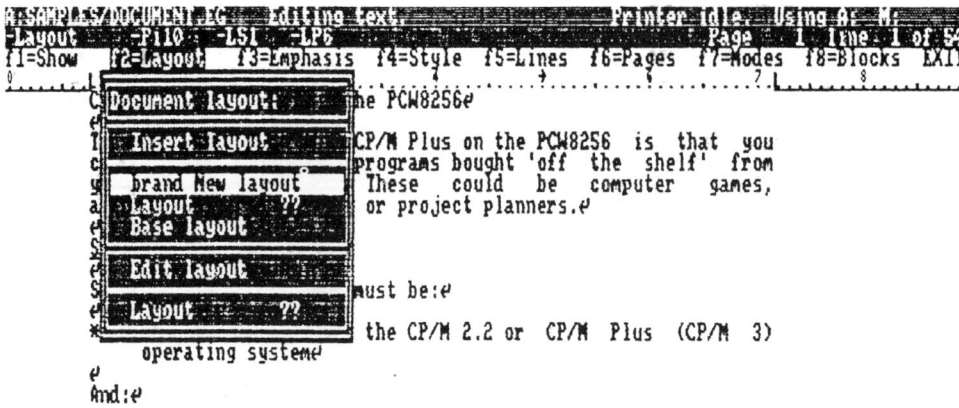

Figure 15.18 Document Layout options.

The task of printing a document is also complicated if selective printing is required. After selecting the document to be printed using the cursor on the main menu, <P> must be pressed. This again puts the details in a highlighted window (Figure 15.19).

Figure 15.19 Print some pages prompt.

Why the cursor is now left at the top of the window isn't clear. However, if selective printing is required the cursor must now be moved to the bottom of the window and

<ENTER> must be pressed. A further window then appears (Figure 15.20). This is helpful in that it shows the first and last page numbers (which could usefully have been shown in the first window, as could the other options).

At this point the program shows that a lot of thought has in fact gone into some aspects of the system. Invalid page numbers are rejected, but no error message is shown.

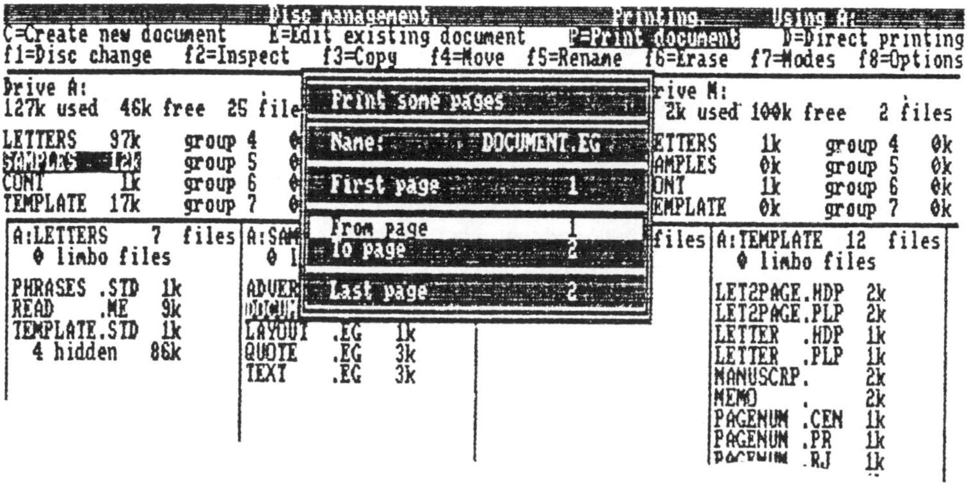

Figure 15.20 Print some pages options.

Similarly, the system will deduce obvious values. For example, if the 'To page' is set to '1', the 'From page' is also automatically set to '1' and you cannot print from, say, page 3 to page 2.

It is therefore somewhat surprising that the cursor doesn't move to the second field once the first field has been entered.

Similarly, the logic by which the system decides when users are satisfied with the values that they have put in is somewhat unusual. Pressing <ENTER> without making a change immediately prior to this is the signal.

Note that until printing actually starts, although the user has been invited to confirm the title of the document, the user hasn't been given a chance to see the document to check that it is in fact the right one.

Conclusion

A great deal more could be said about LocoScript, particularly as far as the impressive facilities which it provides.

There are just two additional basic features that I would like to see as well as a spelling checker. Firstly, a facility to go directly to a particular page of a document, without having to scroll through the document, would be useful, particularly for inserting corrections. Secondly, a facility to page rather than scroll would considerably simplify the task of spotting where corrections have to be inserted. But these are minor details compared with what the system already offers.

Clearly there is a significant amount of room for thought about the HCI of WP systems in general.

It would be nice to be able to say that PSD would solve all the problems, but this is not the case. Nevertheless, it is hoped that what has been said here, coupled with PSD, will help to encourage improvements in this vital area.

Chapter 16

DBMSs and 4GLs

Introduction

There are a large number of systems development aids now available in the form of Data Base Management Systems (DBMSs) and/or 4th Generation Languages (4GLs), as the more modern ones tend to be called. It is suggested that 4GLs are so easy to use that users should design and program systems themselves. However, experience suggests that, in general, this claim, like many others, is highly misleading.

The main features and limitations of 4GLs are examined in this chapter, whilst in the next consideration is given to how to improve 4GLs by applying the PSD methodology.

What Are 4GLs ?

4GLs consist essentially of very high-level coding systems which allow programs to be written using about one-tenth of the instructions necessary for the corresponding COBOL or BASIC program. The commands used are normally plain, but rather cryptic, English (Figure 16.1).

```
BEGIN
1. IN CUSTOMER FIND ALL RECORDS FOR WHICH
   REGION = WESTERN
2. FOR EACH RECORD IN 1
   2.1 NOTE CUSTOMER I/D
   2.2 IN ORDER FIND AND PRINT COUNT
       CUSTOMER NO = VALUE IN 2.1
END
```

Figure 16.1 Sample 4GL program. Locates all customers in the Western region and counts how many Orders there are for each.

Generally, 4GLs are linked to computerised systems for specifying systems. In other words, linked to a computer system which will allow details of fields and field characteristics to be captured. In this form that it is perhaps more appropriate to refer to the systems as DBMSs. However, for convenience the term 4GL will be used throughout.

Clearly, the prospect of simply typing a system specification into a computer and then being able to compile it into a program is attractive. Similarly, the more flexible alternative of the system specification being interpreted at run time is even more attractive, although this will normally result in lower speeds of execution for programs. Whichever alternative is chosen, there are clearly considerable benefits to be gained in terms of both time taken and cost, although it should be appreciated that at present programming accounts for only 10% of the cost of developing a system. So in assessing the overall impact of a 4GL it is important to consider the wider implications of the method on the development process as a whole. In particular, this means considering:

*   The ease with which users can relate to the systems produced by the 4GL.

*   The ability of designers to relate to the 4GL.

Looked at in this light, it becomes clear that the development of an application-system is in itself an application. In other words, a 4GL must be looked upon as a series of application programs for developing further applications (Figure 16.2).

So the same basic principles of good design, that apply to applications, must also apply to 4GLs.

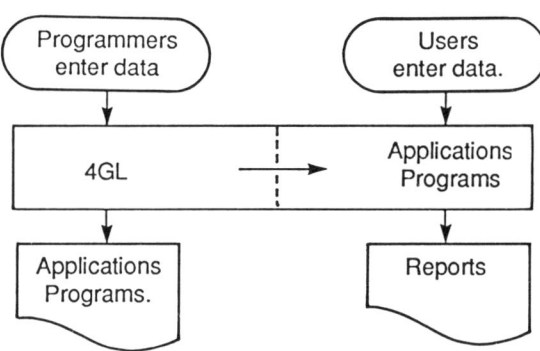

Figure 16.2 A 4GL is a set of application programs for developing further applications.

As was suggested earlier, there are a very large number of 4GLs available and these vary considerably, both in the way in which they operate and the degree to which they satisfy the above criterion. It would, therefore, be inappropriate to select any one 4GL and examine it in detail, particularly since most 4GLs can only be used on a limited range of computers. But the only real way to determine the suitability of a 4GL in any particular circumstances is to actually try it. Suffice it to say that at the time of writing almost all 4GLs left a great deal to be desired, although it is worth noting that those based on the increasingly popular PICK Operating System measure-up most favourably.

The aim of this chapter is to provide a check-list for potential users by illustrating some of the more common HCI problems on 4GLs in general.

User/Designers

One of the claims most commonly made for 4GLs is that they solve the problem of finding out what users really want by allowing users to develop their own programs.

Certainly, most 4GLs have good, easy to use Report Generators, which can readily be run by users to cover new reporting requirements, as and when these arise. Equally certainly there are hidden dangers in producing reports, even where the facilities are limited to ensure that data can only be reported on and not changed.

On multi-user systems, in particular, unskilled users may generate reports of massive proportions. At the same time, the problem of limiting access to confidential data is complicated, and it becomes impossible to control the proliferation of programs.

Where users are given access to facilities to actually change data, or delete files, the problem is even more acute. There can surely be few EDP staff of any standing who are not very much aware of the danger of vital files being 'lost'.

For the one-man-band with a Personal Computer control over developments may not be a problem, but for commercial multi-user systems it is vital that systems should be developed in a controlled manner, that they should perform efficiently in favourable and adverse conditions, and, above all, that they should be secure. To achieve this there is no substitute for the experience of professional programmers, with their intimate knowledge of the workings and foibles of the computer, and indeed of the 4GLs themselves.

By the same token, it is wrong to assume that users are suddenly going to become experts on Systems Design, when a 4GL manual is thrust into their palms. Systems Design is an area where there is no substitute for experience.

Because they tend to become captivated by the computer itself, even first-class programmers rarely make good systems designers. Therefore the conventional team of Users/Designers/Programmers (Figure 16.3) will still give the best results, even with 4GLs.

This doesn't mean that 4GLs cannot bring the three closer together. Certainly, shorter development times will be welcomed by all concerned and if details of the specification can be captured so that the programmer can readily generate code from them, this will also be helpful. But care should be exercised in considering suggestions that users and designers should sit together at a terminal and design a system by drawing up Data Flow Diagrams or Data Base Diagrams. There are many excellent systems to allow diagrams to be captured and amended by the computer, and these are ideal for formalising designs. However, they must not be regarded as a substitute for the large sheet of paper and a pencil, people can detect errors more readily on paper rather than on a VDU screen and it is much easier to get a feel for a system from a single sheet of paper, rather than from zooming from one screen to another.

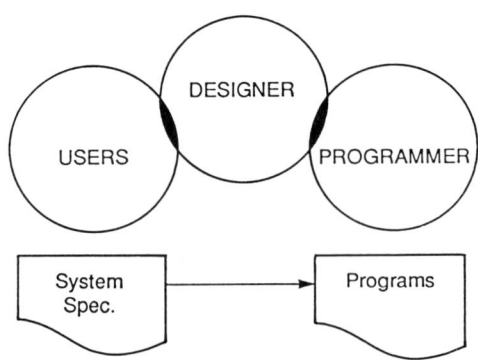

Figure 16.3 A conventional development team seems likely to give the best results, even when a 4GL is used.

To sum up, 4GLs are powerful programming aids, but they must not be regarded as a substitute for a good Designer and a good Programmer, except where no other alternative exists.

Terminology

With one or two notable exceptions, most 4GLs appear to have been designed to impress potential-users with the sheer volume of their obscure terminology. In addition to the terms already in use, new terms are freely introduced, such as Schemas and Sub-schemas, Elements and Components and various degrees of Normalisation. At least two systems insist that an Entity is not just a Record. It can also be a thing, like a lorry or a machine. Unfortunately, how this can possibly affect the design of a system is never made clear.

One thing will become clear later. It is necessary for 4GLs to introduce a number of terms which may be unfamiliar to users. This is particularly so as far as file handling and other programming aspects are concerned. In some cases new terms are clearly defined, but in others they are not. This can quickly lead to confusion, particularly as on some 4GLs the terms Input and Output are used to describe transfers to and from a disc. It is clear, however, that the proliferation of new terms and the duplication of terms which many 4GLs have introduced could and should have been avoided.

Hierarchical Systems

Up to this point the essential simplicity of the task of designing EDP systems has been stressed. However, as was admitted earlier, there is a programming problem as far as finding data on discs is concerned.

In practice, the problems of disc-access are not as difficult as they may appear at first sight, mainly because the disc operating system and the 4GL will take care of them usually by means of an index which points to the disc location of each record (Figure 16.4). Fortunately or otherwise, depending on one's point of view, the concept of indexing opens up a whole new area for thought. Suppose, for example, that a system is to be established to hold the names and addresses, and other details, about the population of the UK. From Figure 16.5, it is not difficult to see that by creating a structure of the form shown using pointers, the task of actually storing the name of the country, county, town and so on, for each person can be avoided. This method of working is usually described as a Hierarchical Structuring.

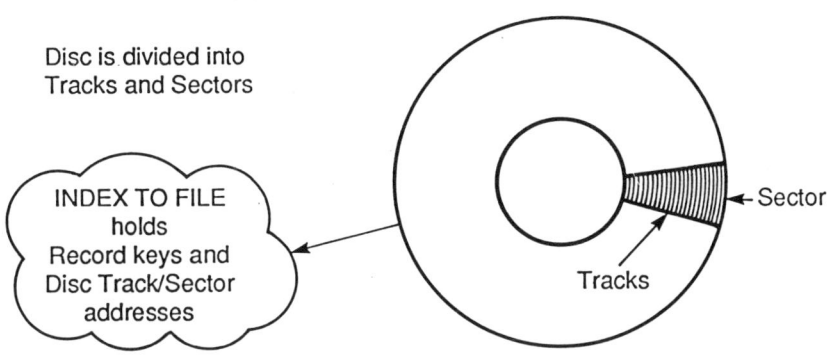

Figure 16.4 Index on disc allows system to go directly to a particular record on a file.

For very large applications, such as the one described, the hierarchical approach has many advantages. Storage requirements can be significantly reduced and, in particular, 'blanket changes' can readily be made. If, for example, the County name of Lancashire is changed to Merseyside, only one record would need to be changed to reflect this on all the appropriate records.

But the hierarchical approach does present problems. In the main, these arise because of the complex nature of the approach and because what users may think is on a file may in fact be spread over several several files. As a result, hierarchical systems usually take a long time to develop and are not normally very flexible. Thus what may be a very simple change on a conventional system will usually prove to be costly on a hierarchical one. Most changes will also require the system to be taken out of service to allow the changes to be introduced.

SPECIMEN OF DETAILS TO BE HELD ON FILE:

SMI.09642
A.SMITH
22 THE BROW
SOUTHFORK
LANCASHIRE
ENGLAND

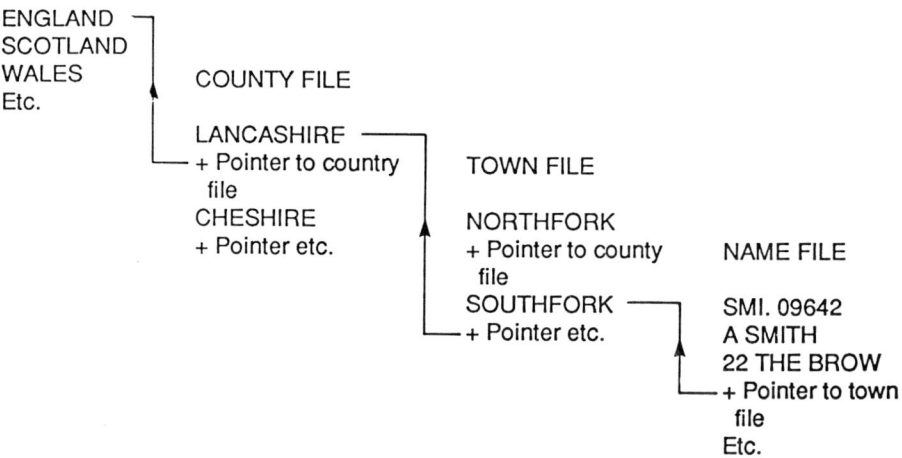

Figure 16.5 A Hierarchical File Structure Files to hold details of all the residents of the UK.

From the systems designers point of view, a more serious problem is that most 4GLs that employ this technique start off by suggesting that Systems are hierarchical and that one of the first steps must be to develop an Entity Model (Figure 16.6). The point that seems to have escaped most suppliers of Hierarchical 4GLs is that it is the method of storing data that is hierarchical; not the systems. As a result, aspiring designers will find that they are forced down a totally illogical development path. In particular, they are asked to consider how data is to be stored before considering what data is to be stored. The ever expanding nature of reporting requirements on systems has already been stressed, as has the secondary nature of Reports. The question of how best to store data must therefore be tertiary - as indeed it is with most other systems.

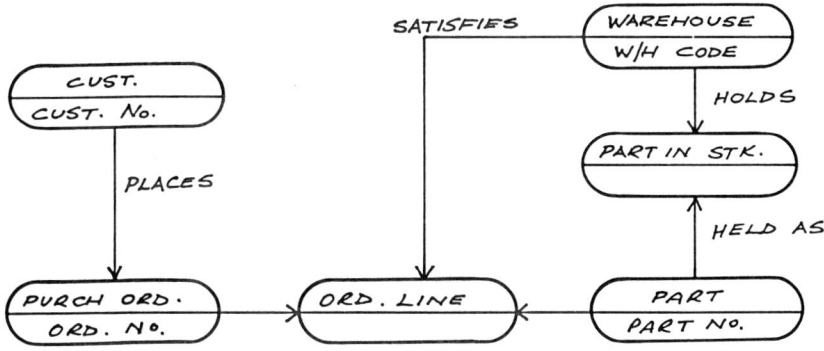

Figure 16.6 Entity Model. Tends to force designers down an illogical development path.

So the net result of using a Hierarchical 4GL is very similar to the situation that arose in the 1960s when IDP was the vogue. There is also a danger that designers will become chair-bound manipulators of models instead of establishing what records are actually used to support a business. Similarly, most exponents of the principles of hierarchical design also devote a great deal of time to the subject of how to get rid of many-to-many relationships (Figure 16.7), whilst, in practice, this is a hypothetical problem.

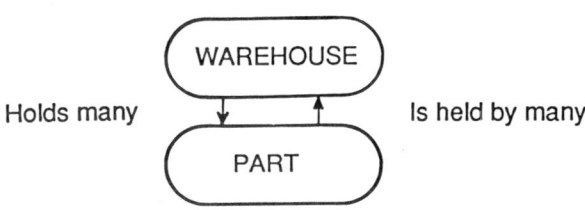

Figure 16.7 'Many-to-Many' Relationship. A hypothetical problem.

For example, in the case illustrated astute analysts would have discovered that each warehouse had a Stock Record long before they were worried by the threat of a many-to-many problem.

Hierachical 4GLs also tend to be the worst offenders as far as terminology is concerned. Even what should be a very simple concept of an Index to Records is made unnecessarily difficult by the use of terms like Sets and Data Sets (Figure 16.8).

It is perhaps fortunate therefore that most users can avoid these problems by opting for simpler more flexible alternatives.

```
              EMPLOYEE DATA SET
              (EMP-NO:
              EMP-NAME:):

              EMPLOYEE-NO-SET OF EMPLOYEE
              KEY EMP-NO ASCENDING
              NO DUPLICATES
              INDEX SEQUENTIAL.
```

Figure 16.8 Sets and Data Sets. More unhelpful terminology in a 4GL program.

Structuring

Very few 4GLs are structured in a way which reflects the way in which designers would logically design systems, and none of the 4GLs examined so far show users systematically where they are in the 4GL system.

Most 4GLs employ menu selection to select the appropriate module of the 4GL. Some do use the PSD numeric-selection method, but many rely on cursor manipulation or the entry of letters. An interesting feature of one 4GL is the inclusion of a final selection on each menu to exit from the menu to the next highest level (Figure 16.9)

```
    Enter selection number ...? [  ]

    1. Diary Sub-system

    2. Calender Sub-system

    3. Exit to calling menu
```

Figure 16.9 Selection menu, with selection number for exit. Not recommended.

This is obviously a serious attempt to improve the HCI of menu selection, but, depending on the number of items on the menu, users will have to enter a different number to exit from each menu.

This problem could be overcome by making the exit-selection the first one on all menus, in other words, selection 1 or perhaps 0. However, on balance, the consistent use of the asterisk to exit from a Field, Record or Menu seems preferable.

Once users have actually selected a module of a 4GL, the variety of approaches which are adopted is considerable. In a few cases the fact that a 4GL is just like any other application has been recognised and the generation of applications is treated as a form-filling exercise (Figure 16.10).

```
INSERT REPORT DEFINITION: STAFF

ENTER FIELD NO TO AMEND (0=OK)
-----------------------------------------

1. Report name              STAFFREPT1
2. Report Heading           PERSONNEL REPORT
3. Sort Keys                DEPT NAME
4. Fields to Print          KEY DEPT (B) DEPTDESC NAME
                            SALARY (T)
5. Printer or Screen (P/S)  S
6. List Totals Only (Y/N)   N
7. Double Spacing (Y/N)     N
9. Label Print (Y/N)        N
10. Label Parameters
11. Select List Name
12. Preferred Heading

13. Footing                 'LL' CONFIDENTIAL
```

Figure 16.10 A few 4GLs use 'form-filling' techniques, to define application systems.

```
+0----+----1----+----2----+----3----+----4----+----5----+----6----+----7----+----+
!                              -  Code Generator                                 !
!           Item Name : ~~~~~~~~~~~~~~~         Program File : ~~~~~~~~~~~~~~~   !
!                        File references and field names                         !
!--------------------------------------------------------------------------------!
!                                                                                !
!  File Reference [~~~~]  Name [~~~~~~~~~~~~~~~~~~~~~~~~]    As at ~~~~~~~~~~    !
!                                                                                !
!      Remarks [~~~~~~~~~~~~~~~~~~~~~~~~~~~~~~~~~~~~~~~~~~~~~~~~~~~~~~~~~]      !
!              [~~~~~~~~~~~~~~~~~~~~~~~~~~~~~~~~~~~~~~~~~~~~~~~~~~~~~~~~~]      !
!              [~~~~~~~~~~~~~~~~~~~~~~~~~~~~~~~~~~~~~~~~~~~~~~~~~~~~~~~~~]      !
!              [~~~~~~~~~~~~~~~~~~~~~~~~~~~~~~~~~~~~~~~~~~~~~~~~~~~~~~~~~]      !
!                                                                                !
!Att      Attribute Name          Conv   L/R  S/M           Comments             !
!~~~  [~~~~~~~~~~~~~~~~~~~~]    [~~~~]  [~]  [~]  [~~~~~~~~~~~~~~~~~~~~~~~~~~]  !
!~~~  [~~~~~~~~~~~~~~~~~~~~]    [~~~~]  [~]  [~]  [~~~~~~~~~~~~~~~~~~~~~~~~~~]  !
!~~~  [~~~~~~~~~~~~~~~~~~~~]    [~~~~]  [~]  [~]  [~~~~~~~~~~~~~~~~~~~~~~~~~~]  !
!~~~  [~~~~~~~~~~~~~~~~~~~~]    [~~~~]  [~]  [~]  [~~~~~~~~~~~~~~~~~~~~~~~~~~]  !
!~~~  [~~~~~~~~~~~~~~~~~~~~]    [~~~~]  [~]  [~]  [~~~~~~~~ ~~~~~~~~~~~~~~~~~]  !
!~~~  [~~~~~~~~~~~~~~~~~~~~]    [~~~~]  [~]  [~]  [~~~~~~~~ ~~~~~~~~~~~~~~~~~]  !
!~~~  [~~~~~~~~~~~~~~~~~~~~]    [~~~~]  [~]  [~]  [~~~~~~~~~ ~~~~~~~~~~~~~~~~]  !
!~~~  [~~~~~~~~~~~~~~~~~~~~]    [~~~~]  [~]  [~]  [~~~~~~~~~ ~~~~~~~~~~~~~~~~]  !
!                                                                                !
!-------------------------------------------------  ----------------------------!
+0----+----1----+----2----+----3----+----4----+----5----+----6----+----7----+----+
```

Figure 16.11 Where 4GLs employ form-filling, the forms are not always well designed.

Unfortunately, even where 4GLs employ a form-filling method for developing applications the design of the forms often leaves much to be desired (Figure 16.11).

Although some 4GLs use down-screen input for forms, many do not and almost all rely on cursor manipulation for corrections. What makes this particularly unfortunate is that designers are likely to be influenced by the standards set in the 4GL and will therefore tend to perpetuate these in applications. There are, though, many other 4GLs where sytems are still defined by Commands, even down to the level of defining what Fields should be on a Record (Figure 16.12).

To many readers, the details shown in the illustration may seem rather sparse; one would normally expect to see details about the length and characteristics of each field. The reason why these are not shown is that the system illustrated is able to store variable length fields of any type.

```
OPEN    EMPFIL

INITIALISE

DEFINE   CLOCK NUMBER (KEY)
DEFINE   LAST NAME
DEFINE   FORENAME
DEFINE   DEPARTMENT (KEY, NUMERIC   RANGE)

CLOSE   EMPFIL
```

Figure 16.12 Commands used to define fields on a record. Not recommended.

The question of defining the characteristics of each field is left until the input screen is defined (Figure 16.13).

The ability of this system to handle variable length records, and to store them efficiently, is quite remarkable, but for EDP applications the problems of trying to accommodate variable length fields on Reports and Pro-formas is such that fixed-length working is normally essential. The system can in fact work in fixed-length mode, so it seems to be a retrograde step to depart from the logical approach of defining the fields on a record together with the characteristics of the fields.

Using the more logical approach allows the positioning of fields on a screen to be treated as a separate task, or, better still, for the task to be eliminated by using PSD.

Returning to the record definition process (Figure 16.12), it will be seen that provision has been made for fields to be designated as 'Key' and 'Numeric Range'. These simple provisions result in an indexes being produced to ensure fast access to data. In the case of Numeric Range, a special indexing feature is invoked to ensure speedy retrieval of values within a range.

Both of the above features are very useful and easy to use. It is a pity therefore that, as in so many other cases, the logical distinction between Records and Reports has been blurred. The numeric-range facility is, for example, obviously a feature associated with reporting on, rather than establishing, records. It could be argued that it is convenient to show this or things like 'Default Report Heading' as part of the definition of a Record. From a purely physical point of view, this is certainly true, but experience suggests that distracting designers from the primary task of establishing Records is highly debilitating.

This form of distraction is rather like trying to write a letter and read a book at the same time. It can be done by writing a line and then reading a line and so on but the results are not very satisfactory.

```
BEGIN

SCREEN NEW.EMP

TITLE '*** FILL IN FOR NEW EMPLOYEES ***'

SKIP 3 LINES

PROMPT    'EMPLOYEE NUMBER:' INPUT EMP.NO LEN 5 NUMERIC
PROMPT    'SURNAME:' INPUT SURNAME LEN 20
PROMPT    'FORENAMES:' INPUT FORENAMES LEN 30
PROMPT    'DEPARTMENT:' INPUT DEPT LEN 4 NUMERIC

END SCREEN
```

Figure 16.13 Commands used to generate input screen. The result is a question and answer type of display. Not recommended.

To sum up, the structuring of most 4GLs leaves a lot to be desired from the HCI point of view, both as far as providing a system to which designers can readily relate is concerned and in leading designers logically through the design process.

Screen Design Facilities

The facilities provided for designing screens vary very considerably from one 4GL to another. In some cases the design is effected by a series of simple instructions defining the line and column and what must be printed or read in (Figure 16.14). On more sophisticated systems the designer simply 'paints' what is required onto the screen and this is captured automatically by the system.

```
        SET HEADER 1 'SPECIAL REPORT HEADING' AT 16
        SET HEADER 3 'AMOUNT' AT 18 AND 'AMOUNT' AT 33
        SET HEADER 4 'CUSTOMER' AND 'ORDERED' AT 18 AND
                     'OUTSTANDING' AT 33
                PRODUCES
```

```
┌─────────────────────────────────────────────────────┐
│              SPECIAL REPORT HEADING                 │
│                                                     │
│                     AMOUNT          AMOUNT          │
│   CUSTOMER          ORDERED         OUTSTANDING     │
└─────────────────────────────────────────────────────┘
```

Figure 16.14 Typical Screen Design program and results.

Generally, the methods are all easy to use, but almost all of the 4GLs have failed to recognise the significant difference between generating screens for Records and Reports. So most of the 4GLs still demand a design for screens for records, even though this should be implicit in most cases. There are occassions where this simplistic approach may be unacceptable, such as in the case of big-fields split between screens, but these occurences should be treated as exceptions. Even where a special screen has to be designed for input, it should not be necessary for the characteristics to be repeated at both the Record Definition and Screen Design Phases. On many 4GLs, though, the same details of the fields have to be repeated.

As far as Prints and Reports are concerned, it would seem to be desirable for provision to be included for standard screen header details to be printed out. However, since none of the 4GLs currently provide for standard headers, this facility is not currently available. Similarly, since none of the 4GLs examined have standard FOS routines, provision for these must be developed by users.

Menus, Views and Security

The screen-painting facility can, of course, be used to paint menus. On most 4GLs this is then backed up by coding to tell the system which menu (or procedure) to go to when a particular selection is made. This is not difficult, but again the process can be simplified, as will become clear in the next chapter, assuming that is that systems are designed to conform to the PSD Structure and Screen I/D's.

As far as Security is concerned most 4GLs tend to omit full details, presumably because this is usually taken care of elsewhere. Often however, security is taken down to Field-level which, as was suggested earlier, leads to something of an over-kill. On other systems security is obtained by removing options from menus when users are not authorised to use the options. At first sight, this seems attractive, as it can be argued that it is wrong to show options to users and then to tell them that they are not authorised to use some of the options. One system even renumbers menu selections to cover-up deleted items. Presumably, this is intended to avoid embarrassing users who are highly restricted. This could well be construed as the ultimate in HCI.

If one considers, as has already been suggested, the problems of trying to keep just one User Guide up to date, let alone a variety of different guides for the same system, then the idea quickly becomes less attractive. Similarly, if Supervisors have different menus from their staff, and have to enter different selection numbers, the problems of training and assisting must be enormous. So on balance, the concept of variable menus does not appear to be attractive.

In the same way, the concept of 'Views' appears to be designed primarily to cause confusion. A View defines what data users can access and in some cases what it will look like. Fields can be masked and/or even re-named within a view. This seems much too complicated, particularly as access to a view normally calls for a password. If the structure of the main system is changed, all the views must be recompiled.

Conclusion

There can be little doubt that most 4GLs represent a significant step forward in computing. However, they differ significantly in terms of their suitability, flexibility and ease of use.

Very few of the 4GLs currently available lead users logically through the design process, although fortunately none of the systems so far examined provide for icons, so perhaps some of the excesses of micro systems will be avoided.

There are many ways in which 4GLs could be made more friendly and exert a powerful influence over the design of applications. Improving 4GLs is, therefore, of major importance as far as improving HCI is concerned. What needs to be done to up-grade 4GLs is considered in the next chapter.

Chapter 17

Outline Specification for a 4GL+ - Record Processing

Introduction

This chapter looks at the way in which the key features of PSD could be incorporated into a 4GL. The specification is incomplete in a number of respects. No reference is made to the commands which should be available and no attempt has been made to cover requirements which may be imposed by a particular host language.

For simplicity, it is assumed throughout that an interpretive language will be used, so that reference to compilation can be omitted. Even so, it is hoped that the details shown will be sufficient, firstly, to show users the type of HCI that they should expect and secondly, to suggest how suppliers should develop their 4GLs into 4GL+s.

I am tempted to suggest that the result should be called a 5GL, since the results should produce a quantum leap forward. However, the term 5GL has already come to imply systems with Artificial Intelligence (AI), whatever that may mean. At present, AI appears to mean a great many different things to different people. In most cases AI systems are what I would call Expert or Diagnostic Systems. Clearly computers are very good at evaluating complex alternatives once they have been properly programmed.

I do not like the use of the term AI, since the word 'intelligence' tends to imply human qualities, which computers do not have. However, this is a subject in itself, so in deference to those who may be more far-sighted than I am, I will simply call a 4GL embodying PSD a 4GL+.

Abbreviations

To try to eliminate some of the confusion that arises between the names of files, records and fields, the following suffixes are used:

_FIL for Files (eg. CUST_FIL).

_REC for Records (eg. CUST_REC).

_FLD for Fields (eg. CUST_NAME_FLD).

These suffixes should be used throughout the specification and programming of any system. The suffixes add to the length of field names and so on, but they also help considerably to make programs and guides more readable (Figure 17.1).

```
BEGIN
1. IN CUSTOMER_FIL FIND ALL RECORDS FOR WHICH
   REGION_FLD = WESTERN
2. FOR EACH RECORD IN 1
   2.1 NOTE CUST.I/D_FLD
   2.2 IN ORDER_FIL FIND AND PRINT 'COUNT'
       CUST.I/D = VALUE IN 2.1
```

Figure 17.1 The use of a suffix can make programs and specifications more readable.

Note that the suffix is connected by an under-line rather than a hyphen. The under-line is acceptable to most host languages, whereas a hyphen is usually interpreted as a minus sign and will not be accepted as part of a file name on many systems. Other connectors, such as full-stops, could be used, but users should ensure that whatever convention is adopted it will not create problems if it is used throughout the system.

Highly restrictive operating systems should be avoided, but if necessary the suffix can be appended directly (eg. CUSTFIL). This reduces the legibility of the name but is better than nothing.

Since a particular type of Record will always be on a particular File, it is most convenient to call them both by the same root name (eg. CUST_FIL holds CUST_RECs). Where programs act as sub-routines and return to the point from which they were initiated, the programs will be called Procedures, usually abbreviated to PROC or PROCs. For want of a better name the proposed system will be called the 4GL+.

Entry to the 4GL+

The 4GL+ should be incorporated into a standard PSD-structure (Figure 17.2). For convenience the system is broken down into two sub-systems Record Processing and Report Processing. This chapter is concerned primarily with the processing of Records. Reports are dealt with in the next chapter.

The first significant part of the record processing is the menu showing the modules available (Figure 17.3). This will be reached by entering the appropriate selection numbers in the conventional way into a standard Menu Selection Program. This will also update the standard Screen Header and the same program will also be used for applications.

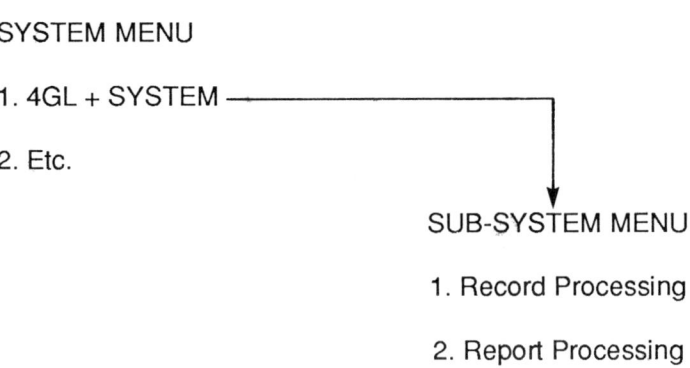

Figure 17.2 Access to the 4GL+ must be via standard PSD menus.

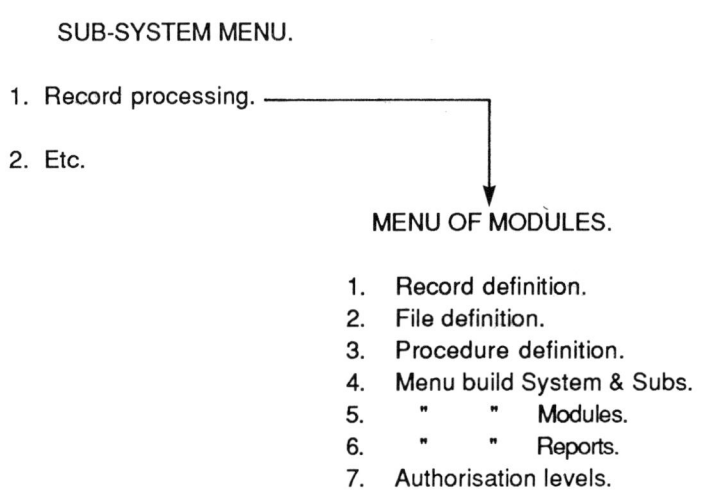

Figure 17.3 Menu of Modules for Record Processing.

Wherever a single selection number is entered at this level, the next screen appearing will normally be the standard Functions Menu (Figure 17.4). Provision should be included for this to be skipped in 'skilled mode', but the effect is the same.

As always, entering a selection number into the Menu of Functions will result in a check to ensure that users are authorised to use the function. If a user is not authorised, a Bell will sound and a flashing message will be displayed on the line reserved for messages, normally line 21.

If the user is authorised, the Screen Header will be updated to show the selection made. Where a REPORT selection is made (selections 6 or 7) the menus of the reports available will be displayed. For other valid selections a master procedure, PROC_MASTER will be initiated.

PROC_MASTER will run in slightly different ways depending on the mode selected from the Menu of Functions. This will be amplified later once the basic method of establishing records has been described. For simplicity, it is assumed initially that the mode selected is CREATE record.

```
MENU OF FUNCTIONS

1. CREATE record
2. AMEND record
3. ERASE record
4. DISPLAY record
5. PRINT record
6. REPORT DISPLAYS
7. REPORT PRINTS
```

Figure 17.4 Standard Menu of Functions - Common to all Modules. (Note that for simplicity the standard Screen Header and the prompt 'Enter selection number' have not been shown on most illustrations.)

Record Definition

When the Record Definition module is selected a screen of the form shown in Figure 17.5 will be displayed after the appropriate mode selection. Designers will then be prompted to enter each field in sequence.

Most of the details to be entered to define the first field of the record for an application should be apparent, from the completed specimen (Figure 17.6). But the points which follow should be noted.

Field number 5, Field type, will need to be adapted to satisfy the requirements of the host programming environment.

Field number 6, Mandatory, is used to indicate whether completion of the field is to be optional or mandatory.

Field number 7, Prime key, allows the designer to indicate whether the field being defined is part (or all) of the primary key to the record. Secondary keys are dealt with later.

```
              RECORD DEFINITION MODULE
     1. Record name...?[_     .     ]
     2. Field number ...[   ]
     3. Field description...[              ]
     4. Field size...[  ]
     5. Field type (A) or (N) ...[ ]
     6. Mandatory (Y) or (N) ... [ ]
     7. Prime key (Y) or (N) ...[N]
     8. Short field name ...[          ]
     9. Retained field (Y) or (N) ...[ ]
     10.Initial value ...[       ]
     11.Procedure ...[       ]
```

Figure 17.5 Initial display for Record Definition Module, in Create mode.

```
              RECORD DEFINITION MODULE
     1. Record name ... CUST_REC
     2. Field number ... 1
     3. Field description ... CUSTOMER I/D
     4. Field size ...6
     5. Field type (A) or (N) ....A
     6. Mandatory (Y) or (N) ...Y
     7. Prime key (Y) or (N) ...N
     8. Short field name ...CUSID_FLD
     9. Retained field (Y) or (N) ...Y
     10.Initial value ...
     11.Procedure ...PRO_CUSR
```

Figure 17.6 Completed definition of the first Field of a Record, to be called CUST_REC

Field number 8, Short field name, may or may not be useful, depending on the host environment.

Field number 9, Retained field, enables the designer to indicate whether or not a field should be retained and displayed after the first record has been filed. For example, in the case shown, where the designer would normally wish to define a number of fields for a particular record, it would be helpful to retain the first field, Record name. In this way designers can simply <ENTER> it, without having to re-type it for each field of the application record.

Field number 10, Initial value, is optional and will allow an initial value to be displayed for the field. In Figure 17.5 field number 7 illustrates the use of this feature within the 4GL+.

Field number 11, Procedure, allows a PROC to be called up when necessary. Note that this is concerned only with any processing that must be done when this particular field is Created or Amended. This will normally be used to allow additional checks to be specified for a field. For example, to check that a Unit of Measure is valid or that a value falls within a particular range.

The field can also be used to call a PROC to display clarifying messages. For example, to show the description of a part when a Part Number is entered.

Simple requirements of this nature should be handled by a few standard commands, such as 'DISPLAY PART_FIL DESC_FLD'. Note that the command shows both the file and the field name. The command could be shortened by insisting that all Field Names should be unique, but the approach shown is thought to be more logical and more flexible. In particular, it allows the same field name, such as DATE_FLD, to be used on any number of files.

When the designer has completed the definition of the first field of the recorda standard FOS routine will be invoked. At this stage suffice it to say that provision will be made for corrections to be made before the details are filed on a REC_DEF_FIL. The designer will then be prompted to enter details of the next field to be defined and so on, until all the fields of the application record have been defined.

File Definition

The File Definition procedure is used to enter details relevant to the files on which the records for an application will be held. It is invoked by a selection of number 2 from the Menu of Modules (Figure 17.3). In this case, the input screen is as shown in Figure 17.7.

The File Definition process is essentially concerned with what should happen when users indicate that a Record is to be Filed or Erased. Most of the processing will be handled automatically by PROC_MASTER. In Create mode, for example, the record will automatically be added to the file, whilst in Erase mode it will be removed once the record to be erased has been displayed for the erasure to be confirmed. However, there are circumstances where additional details are required to enable processing to be carried out efficiently, so the following details are requested.

Field number 2, File description, is used to allow a brief description of the purpose of the file to be recorded. It also illustrates the format recommended for fields which cannot be fitted onto a single line on the VDU.

Field number 3, Record sequence. This allows the designer to specify the sequence in which records will be stored on the file. Normally records will simply be added to a file in the sequence in which they are entered. But where a lot of reporting has to be done the operation of the disc can be speeded-up by holding records in other sequences.

```
                    FILE DEFINITION MODULE
    1. File name ... [          ]
    2. File description:
    [                                           ]
    [                                           ]
    [                                           ]
    3. Record sequence (EO) (SA) (SD) or (HK) ...[ ]
    4. Repetitive processing (Y) or (N) ...[ ]
    5. Record display (S) or 'PROC_' ... [        ]
    6. CREATE procedure 'PROC_' ...[        ]
    7. AMEND procedure 'PROC_' ...[        ]
    8. ERASE procedure 'PRO_' ... [        ]
    9. Secondary key 'FLD. No.' _ 'FLD. No.' ...[         ]
    10.      "            "                   ...[         ]
    11.      "            "                   ...[         ]
    12.      "            "                   ...[         ]
    13.      "            "                   ...[         ]
```

Figure 17.7 Input format for File Definition Module.

The options which are offered are:

    EO - Entry Order.

    SA - Sorted to ascending order.

    SD - Sorted to descending order.

    HK - Hash Key sequence.

Whilst the two 'Sorted' options (SA & SD) have advantages they also have disadvantages, in that the file must be resorted whenever a new record is added. These options are therefore normally only suitable for files of a fairly static nature.

The Hash Key option is a method whereby a record is stored in a fixed position in a file, the position being calculated from the record key. This is a very fast way of accessing records as the system can go directly to any record, but if keys do not follow in sequence large areas of file space will be wasted.

Field number 4, Repetitive processing, is used to indicate whether or not the system should prompt for another record to be entered or displayed in the same mode. Setting this to 'N', for No, will result in the system returning to display the calling menu, after each record has been processed.

So if users can normally be expected to want to work on a number of records of the same type and in the same mode, the repetitive processing option should be set to 'Y' for Yes.

Field number 5, Record display, allows provision to be made for non-standard record displays. If the standard down-screen PSD display is to be used, 'S' for Standard must be entered. For other displays the name of the PROC to be used to produce the display must be entered.

Similarly, fields 6 to 8 allow any special procedures to be used to be identified, for use during Create, Amend and Erase. For example, when a record is created showing a receipt into stock the quantity received must be added to the Actual Stock on the stock record.

Finally, fields 9 to 13 allow upto five fields, or combinations of fields, to be nominated as Secondary Keys. This will result in up to five Index Tables being created to facilitate access to records based on the fields specified.

Procedure Definition

Once the Record and File Definitions have been completed, the next stage is to specify the PROCs that have been named in the definitions.

The way in which this is done will depend very largely on the constraints imposed by the host language. However, it is perhaps appropriate to express surprise at the number of host languages that don't call for lines of programs to be numbered.

It is beyond the scope of this guide to look in detail at programming, but the advantages of being able to key in a line number, and to then go directly to that line, seem to be considerable.

In other words, ideally the 4GL+ should treat programs just like any other PSD record, although in this case field sizes and the number of fields (lines of code) would not have to be defined, that is, the records would be free-format.

However, to return to the subject of systems design. Once all the PROCs have been defined, all that remains to be done, as far as the single record side of the 4GL+ is concerned, is to arrange for the module to be called from a menu.

Before considering how this should be done it is perhaps appropriate to stress that the single record side of each module should be thoroughly tested and demonstrated prior to wasting time on developing reports.

Menu Building

Menu Building provides the facilities necessary to Create (and Amend etc.) menus for applications. It also allows the designer to indicate which PROCs should be run when a particular menu selection is made, and defines the levels of security to be applied.

The approach described assumes throughout that the recommended method for Screen I/Ds is used. In other words, it assumes that a screen is identified by the menu selection numbers needed to access it.

There are three modules for menu definition. These are shown as selections 4, 5 and 6 on the Menu of Modules (Figure 17.3). The module required depends on the level at which the selection is to be included in the finished system. Thus:

> Selection 4, Menu build System and Subs, allows details to be added to System and Sub-system menus.

> Selection 5, Menu build Modules, allows details of modules to be added to the appropriate Menu of Modules.

> Selection 6, Menu build Reports, allows details of reports to be added to Report Display and Report Print menus.

At first it may be thought that one module could handle all menu building, but as will become clear later, different features are required at different levels. So the simplest alternative is to treat these levels separately.

At the top levels, the details required to define a menu item are simply the Screen I/D, the Selection Number and the Title of the Selection (Figure 17.8).

```
MENU-BUILD, SYSTEM & SUBS. MODULE.
1. Screen I/D ... [         ]
2. Selection number ... [ ]
3. Title of selection ... [              ]
```

Figure 17.8 Input format for Menu-build for System and Sub-system menus.

Thus, for example, an entry of the form shown in Figure 17.9 would result in a selection numbered 3 being added to the Sub-system Menu 01 on package A.

During the Create process the 4GL+ will, as always, check that the designer is not trying to create a selection-record that already exists. The system must also check that a path exists from the Menu of Systems down to the menu that is being created. In other words, menus can only be created from the top-down. This is to prevent menus being created with no means of access to them. Note that at this level, it is not necessary to indicate what procedure should be run when a particular selection is made. This is because the Screen I/D and the Selection Number identify the next menu to be displayed.

```
MENU-BUILD, SYSTEM & SUBS. MODULE.

1. Screen I/D ... A01

2. Selection number ... 3

3. Title of selection ... Bill of Materials Sub-system
```

Figure 17.9 Sample input for Menu-build for System and Sub-system menus.

To create Menus of Modules, additional details are required (Figure 17.10). In particular, the name of the file to be accessed upon selection must be defined and Levels of Authority required to run the procedure must be added, assuming that the method of security described earlier is used.

```
MENU-BUILD, MENU OF MODULES.

1. Screen I/D ... [                    ]

2. Selection number ... [    ]

3. Title of selection ... [                              ]

4. File to be accessed ...[              ]

5. Authority required for CREATE ... [ ]

6.      "            "       "   AMEND  ... [ ]

7.      "            "       "   ERASE  ... [ ]

8.      "            "       "   DISPLAY ... [ ]

9.      "            "       "   PRINT  ... [ ]
```

Figure 17.10 Input format for Menu-build for Modules.

The next level in the structuring of a system is the Menu of Functions. This is standard for all applications and therefore does not have to be defined as it will be built into the 4GL+.

The next level of menu-building is the final level of the Menus of Reports (Figure 17.11). This is similar to the modules menu, but in this case the PROC to be run must be identified, and only one level of authority is required for each report selection.

```
MENU-BUILD, MENU OF REPORTS.

1. Screen I/D ... [              ]

2. Selection number ... [    ]

3. Title of selection ... [                    ]

4. Procedure to be run ... [         ]

5. Authority required ... [ ]
```

Figure 17.11 Input format for Menu-build for Reports.

Authorisation Levels

To complete the record processing side of a system it only remains for users to be authorised to use the system. This is achieved by entering a selection number of 8 into the 4GL+s Menu of Modules (Figure 17.3).

The format for the screen display for this module is shown in Figure 17.12. The format assumes that users will already have been allocated a User I/D and Password.

```
AUTHORISATION LEVELS MODULE.

1. Sub-system Screen I/D ... [       ]

2. Level of authority ... [ ]

3. User I/D ... [     ]
```

Figure 17.12 Input format for User Authorisation Levels.

As was suggested earlier, the level of authority for users should be set at Sub-system level. This limits the number of entries that have to be made for each person. At the same time control over what a user can do within the Sub-system is finally governed by the authority levels required for each function. In this case, the first task is to identify the Sub-system by the standard Screen I/D.

It is desirable for the corresponding title of the sub-system to be displayed at this point for checking. Next, the system will prompt for an authority level and finally the users I/D. Again the name of the user should be displayed in the messages area.

This method of working is most suitable where numbers of users have to be authorised to use a new sub-system. The name of the Sub-system and the authority level should be treated as 'Retained Fields'. In many cases, only User I/D's would need to be typed, after the first entry.

Where it is more common for new users to have to be authorised to use a variety of systems this is not so convenient. In other words, the User's I/D should be retained. There is no reason why this could not be done. However, it is a lot simpler if any retained fields are at the start of the record.

Under these circumstances the order of the fields shown in Figure 17.12 should be reversed. Where both conditions are common then both alternatives could be presented as options on the Menu of Modules.

The temptation to include both alternatives should be resisted, because if they are both used, there will be serious confusion about the order in which fields are actually stored.

This completes what is going to be outlined for single Record processing. It should be appreciated, however, that a fuller specification must include details of the Reports associated with this processing. Details of the nature of these Reports will become clearer from the next chapter.

Chapter 18

Outline Specification for a 4GL+ - Report Processing

Introduction

This chapter looks at the facilities, required in a 4GL+ to enable Reports to be defined. Reports can take a variety of forms, ranging from straight file-listings to complex formats, such as Invoices or Accounts. There are also a wide variety of different ways in which reports can be defined.

Many operating systems include powerful reporting routines and where appropriate full use should be made of whatever exists. Occasionally screen-painting facilities are also provided and many designers find these helpful, but they tend to lead to the introduction of 'unusual' methods of processing, involving excessive cursor manipulation and cryptic prompts.

The approach outlined below avoids these problems by using the standard PSD approach. It should be regarded as an indication of the type of facilities required, rather than as an attempt to cover all the possibilities.

In particular, it is intended to show that for most reports the design process can be reduced to a simple form-filling exercise.

From what has been described earlier, it should be appreciated that reports can take the form of either displays or prints and that normally both of these facilities will be required.

Every effort must be made to ensure that what is displayed and what is printed match-up as far as possible. Generally it should only be necessary for the form of the printed report to be defined. The form of the corresponding display should then be implicit. In other words, displays of the report should be in the same form, but divided up into what can conveniently be fitted onto one screen. Namely 16 lines, allowing for standard header and FOS routines.

Note that the temptation to squeeze a few more lines, onto each screen must be avoided. At all times, users must know precisely where the are in a system, and must be in full control of what is happening. This includes stopping the printing of a report in mid-stream.

One further word of caution. Many 4GLs have a default reporting facility. This produces a straight file listing in column form. This is undoubtedly useful, but often the way in which this is achieved is not as helpful as it could be.

The method most commonly used for default reporting is to call for details of column headings, justification and conversions and so on, to be entered as part of the Record Definition phase. The whole process of defining Records, and then defining Reports becomes confused. Since provision must be made for other reporting facilities, it seems to be logical to keep all the provisions for report definition together and thus preserve the essential primary nature of Record Definition.

As was suggested earlier, any miscellaneous multi-record activities associated with an application will be relegated to Reports Menus. These may include facilities to copy files or to generate graphical displays and so on. These facilities will require special coding or additional packages and are beyond the scope of this chapter, which is restricted to looking at conventional commercial reporting.

Types of Reports

Conventional commercial reports not only vary considerably in their form, but also in the facilities that are required. For example, a procedure to print labels for envelopes may be required to print labels for all customers, for only customers in a particular region or for just one customer. These requirements could all be defined in the 4GL+, using a single routine. However, it seems to be more convenient to split the task into a number of steps, firstly, by providing separate routines for defining reports with simple, as opposed to complex formats, secondly, by separating the definition of the format from the definition of the processing. Thus, in the first instance, three basic categories of reports have been identified (Figure 18.1):

* File Listing Reports - where output is in a standard columnar format and where the data to be output is actually on file.

* Simple Reports - which are similar to the above, with output in columns, but in this case provision is required for calculations to be performed and for more sophisticated formatting.

* Complex Reports - which cover any reporting requirements which cannot be handled by the above.

Each category of report will then be divided into two basic modules;

* A Format Definition Module - which will allow the format of the report to be defined.

* A Procedure Definition Module - which will allow the procedures to be used for the report to be defined.

```
┌─────────────────────────────────────────────────────┐
│  TELEPHONE DIRECTORY.                               │
│                                                     │
│  SURNAME     INITIALS      PHONE NUMBER             │
│                                                     │
│  ALLEN       A.B.          01.456.6789              │
│  ALLEN       R.T.Y.        051.789.67890            │
│  BALL        T.            061.887.4563             │
│  Etc.                                               │
└──────────────────────────────┐~~~~~~~~~~~~~~~~~~~~~~
```
a) A File Listing Report

```
┌──────────────────────────────────────────────────────────────┐
│  STOCK VALUATION                                             │
│                                                              │
│  PART NUMBER       QTY IN STOCK     COST PRICE    TOTAL VALUE│
│                                                              │
│  R1236754             100             56.05         5605.00  │
│  S654987             1000              2.00         2000.00  │
│                                                              │
│  TOTAL.                                             7605.00  │
└─────────────────────────────────┐~~~~~~~~~~~~~~~~~~~~~~~~~~~~
```
b) A Simple Report

```
┌──────────────────────────────────────────────────────────────┐
│  DELIVERY NOTE.                                              │
│                                                              │
│  Deliver To:              Invoice To:                        │
│                                                              │
│  B.W. Smiths              B.W. Smiths                        │
│  1 Water Lane             15 The Strand                      │
│  Blackpool                Ipswich                            │
│  B12 6XJ                  17  8LF                            │
│                                                              │
│                                                              │
│  ITEM        CAT          DESCRIPTION          U/M   QUANTITY│
│  No.         No.                                             │
│                                                              │
│  1           T345         ROOFING FELT         ROLL     10   │
│  2           T874         FELT NAILS, 1/2IN GALV. LB    5    │
│  3.          T541         BITUMEN              TUB      2    │
│  Etc.                                                        │
└───────────────────────────┐~~~~~~~~~~~~~~~~~~~~~~~~~~~~~~~~~~
```
c) A Complex Report

Figure 18.1 The three basic categories of Reports.

So the Menu of Modules for the Report Definition Sub-system will take the form shown in Figure 18.2.

The final selection on the menu, 7. Page Layout Definition, is a module which can be used with all three types of reports. It allows details of page size, margins, line spacing and so on to be defined. It will be examined in more detail later.

Figure 18.2 is on the next page

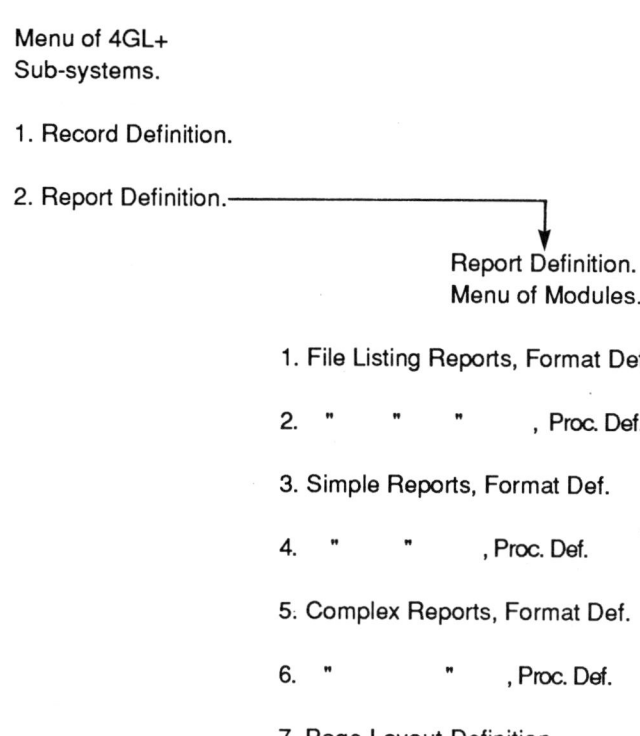

Figure 18.2 Modules of the Report Definition Sub-system.

File Listing Reports - Format Definition

Consider first the first selection on the menu, the File Listing Reports - Format Definition module. This is designed to allow the format for very simple listings to be defined, with minimal effort.

Fields from any number of files can be printed, but only data which is actually on file can be output and this must be in the same form that the fields were put into the system. The output must also be in columns. Since the width of each field is already held on the Record Definition File, all that is necessary to define the format is to name the fields and the column headings required. Again the actual definition will be a form-filling exercise. In this case the the details required are shown in Figure 18.3.

The details to be entered should be self-apparent, apart from the fact that each column will automatically be given a Column Letter (from A to Z). This is to facilitate modifications. (Letters have been used to avoid confusion with field numbers).

The first three fields will be retained. After the first column has been defined, only fields 4 & 5 and the Column Heading need to be typed if all the fields are from the same file. Field 4 shows the field number of the data to be reported and Field 5 indicates whether or not the field is to be used as a selection key. The system will automatically set column widths to whichever is the greater of the column heading or the field size; plus one to allow space between columns.

```
File Listing Reports, Format Definition Module

1. Report format name ... [          ]

2. Column letter ... [ ]

3. File name ... [          ]

4. Field number ... [ ]

5. Key field (Y) or (N) ... [ ]

6. Column heading, Line 1. ... [          ]

7.    "         "      "   2. ... [          ]

8.    "         "      "   3. ... [          ]

9.    "         "      "   4. ... [          ]

10.   "         "      "   5. ... [          ]
```

Figure 18.3 Input format for File Listing Reports, Format Definition module.

Provision has been included for five lines on each Column Heading. The system will adjust the number of lines used on the report to accomodate the longest header plus one blank line to separate the header from the data. Clearly, further details are required to complete the definition of the report. Before leaving this very simple method of defining the format there are two further points to be considered.

Firstly, when a field is first linked to a column heading, the heading should be noted as a default heading. On subsequent reports the default heading must be used when the column heading fields are left blank.

Secondly, there is the problem of reports which exceed the width of the paper, or screen. As has been stressed, every effort must be made to avoid non-standard reports. But the 4GL+ must be able to cope with this problem.

There are a number of alternatives. Using the PICK Operating System, for example, the system switches to down-page, rather than columnar output, when this problem arises. Unlike so many of the excellent features of PICK, this doesn't seem to be the best solution. A better alternative would appear to be to devote a second line to the excess data (Figure 18.4). Note that the second line is indented by two spaces for ease of scanning.

```
{  Col. A. Header. }  {  Col. B. Header. }  {  Col. C. Header. }
  {  Col. D Header.  }  {  Col. E. Header.  }

{ Line 1, Data A. } { Line 1, Data B.    } { Line 1, Data C. }
  { Line 1, Data D,  } { Line 1, Data E.  }

{ Line 2, Data A. } { Line 2, Data B.    } { Line 2, Data C. }
  { Line 2, Data D.  } { Line 2, Data E.  }
Etc.
```

Figure 18.4 Recommended method for handling reports that require more columns than can be fitted onto a single line.

To do justice to PICK, it should be pointed out that PICK allows designers to limit the problems of overflow by defining multi-item fields for details such as names and addresses (Figure 18.5).

A PICK Multi-item Field;

J. Smith & Co.] 10 High St.] Dover] Kent.

Can be listed in a single column as;

J. Smith & Co.
10 High St.
Dover
Kent.

Figure 18.5 An example of the use of the PICK Multi-item Field facility.

There are other advantages to this approach in terms of file space, but, on balance, it seems often better to stick to the simpler concept of single-item fields.

Report Procedure Definition

Once the format for a File Listing Report has been defined, the next step is to define the associated procedure. Again this should be a simple form-filling exercise and the format required is shown in Figure 18.6.

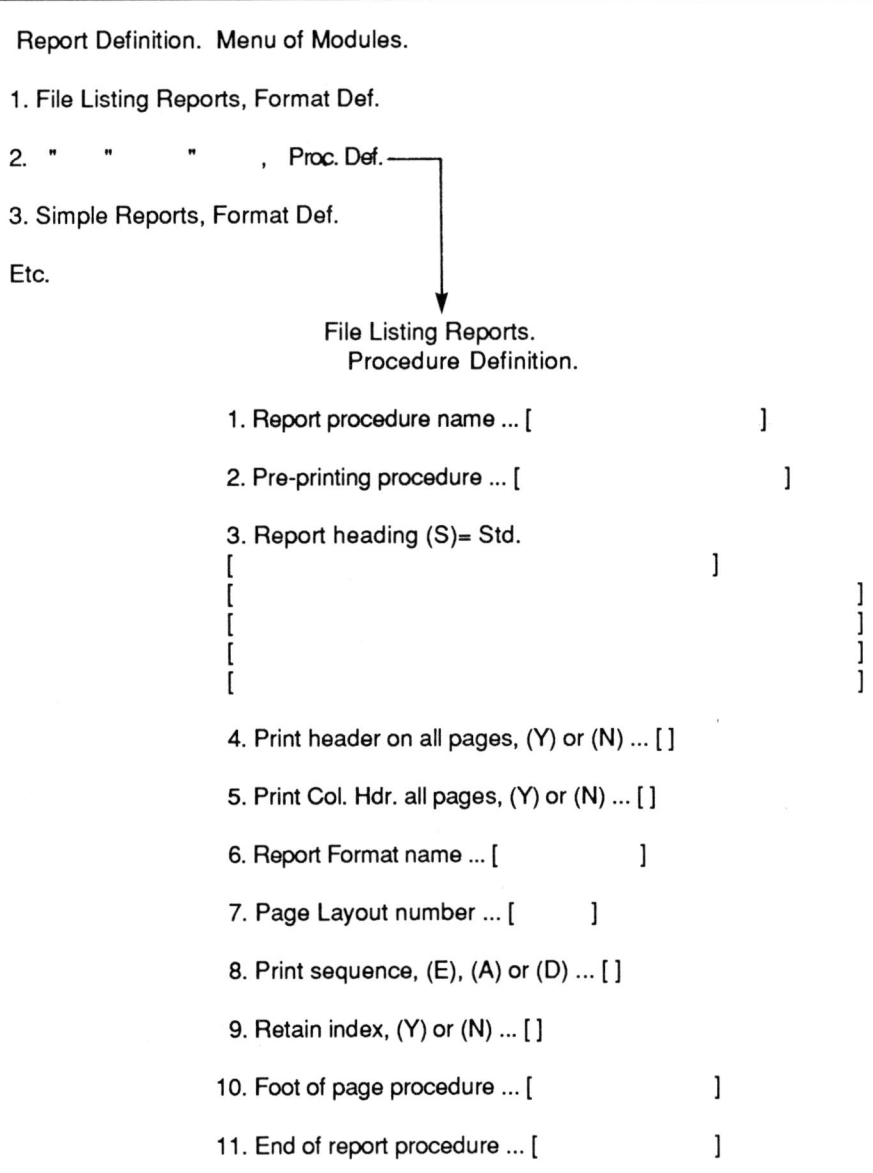

Report Definition. Menu of Modules.

1. File Listing Reports, Format Def.

2. "   "   "   , Proc. Def.

3. Simple Reports, Format Def.

Etc.

File Listing Reports.
Procedure Definition.

1. Report procedure name ... [   ]

2. Pre-printing procedure ... [   ]

3. Report heading (S)= Std.
[   ]
[   ]
[   ]
[   ]
[   ]

4. Print header on all pages, (Y) or (N) ... [ ]

5. Print Col. Hdr. all pages, (Y) or (N) ... [ ]

6. Report Format name ... [   ]

7. Page Layout number ... [   ]

8. Print sequence, (E), (A) or (D) ... [ ]

9. Retain index, (Y) or (N) ... [ ]

10. Foot of page procedure ... [   ]

11. End of report procedure ... [   ]

Figure 18.6 Format for File Listing Reports, Procedure Definition.

At first sight, the amount of detail required may seem to be fairly formidable, but closer examination will show that the details are all straight forward. A simpler format could be devised, but this would impose a corresponding limitation on the flexibility of the reporting system. What is shown is considered to be an equitable compromise between the degree of flexibility of the reporting facilities and the demands placed on designers.

The approach is based on standard procedures being provided for such things as Pre-printing and Foot of Page processing. Ideally, most of those required should be incorporated in the 4GL+, but provision should also be made for users to define their own. The specification of these routines is beyond the scope of this brief outline.

Again, most of the details required should be self-apparent apart from the following:

Field 3, Report heading allows a four line header to be 'painted'. Note that the first line of the header is truncated to allow space for a page number to be printed.

Field 7, Page Layout number. This allows a standard page layout to be imposed on the report, (which will be examined in more detail in the next section of this chapter).

Field 8, Print sequence allows for the report to be sequenced in Entry order, Ascending order or Descending order.

Field 9, Retain index allows the designer to specify whether or not the index required for the report should be saved. In this way, the task of having to sort the index every time a particular sequence is required may be saved.

Page Layout Definition

To complete the definition of a report it is necessary for the computer to know where to print the report on a page and how big the page is and so on. In practice, this may already be taken care of, because a number of standard layouts must be provided with the 4GL+. However, provision must be included for designers to add their own layouts. This is done by means of the Page Layout Definition module.

Once more, the task is a form-filling one (Figure 18.7). Apart from the fact that different details are required, the only major difference between this and the earlier modules described is that layouts can be used by any type of report.

With the details already described and a completed layout, the 4GL+ can now work out the way in which to format and print or display the report. Again most of the details in the layout should be self-explanatory.

The only item which needs clarification is the last field. This is used to indicate to the system how lines of data should be grouped. The '+' sign indicates where a blank line is to be inserted and the sequence shown will be repeated throughout the report. For example, the default value shown would result in a blank line being inserted after 5 lines, then after a further 3 lines and so on. Note that the system must ensure that screens of data are not split on printed pages. If waste is to be avoided, some care must be taken in choosing top and bottom margins and line groupings. (Refer back to Chapter 7 for fuller details.)

```
Report Definition Sub-system.
Page Layout Definition Module.

1. Page layout number ... [ 14]

2. Lines per page ... [ 70]

3. Page width in chars. - Local ... [ 83]

4.   "       "      "    "    - Central ... [ 166]

5. Margins in lines - Top of page ... [ 4]

6.    "       "      "  - Foot of page ... [ 3]

7.    "    in chars. - Left side ... [10]

8.    "       "      "   - Right side ... [ 3]

9. Single sheet or continuous (S) or (C) ... [C]

10.Line spacing,(1),(2) or (3)...[1]

11.Line grouping, 'N+N+N'...[5+3+    ]
```

Figure 18.7 Input format for Page Layout Definition Module.

Where the usable page width, excluding margins, is less than the line length required for a report, excess fields will automatically be put on the next line. In doing this, line spacing instruction will be ignored. In other words, even when double spacing is specified the excess will be single spaced. Note that provision has been made for different widths of paper to be defined for Local and Central printing. This is to enable users to choose which printer to use at run time. Again this means more work for users, but this is felt to be necessary.

Where a From/To option is included in a report program, a particular report can vary in length from a single line to several hundreds of pages. Since the length will be determined by the user at run time, it is appropriate that the printing facility should be chosen at the same time.

Finally, before leaving this section, it is perhaps appropriate to point out that there is clearly a need here for a Report which will summarise briefly the facilities of all the Page Layouts that are on file.

Report Format Definition - Simple Reports

Simple Reports are similar to File Listing Reports and the basic steps in defining them are exactly the same. They are also limited to producing reports in columns, but in this case provision is made for arithmetic to be performed on both lines and columns. More advanced formatting facilities are also required.

Reports of this type are commonly called 'Spreadsheets' and a wide variety of proprietary systems cater for this sort of application. On most of these provision is made for basic data to be type into the Report Format and the system then completes the report.

This is, of course, contrary to the basic philosophy of PSD and is not recommended for general use, although it may be acceptable for ad-hoc reports of a transitory nature. As with all PSD Reports, what follows assumes that the records to be reported on will have been established in the recommended manner. As far as the Report Format Definition is concerned, all that is necessary is to add to the facilities defined earlier for File Listing. This results in the input format shown in Figure 18.8.

With Simple Reports, the values to be printed out may not be on file, instead they may be calculated. In Field 3 provision has been added for this to be indicated by the word 'CALC'. Note that this implies that this is a reserved word which must not be used as a File Name. Where CALC is entered the Field Number (Field 4) becomes redundant. This allows the system to double check that the designer does not intend to call up data from a file. Field 5 allows the actual calculation to be specified. This must allow any normal arithmetic operations to be specified and is most easily achieved by reference to the column letters. For example, when Col. D is being defined an entry in the calculation field of 'B*C' would result in Cols. B & C being multiplied together and placed in Col. D.

Calculations need not necessarily involve other columns. When defining a column, a value taken from a file may be operated on. For example, when Col. E is being defined, a calculation of 'E/100' would result in the value on file being divided by 100 before it is included in the report.

Note that in this case the File Name of the data must be defined, rather than CALC. In other words, CALC must only be used where access to a data file is not required that is, when any data to be operated on is already in a column.

```
Simple Reports, Format Definition Module

1. Report format name ... [            ]

2. Column letter... [ ]

3. File name or (CALC) ... [            ]

4. Field number ... [    ]

5. Key field (Y) or (N) ... [N]

6. Column heading, Line 1. ... [                    ]

7.     "         "         " 2. ... [                    ]

8.     "         "         " 3. ... [                    ]

9.     "         "         " 4. ... [                    ]

10.    "         "         " 5. ... [                    ]

11. Calculation ... [                                    ]

12. Column width in chars. ... [    ]

13. Decimal places displayed ... [    ]

14. Justify to Right, (Y) or (N) ... [Y]

15. Total column, (Y) or (N) ... [N]
```

Figure 18.8 Input format for Simple Reports, Format Definition module.

Because of the effects of calculations on fields, it is no longer possible for the system to predict column-width requirements. Field 12 allows for these to be inserted. Except in the case of CALC columns, a default width is set if no column width is entered. This will be determined as for File Listing Reports. Again the effects of calculations can result in varying numbers of decimal places being generated. Provision must be included to limit the number of places displayed. Field 13 provides for this. Where decimal places occur in a column, they must be aligned. Provision must also be made for data to be justified either to the left or right side of a column. Field 14 enables this to be defined.

Finally, the only other new field is Field 15, Total column. This indicates to the system whether or not the values in a column should be totalled. The full implications of this will become clear when the next section is considered.

Report Procedure Definition - Simple Reports

The process of defining the report procedure for Simple Reports is very similar to the procedure for File Listing Reports. Again more advanced facilities are incorporated (Figure 18.9).

```
Simple Reports
Procedure Definition Module

1.   Report procedure name ...[            ]
2.   Pre-printing procedure ...[           ]
3.   Report heading (S)=Std.
[                                          ]
[                                          ]
[                                          ]
[                                          ]
4.   Print header on all pages, (Y) or (N) ...[ ]
5.   Print Col.Hdr. all pages,  (Y) or (N) ...[ ]
6.   Report Format name ...[          ]
7.   Page layout number ...[    ]
8.   Print sequence, (E), (A) or (D) ...[ ]
9.   Retain index, (Y) or (N) ...[ ]
10.  Foot of page procedure ...[           ]
11.  End of report procedure ...[          ]
12.  Break-on Column ...[ ]
13.  Print side-heading on break, (Y) or (N) ...[ ]
14.  Print totals on break, (Y) or (N) ...[ ]
15.  Print cum-totals on break, (Y) or (N) ...[ ]
16.  New page on break, (Y) or (N) ...[ ]
```

Figure 18.9 Format for Simple Reports, Procedure Definition.

The new fields are fields 12 to 16 inclusive. These are concerned primarily with introducing 'breaks' into reports (Figure 18.10). A 'break' occurs when the value in a defined column changes. In the illustration the break has been introduced on the Prod. Grp. column. The key to defining this procedure is Field 12, Break-on Column. This allows the designer to define which column of the report is to be monitored to induce a break. The fields which follow then allow the designer to define what must be done when a break occurs.

```
STOCK VALUATION

PART NUMBER         PROD.           QTY IN      COST        TOTAL
                    GRP.            STOCK       PRICE       VALUE

PROD.GRP.A.

R1236754            A               100         56.05       5605.00
S654987             A               1000         2.00       2000.00

TOTAL FOR PROD. GRP.A.                                      7605.00

PROD. GRP.B.

W4398765            B                 1          6.00          6.00
W0987623            B               100          4.09        409.00
W983460             B                 2          5.00         10.00

TOTAL FOR PROD. GRP. B.                                      425.00

CUMULATIVE TOTAL.                                           8030.00
```

Figure 18.10 A Simple Report showing 'breaks' for sub-totalling.

Field 13, Print side-heading on break allows the designer to indicate whether or not a side-heading should be printed for each group of data. The side-heading will consist of the column heading plus the value in the column. For example, 'PROD. GRP. A.'

Fields 14 & 15 enable the designer to indicate whether or not totals and/or cumulative totals should be printed. For the total for a group the words 'TOTAL for' followed by the side-heading must be printed.

At first sight, it may be considered unnecessary to repeat the side-heading. However, confusion could arise if only the word 'TOTAL' was printed and a user simply looks at the last page - and assumes that the total is for the whole report.

Since no such confusion can arise with Cumulative Totals, it is not necessary to elaborate on these. Again, however, it is not difficult to think of additional features that could be incorporated. For example, options to underline totals or to box in headings and so on, but the main aim of the Simple Reports Modules is to enable designers to produce functional reports, quickly and cheaply. Over elaboration must therefore be avoided.

Complex Reports

Clearly, it is not possible to reduce all reports to a state where they can be handled by the Simple Reports facilities and provision must be made for Complex Reports, such as Invoices, to be handled.

Often Complex Reports will call for printing onto pre-printed stationery and the facility must provide for virtually anything to be printed anywhere on a report. It is conceivable that the definition of Complex Reports could be handled as a form-filling exercise, but at the time of writing the simplest approach appears to be to use a free-format approach and to define reports in whatever high-level language is available.

Having stated that, it should be appreciated that many complex reports will include sections which could readily be handled by the Simple Reports facilities. For example, the body of an Invoice. It is possible that the definition of Complex Reports could be simplified by using these facilities.

Once the 'simple' part of a report has been taken care of what remains will normally be simple to define, using a BASIC type of definition (Figure 18.11).

```
100 PRINT TAB(10,15) "INVOICE TO "; CUST_NAME_FLD.
```

Figure 18.11 Typical BASIC type of print statement.

The statement starts with a program-line number, very useful for helping to locate the statement for correction purposes. This is followed by the line number and character position where printing is to take place.

The designer can then insert specific text by putting it in 'in-quotes' and/or details of a particular field, or fields, can be called for. This seems to be very simple and straightforward and it is difficult to see how it can be bettered.

However, the intention of this Guide was to avoid the situation where designers become involved in programming problems. Suffice it to say that the production of complex reports is essentially a programming problem.

Conclusion

A great deal more detail is required to translate this very brief outline into a system specification for a 4GL+. The way in which this is done will depend to a large extent on the facilities provided by whatever host language is chosen.

It is hoped that what has been described is sufficient to show firstly, the importance of the role of 4GL+s in future systems design and secondly, that users will readily be able to relate to a 4GL+ if it is designed on the form-filling principles outlined.

Chapter 19

Dos and Don'ts of Systems Design

Introduction

The basic aim of this Guide has been to show that commercial EDP systems can be produced quickly and efficiently - providing that the importance of effective design standards is fully recognised. For transaction processing systems the Record is the logical level at which to standardise and PSD is the way of achieving this.

Using the principles of PSD not only ensures that users can readily relate to systems, it also ensures that systems are helpful to all concerned at all stages in the development, implementation and maintenance of systems.

In this chapter the key features of PSD are summarised in the form of a series of Dos and Don'ts.

Design Standards

* *Do* ensure that effective Design Standards are clearly laid down and applied to all EDP systems.

* *Don't* fail to ensure that all concerned are fully aware of, and adhere rigidly to the Standards.

Keyboards etc.

* *Do* use conventional equipment, unless the need for special features is clear beyond doubt.

* *Don't* restrict the flexibility of the system by introducing special keys or keyboards, unless this is absolutely essential.

At Log-On

* *Do* make sure that as soon as users switch on it is abundantly clear what they must do next.

* *Don't* at any time leave users with a blank screen or cryptic prompt.

* *Do* ensure that any passwords, or other forms of user identification, are entered once only, at log-on time.

* *Don't* confuse users by displaying spurious information.

Structuring

* *Do* provide menus showing the systems, sub-systems, modules and reports that are available.

* *Don't* try to 'save' menus by illogical combinations or by departing from the PSD structure, even if some menus only offer one choice.

* *Do* stick to the shallow structuring of PSD.

* *Don't* forget the secondary nature of reports and that all 'across-record' processing must be treated as a Report.

The Basic Functions

* *Do* ensure that a standard Menu of Functions (Create, Amend, Erase, Display and Print) is common to all modules.

* *Don't* make menu selection difficult by using anything other than 'Enter selection number ... '.

Where am I?

* *Do* make sure that at all times Screen Header details show users precisely where they are in a system.

* *Don't* confuse users by departing from the standard Screen Header.

Screen Formats

* *Do* restrict data input and displays to 16 lines of screen, so that this does not clash with Screen Header and Foot-of-Screen details and ensure that the same key is used throughout to enter data.

* *Don't* allow more than 70 characters per line of input, so that what is displayed can be output directly onto A4 portrait.

Input Formats

* *Do* display descriptions of fields down the left-hand side of the screen, with each field numbered to facilitate correction and cross-referencing to User Guides and so on.

* *Don't* use cryptic descriptions of fields on input screens.

* *Do* show the size of the field expected and a picture of the format where appropriate.

* *Don't* make it difficult to read what is on the screen by using half-inverse video or unnecessary colour and so on.

Error Detection

* *Do* check each field as it is entered and repeat the input prompt if the entry is not valid.

* *Don't* sound a 'Bell' if the data entered is valid. Only sound the Bell when invalid data is detected.

Error Messages

* *Do* ensure that error messages are clear, and that they are always displayed in the same place on the screen.

* *Don't* display messages for a period of time and then remove them. Wait until the user acknowledges the message.

Foot of Screen Processing

* *Do* provide standard foot-of-screen routines to allow a record to be reviewed and corrected before it is filed.

* *Don't* overwrite details on the main files until the system has validated a record and the user has confirmed that the record should be filed or erased.

Reports

* *Do* try to use the same format for all reports from a particular module.

* *Don't* exceed 70 characters per line if this can be avoided, so that reports can be displayed and printed in the same format.

* *Do* make reports as flexible as possible by including From/To options and Effectivity Dates where appropriate.

* *Don't* include too many options on any one report.

* *Do* offer central or local printing as options when this is appropriate.

* *Don't* leave users in the dark about what is happening if their terminals are 'locked-out' during remote printing or extended processing.

* *Do* remember that a report may not be printed correctly the first time. Ensure that the print-out can be repeated.

* *Don't* use pre-printed stationery or multi-part sets if this can be avoided.

* *Do* number screens so that the page on which a particular screen will be printed is the same as the page number on the screen.

* *Don't* forget to discuss proposed records and reports with users as soon as possible.

* *Do* provide facilities for paging from one screen to another, both up and down reports or multi-screen records.

* *Don't* rack or scroll details on a screen.

The Rough Design Phase

* *Do* ensure that existing systems are fully understood before starting to design new ones.

* *Don't* design a new system if a suitable package is already available.

* *Do* make sure that a good supply of large sheets of paper is available, so that designs can be roughed out.

* *Don't* try to design a major system all at once.

* *Do* identify the smallest viable part of a system and concentrate on getting that part live as soon as possible.

* *Don't* allow existing manual records to cause confusion. Manual records will often be complex and there will be no corresponding computer record.

* *Do* search for Rectangular Files, which will be the subject of Modules.

* *Don't* be distracted, at the rough-design stage, by minor details such as field sizes and formats. These can be added later.

* *Do* remember that each record will require a key and that keys must be as simple as possible, but must be unique.

* *Don't* hesitate to split records if confidentiality or security demands it.

* *Do* ensure that the fields to be put onto a record are directly related to its key.

* *Don't* show the same data twice on a records, in the form of a code and its meaning.

* *Do* identify the reports associated with each Module once all the modules have been roughed out.

* *Don't* worry about the actual format of reports at this stage.

* *Do* ensure that all the fields required to produce reports are either already in modules, or are added to the rough-design.

Finalising the Design

* *Don't* attempt to finalise the details of a design, until the rough-design has been completed.

* *Do* document the final design in a standardised way.

* *Don't* forget at each stage to try to anticipate potential problems by asking 'What if ... ?'.

* *Do* be prepared to revise designs in the light of a deeper understanding of a system, or users' comments.

* *Don't* forget to consider how existing data is to be handled when the system goes live.

* *Do* ensure that systems are rigorously tested and that users are fully trained, before a system goes live.

* *Don't* confuse user with obscure terminology or inconsistencies.

Postscript

At the time when the final chapters of this Guide were being completed, my attention was directed to a 'Handbook of Screen Format Design.' (GALITZ, 1982). This book looks at the problems of screen-design in considerable detail, and draws heavily on the work of a wide variety of other researchers.

It was, therefore, most encouraging to find that, in the main, the conclusions reached coincided with the results of my more pragmatic approach, based on some 25 years of field-experience.

Galitz doesn't consider the wider aspects of systems design which are embraced by PSD. As a result, the Handbook misses a number of vital points, such as the importance of Screen-Headers and Field numbering. But, it is extremely lucid, readable and contains references to over 80 other papers on the subject. At first, I was tempted to include some of these references in this Guide. Then I quickly concluded that it would be more appropriate for readers who wished to study this topic in more detail to read both books. In doing so, I hope this will encourage a greater awareness of the importance of HCI and of the impact which HCI can have on the future of computing.

Readers may like to know that the British Computer Society has a section devoted to these aims. This publishes a newsletter and organises conferences and seminars. Further details can be obtained from:

> The British Computer Society (HCI Specialist Group),
> 13 Mansfield St., London W1M 0BP.
>
> Telephone 01-637-0471.

References

BEER, 1979. *'Heart of the Enterprise'* by S. Beer.

BONO, 1969. *'The Mechanism of Mind'* by E. de Bono.

CODD, 1970. *'A Relational Model for Large Shared Data Banks'* by E.F. Codd (Comm. ACM 13, No.6.)

FURST, 1979. *'Origins of the Mind'* by C. Furst.

GALITZ, 1982. *'Handbook of Screen Format Design'* by W.O. Galitz.

JONES, 1985. *'Prototyping for Systems Building'* by R. Jones ('Journal of Data Processing', Vol 27, No.7.)

MARTIN, 1975. *'Computer Data Base Organisation'* by J. Martin.

MARTIN, 1985. *'Fourth Generation Languages'* Vol 2 - Survey of Representative 4GLs by J Martin et al.

WATTS, 1984. *'Introducing Interactive Computing'* by R.A. Watts.

INDEX

4GL+ record processing, 182
4GL+ report processing, 194
4GL+, 182
4GL, entry to, 183
4GLs, what are, 169
4GLs, 169

A4 paper, 55
A4 paper, designing on, 71
abbreviations, 182
access frequencies, 117
across-record processing, 65
across-screen input, 38
amend, 85, 107
amend record, 10
amend record function, 48
Amstrad PCW8256, 157
applications, special, 153
artificial intelligence, 182
authority, levels of, 81, 192
automatic data capture, 94

bar coding, 94
batch processing, 21
batch systems, 2
Beer, 23
bell, 45
box-file, 9
brackets, 41

calculations, 129
cash dispensers, 96
cash-point designs, 154
central printing v local, 69
check-digit, 87
checking data, 19
cluttered screens, 36
codes, 79, 89
colour, 36, 92
column flow chart, 113
command systems v menu, 34
commonality, 9
complex files, 15
complex report, 196, 207
complexity, 129
computer jargon, 3
computer systems, modern, 1
control record, 18, 139
counters, 18, 60
create, 107
create record function, 10, 46
cursor, 22
cursor manipulation, 36, 48
customised devices, 153

data capture, automatic, 94
data checking, 19
data model, 150
data processing, 1, 7
data, transient, 107
data, duplication of, 129

database management systems, 169
DBMSs, 169
de Bono, 23
default values, 60
design phase, rough, 122
design phases, 109
design process, 194
design standards, 208
design, finalising, 144, 150, 212
design, methodology of, 122
design, summarising, 142
designer, systems, 14
designers/users, 171
designing records, 101
designing screens, 41
designs, cash point, 154
designs, re-appraising, 150
details file, 17
display, 85, 107
display record, 10
display record function, 50
displays and prints, report, 65
documentation, 121
documenting, modules, 146
documents, 9
Domains and Tuples, 102
down-screen input, 40, 41
duplication of data, 18, 129

ease of use, design, 75
EDP, 7
effective communication, 7
effectivity date, 75, 76
electronic data processing, 7
entity model, 175
erase, 85, 107
erase record, 10
erase record function, 49
error correction, 39
error detection, 45, 210
error messages, 45, 45, 210
errors, serious, 139
executives, 4

feasibility study, 112
features, miscellaneous, 92
field validation, 148
fields, 9, 41
fields, large, 57
fields, multi-line, 58
fields, typing into, 44
file, 9
file definition, 187
file, details, 17
file listing report, 196
file sizes, 116
file, user/password, 80
files, complex, 15
files, rectangular, 14
files, two-dimensional, 14
first normal form, 103

flexibility, 96, 129, 139
floppy discs, 100
flow chart, 140
flow chart, column, 113
FNF, 103, 103
foot of screen processing, 47, 210
foot-of-screen routines, 47
form-filling, 43, 177, 194
format conventions, 61
format-displays, report, 66
FOS, 47
from/to technique, 76
function levels of authority, 81
functions, 10, 41
functions, basic, 209
functions, menu of, 24, 35
Furst, 23
GALITZ, 213

HCI, 3
HCI specialist group, 213
header, 17
header, screen, 36
headers, PSD, 32
hierarchical systems, 173
high level structuring, PSD, 26

icons, 36
illustrations, 114
implementation, 120
index, 13
inexperienced designers, 5
input and output, voice, 98
input formats, 148, 209
input, across-screen, 38
input, down-screen, 40, 41
input, question and answer, 43
input, random, 42
integrity of the system, 20

Jones, 5
joysticks, 92

key fields, 11
key, repetitive, 59
key, secondary, 12
key-stroke, average time for, 46
keyboard, Maltron, 99
keyboards, 29, 98, 208
keypad, 29
keypad, numeric, 29
keys, special, 96

layout, non-standard, 39
levels of authority, 81
light-pens, 87
local v central printing, 69
Locoscript, 158
log-on, 79, 208

magnetic ink character recognition, 95
maintenance, 120
Maltron keyboard, 99
many-to-many relationship, 175
Martin, 36
menu board, 93
menu building, 190
menu of functions, 24, 35
menu selection, 37, 93

menu v command systems, 34
menus of reports, 25
menus, PSD, 31
menus, 180
messages, error, 45, 45
methodology of design, 122
MICR, 95
miscellaneous features, 92
model, entity, 175
modern computer systems, 1
modern computer, key features of, 21
modularity, 4
module, 10
module menu selection, 64
modules, 125, 184
modules, documenting, 146
monitors, 21
mouse, 92
multi-screen records, 53
multiple record entries, 58

non-standard layout, 39
normalisation, 101, 102
numeric keypad, 29

OCR, 95
on-line, 2
one-to-many relationship, 15
optical character recognition, 95

page layout definition, 201
paging, 56
paper, A4, 55
password control, 79
password/user file, 80
passwords, 82
pattern recognition, 23
patterned systems design, 4, 22
personal identify number (PIN), 155
print, 85, 107
print options, selecting, 70
print record, 10
print record function, 50
printing VDU screens, 55
printing, local v central, 69
print and display, report, 65
prints, report format, 67
prints, report, 68
procedure definition, 189
processing, across-record, 65
processing, batch, 21
processing, repetitive, 58
processing, secondary, 65
processing, transaction, 21
programming terminology, 11
project identification, 111
project initiation, 109
prototype systems, 119
prototyping, 3
PSD, 4, 105
PSD, basic principles of, 21
PSD features, summary, 63
PSD headers, 32
PSD high level structuring, 26
PSD menus, 31
PSD modules, 24
PSD record processing, 38
PSD screen header standard, 32
PSD screen, typical, 51

PSD structure, 29

question and answer input, 43
QWERTY, 29

racking, 56
random input, 42
real-time, 2
record, 9, 10
record definition, 185, 186
record entries, multiple, 58
record function, amend, 48
record function, create, 45, 46
record function, display, 50
record function, erase, 49
record function, print, 50
record keys, 79, 84
record processing, PSD, 38
record processing, 61, 149
record sequencing and access, 12
record split, 83
record, amend, 10
record, control, 18
record, create,
record, display, 10
record, erase, 10
record, print, 10
records, complex, 15
records, designing, 101
rectangular files, 14
references, 214
repetitive processing, 58, 59
report, 10, 65, 210
report displays and prints, 65
report displays, 11
report format - prints, 67
report format definition, 203
report format-displays, 66
report prints, 11, 68
report procedure definition, 200, 205
report selections, 78
report, complex, 196
report, file listing, 196
report, simple, 196
reporting, 11
reports, complex, 207
reports, copies of, 78
reports, menus of, 25
reports, simple, 203, 205
reports, specifying, 149
reports, types of, 195
roller-balls, 92
rough design phase, 122, 211
rough design, refining, 133

screen design facilities, 179
screen formats, 209
screen header standard, PSD, 32
screen header, 36, 209
screen I/D, 33
screen layout, VDU, 54
screen message, 47
screen-painting, 180
screens, cluttered, 36
screens, designing, 41
screens, touch sensitive, 94
screens, touch, 36
scrolling, 56
second normal form, 103, 104

secondary key, 12
secondary processing, 65
security, 180
security levels, 118
security of systems, 79
serious errors, 139
simple report, 196
simple reports, 203, 205
simplicity, 129
skilled users, 35
SNF, 103, 104
special applications, 153
special keys, 29, 96
specification, 3
specifying reports, 149
standardisation, 23
standards, 4, 5
structuring, 176, 209
system specification, 115, 147
system testing, 119
system, integrity of, 20
systems design, what is, 3
systems designer, 14, 124
systems, hierarchical, 173
systems, phototype, 119

tables, 18
teletypes, 43
terminal, 4
terminology, 101, 172
third normal form, (TNF) 104
to/from technique, 76
touch sensitive screens, 94
touch-screens, 36
transaction processing, 2, 21
transparency, 15
Tuples and Domains, 102
two-dimensional files, 14
type sizes, 74
typing into fields, 44

Unnormalised Form, (UNF)102
unskilled users, 43
user guides, 84, 119
user identification, 80
user-friendliness, 2, 3
user/designers, 171
user/password file, 80
users requirements, 4
users, skilled, 35
users, unskilled, 43

VDUs, 21
VDU screen layout, 54
VDU screens, printing, 55
views, 180
visual display units, 21
voice input and output, 98

Watts, 35
what if..?, 20, 145
window-envelopes, 134
word processing, 96, 157
wrap-round, 39